SOCIAL AND EMOTIONAL DEVELOPMENT OF EXCEPTIONAL STUDENTS: HANDICAPPED and GIFTED

SOCIAL AND EMOTIONAL DEVELOPMENT OF EXCEPTIONAL STUDENTS: HANDICAPPED AND GIFTED

By

CARROLL J. JONES, PH.D.

Manager, Faculty Coordination
City Colleges of Chicago–Europe
Wiesbaden, Germany

CHARLES C THOMAS • PUBLISHER
Springfield • Illinois • U.S.A.

Published and Distributed Throughout the World by

CHARLES C THOMAS • PUBLISHER
2600 South First Street
Springfield, Illinois 62794-9265

© *1992 by* CHARLES C THOMAS • PUBLISHER

ISBN 0-398-05781-8

Library of Congress Catalog Card Number: 91-43960

Printed in the United States of America
SC-R-3

Library of Congress Cataloging-in-Publication Data

Jones, Carroll J.
    Social and emotional development of exceptional students :
handicapped and gifted / by Carroll J. Jones.
        p.   cm.
    Includes bibliographical references and index.
    ISBN 0-398-05781-8
    1. Exceptional children—Psychology.   2. Handicapped children—
Psychology.   3. Gifted children—Psychology.   4. Social interaction
in children.   5. Emotions in children.   6. Special education.
I. Title.
BF723.E9J66   1992
155.45—dc20   91-43960
                                                                    CIP

CONTRIBUTOR

Suzanne Jessup, Ph.D.
Associate Dean of Graduate Studies
Southern Arkansas University
Magnolia, Arkansas

To Merrell

FOREWORD

Unfortunately, only a portion of the task of successfully educating exceptional students involves academics. While this alone would be challenging enough, it is further complicated and confounded by the fact that this population of learners is often at a heightened risk for difficulties with social and emotional development as well. No category of exceptional students is exempt from these problems. Whether mentally or physically challenged or academically gifted, all exceptional learners are ripe to encounter difficulties in social interactions with peers and adults, in interpersonal struggles which endanger their chances to use existing abilities to the best advantage, and in emotional roadblocks to successful academic and social functioning.

While social and emotional development is influenced by many factors both intrinsic and extrinsic to the child, there is still ample room in the development of most students for parents and teachers to exercise guiding strategies to heighten successful development opportunities. These efforts should be undertaken by parents and teachers from the advantage point of a thorough understanding of existing research about the social and emotional development of these special learners. This, simply put, is what Carroll Jones has so aptly provided in this text. Dr. Jones, in her characteristically thorough way, has carefully explored, and presented in review fashion to the reader, a status report of the existing knowledge about how students from each major category of exceptionality emerge in both the social and emotional realms. Armed with this valuable resource bank, effective teachers and concerned parents can set about the task of developing and applying ways to insure maximum development in these important areas of their exceptional charges.

VIRGINIA J. DICKENS, PH.D.
Area Coordinator, Special Education
Fayetteville State University
Fayetteville, North Carolina

PREFACE

Today, some sixteen years after the passage of PL94-142, the dream of special educators—to educate handicapped and nonhandicapped children and youth together resulting in increased academic gains and age-appropriate social skills for handicapped children and youth—has not materialized. Mainstreaming or integration and inclusion has resulted in placing handicapped students in the regular classrooms, but often the academic and social gains have not occurred because handicapped children do not automatically make gains by being in a regular classroom with same-aged peers. However, the self-concept related research has indicated that having a caring teacher in a smaller less stressful classroom environment was not, by itself, enough to raise the self-concepts of children who had a history of academic failure.

Mildly handicapped students will not be successful until regular and special education teachers understand normal social, emotional, and self-concept development: the ways in which handicapped students deviate from the norm, the effects of the student's feelings of personal control (metacognition, motivation, attributions) on his/her academic achievement, and the impact of continued academic and social failures on handicapped students and their efforts to learn.

At present a void exists in providing understandable information to regular and special education teachers regarding social, emotional, and self-concept theory, and self-concept research. While the majority of states require that students in teacher-training programs take an introductory course in special education, an informal survey of eight major texts used in Introduction to Exceptional Individuals courses revealed an average of from 0–2 paragraphs on the social and emotional development of the various categories of handicapping conditions. While it is very difficult to specify the social and emotional development of every handicapped child from theory, some generalizations can be made about how various handicapping conditions appear to effect the social, emotional, and self-concept development. Thus, this text could serve as a companion text for Introduction to Exceptional Individuals courses or as the primary text in Psychology of Exceptional Individuals courses.

The book is organized into nine chapters beginning with an introductory chapter on normal social, emotional, and self-concept development (Chapter 1); and eight chapters on exceptional students including vision impaired students (Chapter 2), communication impaired students (Chapter 3), hearing impaired students (Chapter 4), mentally retarded students (Chapter 5), behavior disordered students (Chapter 6), learning disabled students (Chapter 7), physically and other health impaired students (Chapter 8), gifted and talented students (Chapter 9). Each chapter begins with a brief summary of the cognitive and academic learning problems of the various categories of handicapped individuals, then discusses in detail the social and emotional learning problems, feelings of personal control, and self-concepts.

Special thanks to my friend and colleague, Dr. Suzanne Jessup, Associate Dean of Graduate Studies, Southern Arkansas University who served as guest author for the chapter on gifted and talented students. Thanks, also, to my friend and colleague, Dr. Virginia Dickens, Coordinator of Special Education at Fayetteville State University who served as a "sounding board" and provided valuable suggestions.

This book is dedicated to Merrell D. Jones, who has spent 29 years in the service of his country during peace and two wars—Vietnam and the Desert Storm operation in the Persian Gulf. He has twice been presented the Commander's Medal for Meritorious Service. Currently, Jones is stationed at Wiesbaden Air Station, Germany as a Department of the Army civilian advisor on the Apache helicopter. By precept and example, Merrell Jones is an American patriot, one of those unsung American heroes, whose selfless dedication to country has helped to ensure freedom and democracy for his fellow man and for his family.

CONTENTS

SOCIAL AND EMOTIONAL DEVELOPMENT OF EXCEPTIONAL STUDENTS: HANDICAPPED and GIFTED

Chapter One

NORMAL SOCIAL AND EMOTIONAL, AND SELF-CONCEPT DEVELOPMENT

"Social and emotional growth and development are closely linked with all aspects of child development into a synergistic relationship," (Jones, 1988, 241).

Social and emotional development are interrelated psychological perspectives concerned with social relationships, emotional stability, social perspective-taking, social regulation and moral development, social problem-solving, metacognition, and self-concept development.

INFANCY AND EARLY CHILDHOOD DEVELOPMENT

Sensorimotor Stage Social/Emotional Development

Social and emotional growth and development are closely linked with all aspects of child development. Most children follow "normal" range social and emotional developmental patterns in their interactions with adults and children, play skill development, and in self-concept development.

3

Sensorimotor Stage Social Development

Newborns have few ways of expressing their feelings or emotions and show limited discrimination of people and limited social behavior (Fallen & Umansky, 1985). By the age of three months, the infant has begun to be a social individual, smiling in response to mother's face, voice, or smile, and responding to person-to-person contact with adults and other children (Appendix 1). The child's smiling and crying begin to take on social meaning as the child realizes that both can produce desired results in adults—attention. The four- to-nine-month-old child enjoys being near people and responds gaily to attention and play. By about eight months of age, children begin to display stranger anxiety (Appendix 1).

The 8–9-month-old child exhibits influence over the environment by shouting for attention, loudly rejecting confinement in the playpen, and even fighting for a disputed toy (Appendix 1). Social development is enhanced as s/he plays games with adult assistance (e.g., Pat-a-cake) (Appendix 1).

By the time the average child has reached 12 months of age, s/he cognitively understands object concept and object permanence which allows the child to discriminate herself/himself as an individual apart from mother. Communicatively, the 12-month-old child has mastered the adult intonation system which paired with gestures and one understandable word or gibberish conveys his/her primary thoughts and wants or needs (Jones, 1988). S/he is able to interpret the emotional expressions of familiar adults and respond to different tones of voice (Appendix 1).

The 10–12-month-old child begins to participate in social activities, seeking to maintain interactions with an adult, and attempting to play with another child (Appendix 1). S/he fears strange people and places, and suffers separation anxiety when apart from mother (Appendix 1). Play generally involves interactions with adults in learning fine or gross motor skills and language. The one-year-old is developing a sense of humor, and teases and tests parental limits, and feels guilty at wrong doing (Appendix 1).

Much of the social development of children occurs during play. The play of the 13–18-month-old child is characterized by experimentation and rituals in activities such as dropping objects from the highchair and throwing objects from the play pen (Appendix 1). S/he engages in solitary or on-looker play, and initiates and imitates his/her own play. Symbolic play, the last stage of the sensorimotor period (19–24 months), is usually solitary in nature and is the child's attempt to understand reality in ways that are meaningful. S/he is beginning to play with other children and often plays house imitating the adult behaviors that s/he has observed (Appendix 1).

Sensorimotor Stage Emotional Development

The three-month-old infant has begun to develop an emotional repertoire including the ability to express joy and delight, distress, pain or frustration, surprise, and interest (Appendix 1). The nine-month-old's emotional repertoire is becoming more sophisticated to additionally include protest, fear, anger, humor, teasing, and shyness. The one-year-old's emotional expressions are very wide ranged from delight, joy, affection, and humor to anxiety, fear, protest, guilt, and negativism. The year-old child has gradually developed feelings of affection for his/her parents and caregivers. The receiving of affectionate attention by others is very important to emotional growth as the child learns to transfer some of the affection from his/her family to other children and adults outside the home. The average two-year-old child has an almost complete store of emotional expressions (Appendix 1).

Imitation plays an important role in the development of a child's emotional behavior (Crow & Crow, 1953). The child's emotional behavior develops gradually from generalized expressions of emotionalism to focusing emotions on the person or object responsible. The child learns to respond to adult attitudes toward his emotional behaviors. The child of emotionally well-balanced parents usually learns early to control his/her emotions (Crow & Crow, 1953).

Sensorimotor Stage Self-Concept Development

The self-concept begins to develop in infancy and continues throughout one's lifetime, constantly undergoing modification in response to the environment (Lerner & Shea, 1982). Self-concept development during infancy and early childhood involve acquiring an accurate body image which begins with body awareness and initially is manifested as total body responses to sensory stimulation and movement (Appendix 1).

The six-month-old child has begun to give evidence of having formed some definite self-concepts. These early self-concepts or awareness of self characteristics involve understanding of body awareness, recognition of attention, and body image. The concepts of body awareness and body image develop concurrently with cognitive and motor skills. Early self-concept development skills, self-awareness and body image, continue to develop as the child learns to use locomotion to move through space. The child's initial recognition of attention to herself by others is related to the development of negative or positive concepts of self. The young child soon learns to differentiate positive and negative attention and may cry when scolded and laugh when praised (Appendix 1).

The self-concept continues to develop through greater understanding of the body and the skills the child can perform. The two-year-old recognizes herself in a mirror or picture and refers to herself by name. Emerging self-knowledge is increased by the acquisition of category labels including gender categories (e.g., boy, girl) and age categories (e.g., child, grown-up) (Harter, 1988). Body image as related to concepts of maleness and femaleness begin to develop as the young child identifies with the same sex parent and imitates them and their sex role during play activities (Appendix 1).

Preschool Age Social/Emotional Development

Physical, mental, social, and emotional interactive developmental behaviors continue to play an important role in the socialization of preschool children, ages 2–5 years. During this period of rapid growth and development, verbal communication takes on an increasingly important role in the child's social interactions.

Preschool Social Development

The outstanding characteristic of social life at age two-years is parallel play in which two or three children may all be playing with similar materials in close proximity, but without much interaction (Appendix 2). Socially, the 2–3-year-old knows gender identity, participates in simple group activities involving singing and dancing, begins to share automatically, asks for things they want, and defends their possessions (Appendix 2). While social interactions are still very limited, it is not uncommon to make a special friend by age three. Most two-to-three-year-olds begin imaginative play with playing house, and begin to be able to symbolically use themselves and objects in play (e.g., "I am a cowboy and this broom is my horse."). The 2–3-year-old begins cooperative play and participation in simple group games (Appendix 2). However, typical two-year-olds have limited verbal skills and talk mostly to themselves. Their social conversations are usually with adults and are limited to showing something or making a request.

Two-and-one-half-year-olds are involved in considerable interaction, but very little cooperation. Social interactions at this age are primarily aggressive and may be quite violent (Ames & Ilg, 1976). "It is by no means unusual for a child to grab an object from another child, to chase and shout for an object, to push a child out of the way and then grab something, or to hit another child on the head and climb onto him and grab his toy" (Ames & Ilg, 1976, 20).

The three- to four-year-old child finds friends more interesting than adults, shares his/her toys, takes turns with assistance, shows affection for younger siblings; begins to take responsibility (Appendix 2). Three-year-olds often engage in disorganized associative play with other children, but gradually move to organized cooperative play in which children work together for some aim (Biehler & Snowman, 1986). Cooperative play begins as children use turn-taking or sharing spontaneously. Three-year-olds begin dramatic play acting and imaginative play with dolls, and enjoy imaginary companions (Appendix 2). Much conversation is friendly concerning real or imaginary play activity. During play three-year-olds may talk, smile, tantalize, flirt; and boys may, also, engage in clowning and foolish antics (Appendix 2).

Though the four- to five-year-old is still home and mother oriented, s/he is developing a sense of responsibility, enjoys doing things for him/her self, plays outdoors with little supervision, likes to be trusted, and is beginning to learn to take care of their property (Appendix 2). S/he plays and interacts cooperatively in small groups of two to five children, and can be spurred on by rivalry in an activity (Appendix 2). Four-year-old children enjoy the company of each other so much that play time goes smoothly without too much adult interference. Four-year-olds display considerable social maturity in their use of social problem-solving (e.g., if two children want the same toy they may suggest turn-taking) (Appendix 2). They spend considerable time in their play group involved in imaginative cooperative play (e.g., playing house, tea parties). Frequently, they can even organize a cooperative play activity by themselves without adult help or suggestions (Appendix 2). The four-year-old's dramatic play is closer to reality than before, and s/he loves to dress up.

The typical five-year-old wants to do what is expected, respects reasonable authority, shows willingness to play with most children in their class. S/he is not an exceptionally social individual, but may play reasonably well with older siblings and tends to be extremely kind and protective to those who are younger. Five-year-olds engage with others in cooperative and fair play, choose their own friends, and often have one or two best friends of the same sex (Appendix 2). An awareness of sex roles begins, and they are willing to play with other children in a role assignment. Five-year-olds tend to play better in a team of two rather than a group of three or more children. Cognitively, the five-year-old has progressed to a stage where s/he can play games with rules, competitive games, and simple table games; though in free play, due to short attention span, they play in small loosely organized groups and change play frequently (Appendix 2).

Preschool Emotional Development

"The development of the emotional behavior in the growing infant and child from early infancy on reveals that ages of emotional equilibrium tend to alternate with ages of disequilibrium" (Ames & Ilg, 1976a, 15). Developmental equilibrium appears to be characterized by emotional calmness, acceptance of self, and enhanced abilities in motor, verbal, and cognitive abilities (Ames & Ilg, 1976a). Periods of disequilibrium are characterized by less mature behavior such as whining and temper tantrums; regression in language, physical, and cognitive skills. These periods of disintegration are predictable occurrences prior to a growth spurt and result primarily from changes within the child rather than environmental changes (Brazelton, 1990).

Emotionally, the typical two-year-old tends to be gentle, friendly, affectionate, and happy much of the time, enjoying the security of routines. S/he is calm, sure, balanced, lovable, enthusiastic, appreciative, and expresses affection warmly (Appendix 2). The two-and-a-half-year-old, however, is in the "terrible twos." S/he seems to be on an emotional roller coaster, frequently tense, rigid, and explosive (Appendix 2). Characteristic of the two-and-a-half-year-old is their demand for sameness, for ritualism and routine, everything in the house has its place, tasks or activities should always be carried out in the same way, in the same order, and at the same time (Appendix 2). They seem to be easily frustrated and will scream and temper tantrum for little apparent reason (Appendix 2).

Three-year-olds are sensitive to praise, enjoy friendly humor, conform easily, appear calm and collected, and seem emotionally in control having developed some ability to tolerate frustration (Appendix 2). S/he interprets the emotions of others from facial expressions and vocal intonation (Appendix 2). Three-year-olds are beginning to be interested in others' feelings and to empathize. As the pendulum swings, the three-and-a-half-year-old child moves into a period of disequilibrium becoming emotionally and physically insecure as evidenced by stuttering, stumbling, thumb sucking, and nail biting. The three-and-a-half-year-old is characterized by refusing to obey and rebelling at dressing, eating, going to bed, and other routine activities. The child's behavior is marked by inconsistency and emotional extremes ranging from shy withdrawn behavior one minute to overbold behavior the next (Appendix 2).

Emotionally, the secure behavior of the four-year-old disintegrates as the child moves toward four-and-a-half-years old in which his behavior becomes exaggerated by extremes—extreme loves and extreme hates (Appendix 2). S/he tends to be extremely out-of-bounds. S/he laughs almost too hilariously when things please him/her, howls and cries more than too loudly when things go wrong. It is the verbally out-of-bounds expressions that are most conspicuous (Appendix 2).

Five is considered a "golden age" because they enjoy life and look consistently on its sunny side (Appendix 2). Five is an age of emotional equilibrium in which the child feels secure, protects herself from overstimulation, reduces frustration by being self-limiting, likes life the way it is, and is satisfied with herself (Appendix 2). By age five-and-a-half years the emotional smoothness has been replaced by a child who quarrels frequently, expresses emotions freely and openly, engages frequently in anger outbursts, shows jealousy of classmates, and appears ready to disobey (Appendix 2). The five-and-a-half-year-old is characteristically hesitant, dawdling, indecisive, or at the opposite extreme, overdemanding and explosive; and vacillates from one emotional extreme to another (Appendix 2).

Preschool Self-Concept Development

"Consciousness of self is among the many characteristics said to distinguish human beings from other species and two-year-olds from younger children" (Cole & Cole, 1989, 238). This new sense of self-consciousness is manifested in the following: "(1) A growing sensitivity to adult standards, (2) Concern about living up to those standards, (3) A new ability to set one's own goals and standards, (4) Self-reference in language, (5) Immediate recognition of one's image in a mirror" (Cole & Cole, 1989, 241).

By three, many children seem to be developing a rather good self-concept and seem to have a solid set of feelings about themselves (Appendix 2). The four-year-old exhibits a definite personality, and shows concern and empathy for others, begins to evaluate the behavior of other children, but is unable to critically observe and evaluate herself (Harter, 1988).

Through social interactions the preschool-aged child continues to develop the self-concept. The young child cannot differentiate the real from the ideal self-image as s/he does not have the cognitive ability to test or logically determine if the judgments are realistic (Harter, 1988). The child typically evaluates the self as more skillful than does the teacher because he is unable to evaluate his/her competence. In general, the preschool-aged child inflates their ability and is very positive about the things that s/he can do.

MIDDLE CHILDHOOD DEVELOPMENT

Middle childhood spans the elementary school years including the primary grade years (grades 1–3), and the intermediate grade years (grades 4–6). During this period, ages 6–12, the child makes significant growth in cognitive, physical, communicative, social, and emotional abilities. Social and emotional development is demonstrated through increased problem-solving and perspective-taking abilities, increased responsibility for self-control, and the development of social relationships and moral understandings.

Primary Grade Social/Emotional Development

Adults expect primary grade children, ages 6–8 years, to assume some responsibility for behaving themselves in a variety of situations (solitary, instructional, with peers) (Cole & Cole, 1989). The ability to assume increased responsibility for their own behavior stems from cognitive advances that result in more logical thinking, greater attention to task, and the ability to keep track of more than one aspect of a situation at a time (Cole & Cole, 1989).

Social and Emotional Development

Six-Year-Old. Socially, family relationships cause much difficulty for the six-year-old who is competitive, combative, and quarrelsome with older siblings and bossy with younger siblings (Appendix 3). The six-year-old is at his/her best and worst with the primary caregivers, especially mother, as the child tries to be more independent. The "typical six-year-old is a paradoxical little person, and bipolarity is the name of his game. Whatever he does, he does the opposite just as readily" (Ames & Ilg, 1979, 1). Emotionally, the six-year-old is very trying for himself and for others wanting both of any two opposites, and in finding it difficult to make-up or change his mind (Appendix 3). The six-year-old is demanding and difficult, the center of his own universe, and wants to be first and best in everything; so tantrums, argues, and is oppositional to get his own way (Appendix 3). S/he is insecure, sensitive to criticism or ridicule, and finds adjusting to failure very difficult.

The six-and-a-half-year-old is delightful, amusing with a wonderful sense of humor, lively intellectually, and loves to play guessing games (Appendix 3). The six-and-a-half-year-old shows boundless enthusiasm for any prospect or proposal; loves physical and intellectual exploration; loves new places, new ideas, new bits of information, and his own new accomplishments (Ames & Ilg, 1979). "When happy, he not only smiles and laughs, he fairly dances with joy. His enthusiasm is contagious" (Ames & Ilg, 1979, 8).

Seven-Year-Old. The seven-year-old usually gets along well with mother, but may engage in a battle of wills with her (Appendix 3). Seven is anxious to be accepted by the peer group and plays more harmoniously than at age six usually preferring to withdraw than to fight (Appendix 3). The seven-year-old is better with much older and much younger siblings, than those nearer his own age. At this age boys generally begin to discriminate against girls. The seven-year-old, however, is highly sociable and causes little trouble in organized social situations (Appendix 3).

Seven is an age of emotional withdrawal in which the child is often moody, morose, and melancholy feeling that people do not like him and are mean, especially teachers (Appendix 3). Fairness is very important to the seven-year-old who feels that his "parents like his brothers and sisters better than they like him and that they do more for others in the family than they do for him" (Ames & Haber, 1985, 5). Seven is extremely self-absorbed, easily disappointed, and in addition to having many worries and fears, feels that s/he has "all the bad luck" (Appendix 2). The seven-year-old child is making emotional strides in gaining control of his/her temper, in becoming sensitive to friends' attitudes, in becoming more reasonable and willing to listen to someone else's side of the story.

The typical Seven is developing ethical standards and wants to do things right (Appendix 3).

Eight-Year-Old. Eight is an age of equilibrium—emotional calmness, acceptance of self, gentle, affectionate, and happy much of the time (Appendix 3). Socially Eights are somewhat more selective in their choice of friends, and may have a permanent best friend and a semipermanent enemy (Biehler & Hudson, 1986). They like organized games in small groups, but may become overly concerned with the rules of the game or get carried away with team spirit. The eight-year-old's literal interpretation of game rules as edicts handed down by authority may cause him/her to be a tattletale in an effort to get others to follow the rules (Appendix 3). Eight-year-olds use language as their medium of social interaction (Kegan, 1985), and frequently use words during quarrels more often than physical aggression (Biehler & Hudson, 1986).

Emotionally, the eight-year-old is sensitive to criticism and ridicule, and may have difficulty adjusting to failure (Appendix 3). Since primary grade students are frequently forced to participate in sedentary pursuits, energy is often released in the form of nervous habits (e.g., pencil chewing, fingernail biting, hair twirling, and general fidgeting) (Biehler & Hudson, 1986). Most primary grade children are eager to please their teacher, and are becoming sensitive to the feelings of others. About age eight, children have developed the idea that each person has a private, subjective self that is not always easily read from behavior (Cole & Cole, 1989).

Primary Grade Social Interactions

"School-age children live in at least three separate worlds, each with its own rules and styles of behavior: the family, the school, and the peer group" (Skolnick, 1986, 414).

Family Interactions. Socialization of the child is of primary importance to the family as the child learns to interact with adults and children of all ages. During middle childhood years, children learn about their parents' social position in the community. They learn about social system hierarchies and the types of occupations, levels of income, styles of dress and speech, and acceptable behaviors of each hierarchial level. They learn about the social system level in which they are expected to function.

Children's new, more independent status during middle childhood influences the quality of their relationships with their parents. Parents rely on their children's use of higher level cognitive skills and their "greater understanding of the consequences of their actions and on their desire to comply with adult standards" (Cole & Cole, 1989, 478). As children's level of logical reasoning increases parents use indirect socialization techniques such as discussion and explanation rather than using physical force such as spanking and physical restraint to influence their children's behavior (Cole & Cole, 1989).

Peer Interactions. Friendship and peer relations make valuable contributions to a child's social and emotional development. "Unlike adult-child relationships, peers relate to one another on a reciprocal, egalitarian basis. This kind of interaction helps to lay the groundwork for adult relationships" (Skolnick, 1986, 423).

During the primary grades friendships become increasingly important and children's understanding of friendship becomes increasingly complex (Berger, 1986). The formation and maintenance of peer relationships involves facility with a number of high-level abilities including the following: (1) self-knowledge, (2) perspective-taking ability, (3) friendship expectations, (4) knowledge of appropriate behavior in various social situations, (5) social evaluation—ability to evaluate one's own and others' behaviors, (6) knowledge of peer group norms, and (7) social problem-solving (Oden, 1988). These factors in turn facilitate the development of the self-concept. Research has indicated that primary school-aged children value kindness, sharing, and helping as characteristics of their best friends (Youniss, 1978).

Self-Concept of the Primary Grade Student

During middle childhood when children spend more time among their peers, the sense of self they acquired in their families no longer suffices and they must learn to reconcile their old identities with the new ones they begin to form (Cole & Cole, 1989). A number of social-cognition abilities developing within the primary grade student effect this self-concept reconstruction including self-knowledge, perspective-taking, and social evaluation.

Self-Knowledge. Self-descriptions begin to include trait labels such as popular, helpful, smart, and references to athletic ability and physical attractiveness. Self-description at this stage uses social comparison as a means of determining the competence or adequacy of the self as the child combines a number of specific behaviors into a more generalized concept about the self (Harter, 1988). A significant amount of evidence suggests that by the time children are about 6 or 7 years old, they have formed a stable concept of their own identity as male or female (Cole & Cole, 1989).

Perspective-Taking Ability. During middle childhood children develop social cognition which involves role-taking, the ability to see things from another person's point of view; personality perception, the child's conceptions of other people; and moral judgment, the understanding of society's rules and conventions (Skolnick, 1986). During middle childhood, children become increasingly skilled at the metacognitive aspects of social cognition, the ability to think about what another person is thinking and anticipate their behavior (Skolnick, 1986). Thus, there appears to be a reciprocal relationship between the development of perspective-taking ability, and social and cognitive development.

Social Evaluation. Social evaluation, the ability to observe, evaluate, and criticize the self is developmental in nature, progressing through a series of stages that ultimately enables children to compare their self to their peer group. The first stage leading to self-evaluation begins at age 5 years when the child can observe other children and evaluate their behavior, but is unable to recognize that other children are also observing and evaluating them (Harter, 1985). During the second stage, the child begins to understand that other children are evaluating him/her, but s/he cannot determine the accuracy of their perceptions because s/he cannot yet critically observe the self (Harter, 1985). Harter's (1985) third stage in the development of social evaluation emerges around the age of 8 years, when children begin to incorporate the observations of others into their own self-perceptions, and directly evaluate themselves.

As children become interested in evaluating their own performance based on the standards others have for them, they internalize these expectations into self-standards and develop the capacity for self-criticism (Harter, 1985). "The child can now simultaneously observe both self and others, and this ability to engage in social comparison in cognitive competence, social competence, and physical competence provides a major index of the self's adequacy" (Harter, 1988, 61). Prior to age 8 years, children are not capable of constructing a global concept of themselves as a person that can be evaluated in terms of overall worth (Harter, 1985), thus, a major achievement during the primary grade years is to begin to develop a global self-worth or global self-concept.

Intermediate Grade Social/Emotional Development

Later Middle Childhood occurs during the intermediate grades (4th–6th) or ages 9–12 years. Social and emotional developmental gains are evident in increased self-knowledge, social evaluation and comparison, perspective-taking abilities, and social problem-solving abilities. During later middle childhood, as the child's abilities in cognitive integration expand, it becomes increasingly difficult to discuss and/or analyze social, emotional, and self-concept development as separate entities.

Intermediate Grade Social Skills

During the intermediate grade years social and emotional development is concerned with acquiring new levels of self-knowledge, awareness of one's own moral beliefs, increased abilities in perspective-taking, utilizing social problem-solving, understanding social evaluation and comparison especially in relationship to peer group norms.

Social Perspective-Taking. Intermediate grade children develop increasingly sophisticated social-cognitive and metacognitive skills which allow them to infer characteristics of others and to anticipate how these characteristics will affect the person's behavior (Appendix 4). This ability to make social inferences about others and their reactions enables the child to make modifications in their own behavior.

The intermediate grade child becomes able to simultaneously observe his/her self and others, and to engage in social comparison (Appendix 4). This ability to engage in social comparison provides awareness that others have similarities and differences to themselves and assists them in adjusting their behavior to interact appropriately with others (Berger, 1986). Social comparison enables the child to check on his/her beliefs or assumptions about another's perspective through behavioral or conversational strategies (Cole & Cole, 1989). This increased ability of an intermediate grade child to evaluate their self and to evaluate their relationships appears to increase his/her ability to understand other persons through social perspective-taking.

The process of making social inferences and social comparisons contributes to the child's understanding about the reciprocal nature of social interactions (Appendix 4). Intermediate grade youngsters begin to understand reciprocity in a relationship, and see a relationship between their treatment of peers and the resultant reactions of peers. Thus, through social inferences, social comparison, social evaluation, and interpersonal development, intermediate grade children develop an awareness of the many social roles that an individual may play (Jones, 1992).

Social Regulation/Moral Development. The intermediate grade child understands society's expectations to conform simultaneously to several sets of rules regarding moral codes and behaviors (Appendix 4). They understand basic principles of justice and welfare; social norms (e.g., school rules, forms of address, appropriate behavior for males and females, dress codes, etiquette); moral rules (e.g., society's regulations against doing physical or psychological harm to others, rules of fairness and rights of others, and the expectancy to engage in prosocial behaviors) (Turiel et al., 1987).

The intermediate grade child is becoming increasingly more capable of regulating his/her own behavior according to agreed-upon social rules and/or rule-governed play (Appendix 4). The intermediate grade child with a basic understanding of social and moral rules learns social regulation through indirect socialization techniques such as discussion and explanation, and becomes increasingly aware of the nuances of written and unwritten rules and codes of conduct (Appendix 4). This growing understanding of the self and others in social interactions results in an increased ability to get along with people, and to understand that appropriate behavior differs in various social settings (Appendix 4).

Social Problem-Solving. Continued development in the area of social problem-solving skills during later middle childhood requires knowledge of basic social and moral rules of society, perspective-taking abilities to note changes in others' reactions that signal a breach in social behavior, and higher-level cognitive thinking abilities (Appendix 4). The child must have knowledge of his/her social self through social comparison and knowledge of the social self of others to engage in complex social problem-solving. S/he must become sensitive not only to social problems but, also, to social consequences usually gained through social comparison and perspective-taking (Appendix 4). Metacognitive skills enable an individual to monitor and analyze their social problem-solving situations and determine a course of action (goal-setting). Older middle childhood youth become increasingly sophisticated in the social problem-solving process and practice it in their peer/adult relationships.

Intermediate Grade Social Interactions

Important tasks during later middle childhood involve re-establishing the self-concept in relation to peers rather than family, and an emerging emotional independence from parents and growing dependence on peers (Appendix 4). The accomplishment of this task is possible due to cognitive, social, and emotional advances that enable youth to understand society's moral and social rules; to use social skills such as social perspective-taking, social comparison and evaluation, and social problem-solving.

Peer Relationships. "A universal social contribution to the changes that occur in middle childhood is the rise of the peer group as a major context for development" (Cole & Cole, 1989, 510). The peer group typically specifies codes of behavior which frequently demand independence from adults, a special vocabulary, dress code, appropriate things to do and places to go, "in" clubs and organizations. From a developmental perspective, peer clubs or gangs serve many functions including building self-esteem, sharpening social skills, and teaching social cooperation (Berger, 1986). In addition to learning the arts of social interaction and making friends, there is evidence that children learn from their peers how to cope with aggression and sex (Skolnick, 1986). The peer group is important because, for the first time, children are in the position of achieving their status within a group of those with relatively equal power and status without the intervention of adults (Cole & Cole, 1989).

Family Relationships. Parental standards for their children's behavior continues to increase throughout middle childhood. Parents expect children to show increased ability to function according to moral rules and society's rules, and family rules and regulations without constant adult monitoring. They use coregulation (Maccoby, 1980) techniques to share the responsibility for controlling their children with the children themselves. Parents expect children to become dependable and reliable, to show initiative in problem-solving by viewing different aspects of a problem or weighing different points of view simultaneously, and in general to display skills valuable in citizenship and adulthood.

During middle childhood, boys and girls, even when both parents work outside the home, begin turning to father more than mother when they need information about things outside the home. Mother continues to maintain influence in the home, in their social and club activities, and in children's school and church activities, especially as a sponsor and provider of "refreshments." Relationships with grandparents continue to be reciprocally warm and admiring as they provide noncontingent positive regard, which is extremely important in self-concept development. Sibling relationships tend to be better with siblings much older or younger than near the same age. Disagreements tend to be settled verbally rather than physically, and often without parental intervention.

Intermediate Grade Emotional Abilities

Self-Evaluation. Later middle childhood is characterized by an increased understanding of the self and development of a self-theory or self-definition (Appendix 4). This new self-understanding occurs in part because new cognitive advances enhance the child's ability to classify, organize, and place concepts in hierarchial sequence. Using these abilities the child can organize the observable behaviors of the self into trait labels, and consider trait stability and consistency of the attributes that define the self (Appendix 4). For example, a fifth grade student may indicate that she's been good at reading since first grade, has always had problems in math, and anticipates this pattern to continue in the future. Thus, the child is able to compare herself in the present with herself in the past and observe the continuity of the self.

Intermediate grade children have evaluated their competence in at least three areas—social competence, cognitive competence, and physical competence (Harter, 1988). Feelings of competence appear to be closely related to the child's feelings of control, feelings of responsibility for successes, personal initiative, feelings of self-worth, and understanding of what controls successes as opposed to failures. The child with overall positive self-worth feels competent in areas of importance to significant others. The child with feelings of low self-worth does not perceive positive regard from significant others regarding their abilities (Harter, 1988). Thus, during the intermediate grades, youth use their higher cognitive skills in self-evaluation to determine competence and create global evaluations of self worth.

During later middle childhood, children make strides in understanding their emotional characteristics which leads to an increased ability to control their emotions and related behaviors, particularly anger. While young children may experience a full range of emotional expressions, they are unable to consistently control their responses and they do not see self-control as a characteristic of the self (Harter, 1985). The emergence of self-control as an evaluation criteria indicates higher-level cognitive functioning. The ability to express emotions directed toward the self in terms of self-shame for not controlling one's behaviors or self-pride for athletic skill emerge during middle childhood.

Self-Concept of Intermediate Grade Children

Children develop complex theories about themselves and their behavior based on their past experiences, the opinions of others, and assumptions about themselves. Relationships to others, particularly peers and close friends, are internalized and become salient dimensions of the self (Rosenberg, 1979). The development of children's conceptions of themselves parallel the development of the ways they conceive of other people (Skolnick, 1986). Thus, social perspective-taking, social comparison, and social evaluation play an important role in redefining the self-theory in late middle childhood.

Numerous researchers have indicated that the self-concept of the intermediate grade child includes the following competence domains: (1) intellectual or cognitive skills, (2) achievement or academic skills, (3) physical or athletic competence, (4) social competence in peer relationships, (5) moral beliefs and/or interpersonal social skills (Appendix 4). The self-concept or overall feelings of self-worth emerge as the child uses social perspective-taking and social comparison to determine his/her adequacy in each area in comparison to others and in comparison to their performance in each of the other domains. Generally, we conceive that the child may concurrently hold both negative and positive conceptions of self in various domains or areas. The degree of importance to the child will determine the degree to which success or failure affects one's overall self-evaluation.

By late middle childhood, the child has become efficient in using social perspective-taking, social competence, self-comparison/self-evaluation, self-regulation, and problem-solving strategies (Appendix 4). S/he organized various trait labels into categories of competence internalizing the values of significant others and emerging with a much better defined self-concept. As children grow older, the self is increasingly described as a private, unique world of thought and experience (Skolnick, 1986).

ADOLESCENT SOCIAL/EMOTIONAL DEVELOPMENT

The transition from middle childhood to adolescence is marked by a number of significant biological and cognitive changes. Cognitive changes in the adolescent include the acquisition of abstract thought processes, logical reasoning, hypothesizing, and metacognitive thinking skills. These higher-level cognitive abilities provide the adolescent the ability to engage in complex perspective-taking in fundamental issues such as social relations, morality, politics, and religion (Jones, 1992). The final task of adolescence is to complete the integration of the developmental changes (biological, social, psychological, cognitive) into a well-adjusted young adult.

Developmental Tasks of Adolescents

Mature Socially and Physically

The average adolescent understands and accepts the biological changes playing havoc with their bodies forcing the development of a new adult physical self-image. Social maturation requires that adolescents understand the parameters of maleness and femaleness, become cognizant of adult responsibilities associated with their sexuality, and define their future goals in regard to work, marriage, and parenthood.

The focus of psychosocial development in adolescence is identity vs. identity confusion (Erikson, 1968). Adolescents establish their identity through reconciling their biological and self-image changes with social expectations of adults and peers, with their own individual preferences, and with developmental patterns (Appendix 5). Thus, the adolescent resolves identity and identity confusion, and defines himself/herself.

Function as a Responsible Citizen

Society demands that adolescents begin functioning as responsible citizens through: (1) Developing moral standards, (2) Fulfilling duties to one's conscience and to society's demands, (3) Assuming responsibility for one's own beliefs, commitments, and attitudes, (4) Learning adult autonomy and responsibility, and (5) Getting a job or doing volunteer work (Appendix 5). Most individuals reach the conventional level of moral development during adolescence (Kohlberg, 1976), when they are able to perceive problems from the viewpoints of others and to identify with society at large. The conventional level of moral development requires adolescents to evaluate, discriminate, and refine their beliefs and to incorporate some of the expectations of society into their own moral code. Adolescents must for the first time take responsibility for their commitments, life-style, beliefs, and attitudes (Appendix 5).

Adolescents learn skills and develop abilities which will enable them to become autonomous and responsible adults, accepting the responsibility for themselves socially, politically, and economically (Appendix 5). Social autonomy refers to being able to conduct oneself in socially prescribed ways, able to vary conduct as to be acceptable in the various settings in which they wish to participate. Political autonomy requires a knowledge of our political system, keeping currently informed on issues, and an ability to make decisions regarding the common good when voting in elections. Many youth begin development toward economic autonomy through part-time employment.

Making Career/Vocational Choices

A primary task of adolescence is to select a career or vocation to pursue. The adolescent needs to be cognizant of the numerous social factors which impact this decision including the following: (1) socio-economic status of the family, (2) the education level of the parents, (3) the school-community environment, (4) the degree of the adolescent's status seeking among peers, (5) the adolescent's own personal aptitude and achievement, and (6) the adolescent's desire for economic indepen-dence (Jones, 1992).

Though parental socio-economic status and life-style play an impor-tant part in the adolescent's career decision, the adolescent's own charac-teristics significantly influence any decision. Aptitude particularly average and low serves to eliminate many occupational choices from considera-tion due to inability to attain the academic requirements. The student's personal achievement level in terms of grades and skills mastered, attitude, courses taken, study habits, organizational skills, willingness to study, concern for grades, acceptance of delayed gratification, and the educa-tional level to which s/he is willing to strive all actively influence the career/vocational choice (Jones, 1992). Additionally, if the student wishes to be an autonomous adult with economic independence immediately or within a year after high school they greatly narrow their career/job possibilities (Appendix 5). Students who are willing to delay adult auton-omy and economic independence usually pursue careers which require more formal education.

Social Interactions: Peer Group and Friendships

School is the major arena in which adolescents earn status. School provides the setting in which adolescents practice casual social interac-tions and complex social interrelationships. Primary social interactions during adolescence center around the peer group, and the more intimate friendship group. Good peer relationships appear to be necessary for normal social development in adolescence. The peer group becomes the general source of rules of appropriate behavior and the pressure to conform to a certain peer group (e.g., jocks, trendies, nerds, etc.) becomes very strong (Jones, 1992). In order to function in a peer group, adolescents must adopt that subculture's standards and moral values.

Peer groups are comprised of voluntary memberships. The element of choice in peer group membership reflects the increased control adolescents have in choosing the settings in which they find themselves, the people with whom they associate, and the things they do (Appendix 5). Developing one's own code of behavior is a move toward adult independence (Biehler & Snowman, 1986).

Friendships become increasingly important during adolescence as friends help each other confront and make sense of uncertain and often anxiety provoking situations. Friendships serve a number of important functions including the companionship of a familiar partner, source of interesting information, physical support and assistance, ego support in terms of encouragement, social comparison, and an intimate trusting relationship (Santrock, 1990). Adolescents tend to form friendships with others from the same socio-economic background, and friends and dates are likely to share similar intelligence, attitudes, behaviors, life-styles, and values (Appendix 5). "Adolescents are motivated to form close relationships with others who are similar to them because similarity provides consensual validation of the adolescent's own attitudes and behaviors" (Santrock, 1990, 275).

In the long run, the adolescent's success in social development, in peer group social situations, and in friendship-making influence mate selection, occupational choice, sense of self, and the quality of adult social life (Manaster, 1989). For numerous adolescents in industrialized societies who continue their education beyond high school, the period of adolescence is extended another four or five years before reaching adult status and autonomy.

Desatellization from Home

A major task of adolescence is desatellization from home or gradual weaning from physical, emotional, and psychological dependence on parents (Appendix 5). Adolescents must learn to provide their physical needs by learning to cook, clean, launder; and financially providing their needs of food, shelter, and transportation. Psychologically and emotionally, adolescents begin to rely on their peers for support regarding personal and career decisions.

The desatellization process is more successful for adolescents who have been provided achievement and independence training. Achievement involves learning strategies of approaching a task, regrouping for secondary attempts, courage to attempt difficult tasks, and learning problem-solving techniques. Independence skills are predicated upon a good self-concept, confidence in ability to perform required tasks, and acceptance of responsibility.

A prerequisite to desatellization is the adolescent's knowledge that s/he possesses noncontingent positive regard or acceptance as valued regardless of behavior, attitudes, and appearance, from teachers and parents (Appendix 5). Noncontingent positive regard contributes to the development of a positive self-concept, and confidence in ability to achieve and to be independent.

Adolescent Self-Concept

For the adolescent, self-concept development involves constructing a self-portrait which integrates the different characteristics of the self. This process includes realistically evaluating his/her intellectual competence, physical competence, physical attractiveness, social competence, leadership abilities, moral beliefs, and sense of humor (Appendix 5). The adolescent uses the perspective of a "universal person" to recognize that the self is known in different ways by different people, to view the self as varying across situations and time, and to integrate conflicting qualities in the self (Leahy & Shirk, 1985). The self-concept of the adolescent includes a view of self as an intimate, sensitive, and spontaneous being (Smollar & Youniss, 1985).

For the adolescent, the self-concept now functions as a standard for evaluating and predicting performance socially, objectively, personally; and functions to limit performance for the purpose of maintaining and enhancing itself (Manaster, 1986). "Compared to younger children, early adolescents are highly self-conscious and have uncertain, shaky images of themselves. They have lower overall self-esteem, and lesser opinions of themselves with regard to certain qualities they value" (Skolnick, 1986, 463). Adolescents are able to maintain a reasonably positive self-image by identifying positive attributes as core constructs in their self-portrait and considering negative attributes or behaviors as foreign to their true self (Harter, 1986).

IMPACT ON ACHIEVEMENT

Analyses of research studies in psychiatry and psychology indicate essentially that the student's ability to utilize the power to learn is determined by their self-concept or their perception of their world including personal goals, purposes, and values (Jones, 1992). Research evidence clearly indicates a persistent and significant relationship between the self-concept and academic achievement (Purkey, 1970). Self-concept of academic ability seems to be associated with academic achievement at each grade level. Teachers have long noted that children with a positive self-concept achieve better and perform the role of student better than a child with a negative self-concept. Students with negative self-concepts often become underachievers in school, and may even become so frustrated and depressed that they drop out of school cognitively and emotionally even if they physically attend school.

Among the self-concepts it appears that the academic self-concept composed of a classroom self-concept, an ability self-concept, and an achievement self-concept have the greatest impact on a child's academic achievement (Song & Hattie, 1984). In examining the self-concept factors of academic ability and academic achievement, it is necessary to consider the sense of personal control the child feels over his/her learning. "A considerable body of research indicates that those children who possess an awareness that they must be responsible for their own learning by taking an active role in that process are the most successful students" (Reid, 1988, 41).

The child's sense of personal control is developmental and highly related to cognitive advances, and is often determined by assessing his/her abilities and perspectives in metacognition, motivation, and attribution. Metacognition refers to both the knowledge about cognition and the regulation of cognition (Reid, 1988). "In school situations, metacognitive awareness refers to a pupil's knowledge of tasks assigned, the solutions to be achieved, the ways to achieve it, and the cognitive strengths and weaknesses" (Mann & Sabatino, 1985, 222). A number of self-control factors found in successful students includes possession of metacognitive skills or the ability to self-plan, self-organize, and self-monitor during the learning process.

"The relationship between self-concept, motivation, and achievement has long been an integral part of humanistic and open education programs" (Biehler & Snowman, 1986, 519). "Motivation is the inner force that moves a person to take action toward a specific end" (Levine, 1989, 210). The self-knowledge aspect of motivation serves as a significant regulator of on-going behavior and provides a set of interpretative frameworks for making sense of past behavior and means-ends patterns for new behavior (Cantor et al., 1986). Motivation and metacognition interact to assist the student in evaluating their own behavior in numerous situations through perspective-taking and social comparisons, and in providing patterns of behavior to allow them to function in socially appropriate ways.

In school settings attributions are children's explanations and/or inferences about the causes of their academic, behavioral, or social performances and their evaluations (Reid, 1988). Attributions are formed over time and result from experiences within learning contexts and represent students' ideas about their control over their learning as well as achievement (Reid, 1988). In school settings children tend to attribute their successes or failures to a number of circumstances. Successful students usually attribute success to their effort and ability, while underachieving students attribute success to luck. Successful students attribute their failures to lack of effort and renew their efforts to master the task, while unsuccessful students generally attribute their failure to bad luck or task difficulty. Success due to internal causes such as ability and effort produces pride and positive self-esteem. Failure due to low ability results in humiliation, and failure due to lack of effort produces guilt.

Since school achievement is a primary means by which a child validates himself, a child who is achieving successfully tends to have a positive self-concept and achievement motivation. Successful students have learned to interpret success as evidence of ability. In the classroom achievers establish their own goals, use good study and organizational skills, show a sense of personal control, possess a desire to achieve, and understand their own learning style.

Unsuccessful student's negative academic self-concept is validated by a negative classroom self-concept, negative ability self-concept, and a negative achievement self-concept. The underachiever appears to be threatened on all sides experiencing difficulty in adult and peer relationships and lacking in the academic and social skills for success in the classroom. These serve as constant reinforcement to his already negative self-concept. Underachievers experience enormous anxiety and frustration within the classroom and about the tasks required. These emotional feelings coupled with academic failure reinforce that he is inadequate and inferior, and may result in self-hatred.

SUMMARY

Social and emotional development begin in infancy and continue throughout a lifetime. Most children follow similar social and emotional developmental patterns in their social interactions with adults and children, and in self-concept development. The young child's bonding with parents provides their first social interactions which are responsive in nature. During preschool years children learn to cooperate, take turns, share, and use social problem-solving and social communication, as s/he plays and socially interacts with peers and adults.

Socially during middle childhood, the child learns to function in three separate worlds — the family, the school, and the peer group — each with its own rules and styles of behavior. By the end of middle childhood, children understand society's moral rules, social conventions, various peer group norms; and use social-cognition, social problem-solving, social inferences. Major social interactions during adolescence center around peers and friends. Peer groups serve as a socializing agent and friends provide the support needed during this period of self-concept building. Adolescents tend to form friendships with others from the same socio-economic backgrounds.

The emotional development of children from infancy through adolescence appears to be characterized by alternating periods of equilibrium (friendly, affectionate, happy periods), and disequilibrium (emotional turmoil). Often, the early months of any age are marked by calmness, while the later months of an age may evidence explosive behavior marked by insecurity and low frustration tolerance. By the time the average child has reached two years of age, s/he has an almost complete store of emotional expressions including fear, anger, teasing, enjoyment, persuasion, protest, guilt, anxiety, and affection. During early and middle childhood and adolescence, the child gradually gains self-control over these emotional expressions.

The development of the self-concept begins in infancy with self-awareness and developing a body image. By age 4 years, the child exhibits a definite personality and shows concern and empathy for others. The major achievement during the primary grades is to develop a global self-concept. By late middle childhood, the child has become efficient in using social perspective-taking, social competence, self-evaluation, self-regulation, and social problem-solving. Self-concept development during adolescence involves constructing a self-portrait in which the different characteristics of the self are integrated. This process includes realistically evaluating his/her intellectual competence, physical competence, physical attractiveness, social competence, leadership abilities, moral beliefs, and sense of humor. The adolescent develops the ability to use the perspective of a universal person, and to use the self-concept as a standard for evaluating and predicting performance and enhancing itself.

Chapter Two

VISION IMPAIRED STUDENTS

Visually Impaired children and youth tend to remain egocentric longer, to be more socially immature, to be more self-conscious than their sighted peers (Tuttle, 1988).

Visually impaired children and youth vary considerably from each other with respect to the type of visual disorder, degree of visual limitation, and extent to which the reduced visual capacity interferes with daily functioning (Tuttle, 1988). The term visual handicap covers a wide range of children including those who have never had any visual function, those who had normal vision for some years before becoming gradually or suddenly partially or totally blind, those with handicaps in addition to the visual loss, those with selective impairment of parts of the visual field, and those with a general degradation of acuity across the visual field (Warren, 1989).

Educators often differentiate between blind and low vision students. "A blind child is totally without sight or has so little vision that she learns primarily through the other senses. Most blind children, for example, use their sense of touch to read braille" (Heward & Orlansky, 1988, 287–288). A low vision student is one who has sufficient residual vision to be able to use it as a primary learning channel, and generally learns to read print through the use of optical aids or other modifications or techniques (Tuttle, 1988).

COGNITIVE AND ACADEMIC FUNCTIONING

Visual input plays a primary role in the development of concepts, and in the provision of information for a child who is sighted to organize the outside world in his or her own thoughts (Cartwright, 1989). Blindness or limited visual abilities often cause some delay in cognitive, language, motor, and social development (Warren, 1989). The impact of the delay will depend on many factors including the degree of visual impairment, the age of onset, functional use of residual vision, the presence of other handicapping conditions such as mental retardation, and the availability and success of preschool intervention.

Cognitive Learning Problems

"Most studies indicate that blind people are not markedly lower than sighted people in IQ as measured by standard verbal intelligence tests" (Hallahan & Kauffman, 1988, 317). However, the lack of vision can hamper cognitive development because it limits the verifying, integrating, and organizing functions of vision; and the variety and number of environmental experiences.

During infancy severe visual deficits may precipitate problems in the acquisition of sensorimotor stage cognitive skills, concept labeling, reach and grasp skills, exploration, fine motor skills, and symbolic play (Jones, 1992). The automatic acquisition of sensorimotor stage cognitive skills including object concept, object constancy, object permanence, means-ends, causality, anticipation, imitation are dependent on normal visual functioning. For the severely vision impaired child, early intervention must provide an alternative means of attaining these cognitive skills. Severe visual impairment reduces the effectiveness of the joint attending-linguistic labeling activity with caregivers in learning the labels for concepts and, thus, may also delay language acquisition. "If formulation of the initial object concept is delayed, acquisition of other concepts such as object permanence, causality, and spatial relationships will also be delayed as will acquisition of higher-order skills such as classification and conservation" (Sacks et al., 1990, 414). "Many studies have found that severely visually handicapped children show developmental lags in the acquisition of more mature conservation concepts" (Warren, 1989, 162).

"There are clearly areas of cognitive development in which visually handicapped children lag developmentally behind sighted children"

(Warren, 1989, 162). Children who are totally blind may never grasp such concepts as color; and may experience difficulty in acquiring concepts of spatial distance and relationships (Sacks et al., 1990). Research suggests that when vision is lacking much of the information needed for spatial organization is reduced, but it can be gained through other senses (Millar, 1981). Visually impaired children are more likely to do poorly on tasks requiring abstract thinking and are more likely to deal with their environment in concrete terms than nonhandicapped students (Stephens & Grube, 1982).

"The more severe the visual impairment is, the less the child can rely on the accuracy and efficiency of the organizational function of vision, and without appropriate intervention, the more significant are the potential lags or gaps in conceptualization" (Tuttle, 1988, 365). Children whose visual input is limited, distorted, or essentially nonexistent must rely on other sensory systems to provide information to construct ideas of their environment and activities within it. The range and variety of the experiences of blind students may be quite limited in both number and quality compared with sighted or low vision children. Therefore, early intervention is of supreme importance to visually impaired children.

Information Processing

A visual limitation by itself does not impair the brain's ability to process information, however, there is less information to process which may result in incomplete or distorted ideas about objects and events in one's environment (Tuttle, 1988). The information processing skills of severely vision impaired children may be significantly different from that of nonhandicapped children. Stimuli bombards the student continuously, however, the visually impaired child may have difficulty processing information at the very onset due to lack of attention to critical details, activities, or tasks. Once stimuli enter the information processing system, the visual stimuli may range from significantly reduced to none in number, be distorted or blurry, or in some way inaccurate or incomplete. This distorted or inaccurate information is coded and integrated with the perceptions from other sensory systems to provide a concept of the object, activity, or task. This incomplete or inaccurate information is then stored in long-term memory for future reference and use. It may be difficult for the visually impaired child to rely on distorted images or reduced visual information for learning new concepts, in recognizing previously learned concepts, and in describing characteristics of objects. Visually impaired children may experience difficulty in demonstrating their knowledge or mastery of information or activities in visual-motor tasks including fine and gross motor skills, and written language.

Hearing and touch cannot compensate for a lack of vision as auditory and tactile cues do not always provide the same stimulus as vision (Sacks et al., 1990, 41).

> Further, the information conveyed by touch and hearing is largely sequential compared to the simultaneous presentation of information possible by vision. Vision enables a child to perceive the whole of an object and subsequently its parts, noting the relationship of parts to each other and to the whole. Touch and hearing, on the other hand, require that the child examine the parts and then integrate them into a whole through mental imagery. This latter conceptualization process is much less efficient and much more susceptible to incomplete or erroneous concepts (Sacks et al., 1990, 415).

Academic Learning Problems

The visual system provides students with a continuous source of information both relevant and irrelevant to task completion. Individuals depend on vision to orient themselves, to identify people and objects, to regulate motor and social behaviors. Those individuals without vision must rely on their other senses to provide this information (Kirk & Gallagher, 1989).

Language Development

"Most authorities believe that lack of vision does not alter ability to understand and use language" (Hallahan & Kauffman, 1988, 315). "The process of acquiring speech and language is the same for sighted and visually impaired children. In general, the early vocabulary of children who are visually handicapped parallels that of sighted children in terms of age and speed of acquisition" (Sacks et al., 1990, 416). Blind children develop their mental images or concepts of objects from their unique experiences with the world, and the language they use reflects that experience and their form of mental representation (Anderson et al., 1984). Research suggests that with adequate supportive nonvisual experiences, the concepts or mental images developed by congenitally blind children are not significantly different from those acquired by sighted children (Tuttle, 1988). "Because auditory more than visual perception is the sensory modality through which we learn language, it is not surprising that studies have found blind people to be relatively unimpaired in terms of language functioning" (Hallahan & Kauffman, 1988, 315).

Though research does not indicate significant major differences in the language development of vision impaired students, some specific differences may exist in areas such as color, spatial relationships, and abstract concepts. Young children with visual impairments tend to ask many more questions and make more demands in their use of language with peers and adults than do their sighted peers (Anderson et al., 1984). Pragmatics or social conversation among visually impaired children and youth of all ages is a concern. Research suggests that the social conversation of young visually impaired children was inferior to nonhandicapped children, that the visually impaired children were unable to keep their peers' interest, and that social encounters were egocentric (Kekelis & Sacks, 1988). During adolescence social interactions and social conversation are frequently areas of considerable concern. Blind individuals may also engage in verbalism or the use of concepts for which the visually impaired individual has no first hand experience (e.g., The clouds were fluffy and white.).

Motor Skills

"During the first few months of life when children are learning head control, sitting upright and rolling, there are no significant differences in the development of visually impaired and sighted children" (Sacks et al., 1990, 414). Motor skills delays among congenitally and severely visually handicapped infants are noticeable with the onset of crawling and walking. Visual skills are important for independent locomotion providing the nonhandicapped child with information regarding the position of his/her body in space, and position in relation to other people and objects in the room; information about balance, whether the head is held upright, and where to move an arm/leg for best balance. If children do not have a reasonably verdical concept or image of their own bodies, or if they cannot maintain a suitable posture, then they will be disadvantaged in their attempts to control their bodies within the external environment and will have poor mobility (Warren, 1989).

Vision also provides the child with the motivation to learn to crawl or walk in order to explore the environment, to get a toy, to find mother. A severe vision impairment can negatively influence motor development due to lack of an opportunity for a variety of motor activities, or an inability to use imitative learning. Other factors negatively affecting motor development include low muscle tone, and poor proprioception or sensory awareness of the body's position in space (Sacks et al., 1990).

Physical fitness and motor skills are concerns for visually impaired individuals. Research indicates that many visually impaired students have poor physical fitness (Jankowski & Evans, 1981). Good physical fitness including body image and posture serves as prerequisite skills for mobility training.

Academic Achievement

Very few studies have been conducted on the academic achievement of visually impaired students as compared to sighted students because the learning conditions are not directly comparable. For vision-impaired students reading large print or Braille is a much slower process than for sighted students reading print. Few achievement tests have been normed on strictly vision impaired populations, so timed tests pose problems in determining how much extra time should be allowed for the vision impaired student to complete various subtests. The time element is of considerable concern on any activity requiring a written response or even circling the correct answer. Standardized tests requiring the student to "bubble in" the number choice requires visual skills such as tracking and comparisons that are difficult for vision impaired students and may significantly increase the time needed to complete the test.

Several generally accepted conclusions about the academic achievement of visually impaired students include the following: (1) Both partially sighted and blind children are behind their sighted peers when equated on mental age (Suppes, 1971), and (2) the academic achievement of visually impaired children is not affected as greatly as that of hearing-impaired children (Hallahan & Kauffman, 1988). Generalizations about the academic functioning of vision impaired children are difficult to make because approximately one third of all school-age children with visual impairments have at least one additional handicapping condition (Scholl, 1986). Vision impaired students who are multihandicapped, deaf, and or mentally retarded may not be able to perform traditional academics and must be assessed in functional skills and adaptive behaviors using observational assessments.

Maximum progress of visually impaired students also depends on the adaptations and compensatory strategies utilized in the mainstreamed or self-contained classrooms. "A significant educational problem for these students is visual fatigue; they must put forth a great deal of effort to distinguish the details of print" (Sacks et al., 1990, 424). A number of modifications can be used to facilitate progress of low vision students: taking frequent short breaks; mixing visual activities with auditory and motor activities; using thicker chalk on the chalkboard and thick grease pencils and pencils on acetate and paper; using low vision nonoptical aids such as yellow acetate, felt-tip markers, bold line paper, book stands, large-print books (Sacks et al., 1990).

Numerous technological devices can be used to enhance the learning of blind students such as versabraille (portable, paperless braille word processor) and speech-activated computers, viewscan (portable electronic magnifying system), optacon (optical-to-tactual-converter), Kurzweil Reading Machines, as well as taped material, tactual maps and globes, scientific aids, speech-activated hand calculators, and electronic travel aids (Sacks et al., 1990; Tuttle, 1989; Kirk & Gallagher, 1989). Thus, the academic progress of low vision and blind students depends on numerous factors that may not be comparable in assessment situations due to the unique circumstances, visual condition, and visual aids available and utilized by each student. However, "Braille reading is much slower than regular reading, which affects the academic output of students with profound visual impairments" (Kirk & Gallagher, 1989, 392).

SOCIAL AND EMOTIONAL FUNCTIONING

The social development of persons who are blind and visually impaired does not always parallel that of sighted individuals because social learning is highly dependent on visual modeling and imitation (Sacks et al., 1990). Wide differences in personality characteristics can be observed among children who are both low vision and blind, just as in the sighted population (Cartwright et al., 1989).

Social and Emotional Problems

"There are no personal or social problems that inevitably follow from being visually handicapped. However, the restricted mobility and consequent limited experiences of children who are visually handicapped appear to cause in many a state of passivity and dependency—a learned helplessness" (Kirk & Gallagher, 1989, 359).

Early Childhood

Social Interactions with Adults. A severe vision impairment in early childhood may interfere with the child's social interactions with adults by reducing the child's responsiveness to the caregiver's signals, by reducing the likelihood of spontaneous smiling, by interfering with visual attending to adults, by delaying discrimination of familiar and unfamiliar people, and by delaying bonding which appears to be linked to eye contact. The severely vision impaired child's social interactions with adults may be significantly reduced by the child's lack of curiosity and motivation to interact and by delayed recognition of family members. The formation of enduring attachment bonds with parents is severely influenced by the absences of visual responses and cues. Blind children do not automatically initiate interactions by reaching their arms up toward mother as mother reaches down toward them which may delay bonding (Cole & Cole, 1989). Severe visual impairment interferes with imitation of simple actions of adults, makes adult manipulations through action songs confusing, retards bonding with secondary adults, and delays initiation of activities with an adult.

Blind infants cannot explore the world visually, and hence may not establish the feedback loop they need in order to develop social smiling; also, their sighted parents cannot use their baby's facial expressions to evaluate the success of social interactions and to determine the infant's emotional feelings (Cole & Cole, 1989). The intuitive solution that some parents of blind children work out is to establish communication through touching (Cole & Cole, 1989).

Interactions with Peers. A severe visual impairment in young children delays interactions with peers by reducing responsiveness to other children in the following ways: delays spontaneous smiling to other children, delays recognition and response to familiar children, delays responsiveness to another child's attempts to play, and delays acquisition of understanding the body language associated with guilt, pity, affection, sympathy. A severely visually impaired child is hampered in attempts to interact with other children because of delayed interest in another child's toy, delayed initiation of play with another child, delay in showing or offering a toy, delayed ability to reverse roles with another child, and by making games such as peek-a-boo very confusing.

Play skill development is interrupted or delayed in a young child with severe visual impairment in a number of ways. The practice stage of play may be retarded as the visually impaired child does not see the repetitive reactions of toys as s/he interacts with them. A severe visual deficit reduces the child's curiosity, exploration, and manipulation of toys. The delay in acquisition of reach and grasp skills delays learning that actions affect objects, and delays understanding of causality. Delayed fine motor skills interfere with the acquisition of all visually directed activities such as putting pegs in a pegboard or rings on a stick. A severe visual impairment delays the acquisition of symbolic play.

Interactions with the Environment. A severe visual impairment in young children will reduce or delay the child's interactions with the environment by delaying acquisition of the understanding of time relationships and eating/sleeping schedules, by delaying awareness and discrimination of sensory stimulation, by delaying differentiation of familiar and unfamiliar environments and changes in the environment, and by delaying the child's ability to anticipate familiar events from cues and respond accordingly. Interaction with the environment is delayed in showing interest in objects, in engaging in exploratory behaviors, in using objects for their specific function, in ambulation and the location of permanent objects in a room (orientation), in playing on large outdoor toys, and in the acquisition of socially appropriate behavior.

Middle Childhood and Adolescence

Blindness and low vision denote no unique psychology or distinct personality, however, some psychosocial concerns are directly linked to a visual limitation (Tuttle, 1988). Visually impaired children and youth tend to remain egocentric longer, to be socially immature, to be more self-conscious than their sighted peers (Tuttle, 1988).

Social Perspective-Taking. Visually impaired children experience difficulty in acquiring social perspective-taking skills. Nonhandicapped children gain numerous cues regarding a person's emotions from their facial expressions, gestures, stance, and other nonlinguistic body language in combination with vocal intonation and actual verbal language used in communication. The visually impaired child receives reduced to no body language cues. Thus, the visually impaired child may experience difficulty in understanding and making inferences about characteristics of people, in making social inferences or predictions about the behaviors of others. The visually impaired child may be significantly delayed in developing insight into the appropriate behavior required for specific social situations because s/he can not simultaneously observe himself and others and engage in social comparisons.

Social Regulation. Visually impaired individuals may experience difficulty with social regulation of their behavior due to the nuances of unwritten rules and codes of conduct that nonhandicapped children and youth gain through visual comparisons and perspective-taking. They experience significant difficulty learning socialization skills indirectly. "Visually impaired children and youth have more limited exposure to appropriate social role models than do their sighted peers" (Tuttle, 1988, 371). Learning about human sexuality, dating, and adult relationships are extremely difficult for visually impaired youth because they have not observed parents, friends, strangers, and television characters in various relationships and internalized expected behaviors.

Social Relationships. The visually impaired youth may experience difficulty in establishing social relationships. They experience more problems in gaining independence from parents. It is difficult for visually impaired youth to dress appropriately for their social group and for girls to have acceptable hairstyles and makeup. Learning sex-role parameters in social situations is very difficult for visually impaired youth who cannot observe the successes or social failures of peers.

Social interactions are more difficult for visually impaired than for nonhandicapped children and youth. "The visually impaired person may not be able to locate a friend in a crowded room, determine who is talking to whom in a small group, or receive complete or correct messages, because the availability of nonverbal communication is more limited" (Tuttle, 1988, 371).

Social Competence and Problem-Solving. Visually impaired youth experience more difficulty than nonhandicapped youth in acquiring social competence. "Visually impaired children and youth tend to be more passive, more dependent than their sighted peers. Far too often they are rewarded for being docile and compliant" (Tuttle, 1988, 371). Decisions are often made for visually impaired children and youth rather than their being involved in exploring alternative courses of action and making choices; thus, their problem-solving skills may be deficient. Social problem-solving abilities may be reduced by severe vision impairment because of difficulty in being sensitive to social problems and social consequences, and in developing a social strategy repertoire.

Stereotypic Behaviors. Occasionally, visually impaired children engage in self-stimulating activities, behaviors known as blindisms. These activities include rocking, finger poking, spinning about, and the imitation of strange noises (Lerner et al., 1987). Although not necessarily harmful in themselves, these mannerisms can place a visually impaired person at a social disadvantage, because such actions are conspicuous and call attention to the person as different or handicapped (Heward & Orlansky, 1988).

There are a number of speculations regarding why visually impaired students engage in these stereotypic, repetitive behaviors including sensory deprivation, social deprivation, isolation, and retreating to less mature patterns of behavior under stress (Hallahan & Kauffman, 1988). Severely and profoundly mentally retarded individuals, and normal infants also engage in stereotypic behaviors.

Feelings of Personal Control

A blind person's self-esteem is affected by the recognition that he is not totally self-sufficient, that he is dependent on the sighted to meet some of his needs even with the best adaptive behaviors and coping skills (Tuttle, 1984).

Metacognitive Deficits

Vision-impaired children and youth experience numerous social, emotional, and cognitive deficits that interfere with adequate functioning. They may experience difficulties with the metacognitive aspects of self-planning, self-evaluation, self-monitoring. The metacognitive skills allow one to take charge of their environment, but this is difficult when the natural mediating, verifying, and organizing function of vision is severely deficit or completely nonfunctional.

In social situations vision provides nonlinguistic information (body language, gestures, facial expressions) that when paired with linguistic cues and voice intonation allow us to "read" the emotions, intentions, and beliefs of persons with whom we are socially engaged and those within our visual range. Vision provides us feedback information regarding the adequacy of our behaviors, verbal and physical, by observing the reactions of significant others as well as casual acquaintances.

Academically, vision is crucial to monitoring ones' mistakes in comparisons of answers, to an answer key or direction guide and comparing products to the projects or works of others. Vision provides an overview of an entire task, project, or situation while a vision impairment narrows or significantly reduces one's ability to "see" the whole to a focus on the parts. Sometimes the sum of the parts does not equal the whole; thus, the vision-impaired person may arrive at erroneous conclusions.

In order to function efficiently, vision-impaired persons need very specific planning and organizing skills such as money folded in a certain order, possessions always kept in a specific location, clothes labeled by color codes. Since reading braille and/or large print in academics is much slower and requires more effort in order to complete assignments, visually impaired persons must plan to allow more time to complete assignments than would be necessary for a nonhandicapped child. These particular planning and organizing deficiencies in academics can often be overcome by training in specific compensatory strategies.

Social metacognitive deficiencies may be much more difficult to remedy. The vision impairment narrows the boundaries of the visually handicapped person's life, reduces exploring even as an adult for safety reasons. Significant others are often reluctant to discuss social blunders with the vision impaired individual so as not to hurt their feelings, but this causes them to believe that their behavior is appropriate. Thus, the vision-impaired person may remain egocentric and socially immature longer than nonhandicapped students due to limited self-evaluation and self-monitoring abilities.

Motivation Deficits

Of enormous concern in the development of visually impaired children is developing sufficient self-confidence and motivation to explore their environment and to become effectively mobile. A vision impairment during early childhood may significantly reduce the child's curiosity and motivation to interact, to explore, to bond with significant others, to develop reach and grasp skills, to use toys appropriately and to play with others, and to learn to walk. The establishment of auditorially directed reaching is a prerequisite to independent creeping and motor movements in blind children (Cole & Cole, 1989).

Among young vision-impaired children motivation may be limited, and passivity and dependency promoted by the fact that others must intervene to elicit behavior from the child (Cole & Cole, 1989). Close social ties with significant others provide the personal security to develop spatial relations concepts, foster a sense of self-help capability, and motivation that lead to effective mobility (Warren, 1989). "If parents, older siblings, or others repeatedly do things for the visually handicapped child that children would normally be expected to do for themselves, habit patterns of reliance on others will develop and prevent the emergence of appropriate independence" (Warren, 1989, 160). In order to foster self-sufficiency, independence, and motivation in mastering the environment, the visually impaired child must be encouraged to investigate and travel within his environment. Thus, the child's level of motivation is a social-related skill.

Attribution Deficits

Locus of control concerns people's implicit perception of whether they are in command of the events that affect their lives. Those children possessing an internal locus of control tend to see themselves as exercising substantial control over events in their lives, whereas those possessing an external locus of control describe themselves as being highly controlled by other people or events (Warren, 1989, 166). Research (Land & Vineberg, 1965) indicated that vision impaired showed a significantly more external control than a comparison group of sighted children. This is to be expected since visually impaired and blind persons are dependent to some degree on sighted people. Attribution becomes a significant concern if the visually impaired person attributes all of his problems to blindness (Tuttle, 1984). The visually impaired person may not accept responsibility for academic, social, and/or physical functioning; thus, motivation to attempt new tasks may be low because of expectancy of failure.

Evaluation of locus of control for academic achievement and correlated competencies in adaptive behavior with 17 blind or partially sighted children (ages 6–19 years) indicated that responsibility for positive intellectual achievement events correlated significantly with increased adaptive behavior scores (Parsons, 1987). Thus, motivation and amount of effort expended to be successful in visually impaired students depends on how successful they feel they are in other areas of their life such as travel (orientation and mobility), competency with home chores, and self-care skills.

Self-Concepts of Visually Impaired Students

The self-concept and self-esteem of a person who is visually impaired emerge from his interactions with the physical and social environment;

however, self-esteem does not need to be any more of a problem for a blind person than anyone else in society (Tuttle, 1984).

General Self-Concept

Results of studies comparing the self-concepts of visually handicapped and seeing adolescents showed no essential and consistent differences (Zunich and Ledwith, 1965). Coker (1979) investigated the self-concepts of visually handicapped children enrolled in day schools compared to those enrolled in residential schools and determined that the overall self-concept of both groups did not differ; and that the visually impaired children had an overall positive image of themselves regardless of the type of school they attend. Results of most studies show no inevitable link between blindness and specific personality patterns or maladjustment in the individual; in other words, "there is no such thing as a blind personality" (Lowenfeld, 1973).

Tuttle (1984) suggested that many visually impaired young adults have a poorly developed self-concept and inadequate self-esteem, however, the problem is not inherent in the visual impairment but results from the student's interaction with significant others in their environment. Since the child's self-concept and self-esteem are rooted in the reflections s/he receives from others, negative reflections from significant others can depress the self-concept. Blindness requires alterations in the life-style of an individual meeting the practical day-to-day demands of living and can increase the stress level of the visually impaired child as s/he acquires coping skills and compensatory strategies. Even after acquiring good coping skills, visually impaired persons are at a disadvantage, because others frequently tell them what to do, solve problems for them, and make decisions on their behalf (Tuttle, 1984). The impact of blindness on the self-esteem should be of a temporary nature and can be alleviated by the positive treatment of significant others and training in self-sufficiency.

Low-vision persons tend to have more difficulty than blind in establishing their personal identity because of their ambiguous, poorly defined role within the sighted world (Tuttle, 1984). From a psychosocial perspective, the low-vision person tends to find the adjustment process more difficult; and s/he experiences self-consciousness, social isolation, and embarrassments in social situations (Tuttle, 1984).

Recent research compared the self-concepts of visually impaired students and normally sighted students in grades 6 through 8 and the results indicated that differences in self-concept scores for normally sighted and visually impaired students were small and not influenced significantly by such factors as grade level, test format, or testing procedure and provided little support for the notion that visually impaired students have lower self-concepts than sighted peers (Obiakor et al., 1987). After surveying the literature on self-concepts of the blind, Warren (1989) indicated that the studies have found no overall differences among the self-concepts of vision-impaired and sighted individuals.

Self-Concept of Academic Achievement

As indicated previously very little research investigated the academic achievement of visually impaired students. It is to be surmised that visually impaired underachievers will have a self-concept similar to other children who are underachieving, as will visually impaired achievers have an academic self-concept similar to other successful achieving students. The many technological advances in the past decade have made successful near-grade level academic functioning a reality for many average and above-average intelligence visually impaired children and youth. As with other children, success in academics stimulates and motivates the visually impaired child and youth to strive for greater achievement.

A strong relationship exists between a blind person's ability to travel independently and his self-esteem (Tuttle, 1984). A focus of the curriculum of the visually impaired child and youth is instruction in orientation and mobility. Mastery over daily home chores and personal-care responsibilities provide a sense of self accomplishment and personal satisfaction for visually impaired students. These skills are also included in the curriculum of the visually impaired student.

SUMMARY

Vision impairment is a low-prevalence handicapping condition including children who have never had any visual functioning, those who had normal vision prior to the severe impairment, those who have other handicapping conditions, and those with selective impairments of parts of the visual field. Educators differentiate between blind (reads braille) and low-vision (reads print) students.

Vision impairment may cause delays in developmental areas and concepts in early childhood, but by school age significant differences on intelligence tests are not noted. During infancy a severe visual deficit may delay acquisition of sensorimotor stage cognitive skills, concept labeling, reach and grasp skills, exploration, fine motor skills, and symbolic play. Research suggests that with adequate supportive nonvisual experiences, the concepts or mental images developed by congenitally blind children are not significantly different from those acquired by sighted children. Motor delays among visually impaired children are common. Physical fitness including body image and posture serves as prerequisite skills for mobility training.

Very few studies have been conducted on the academic achievement of visually impaired students as compared to sighted students because the learning conditions are not directly comparable. Reading braille or large print is a much slower process than for sighted students reading print. Numerous technological devices currently available for vision impaired students significantly enhances their ability to make adequate academic progress.

Visually impaired students may experience some difficulties in social skill development. The severe visual restriction may interfere with initial bonding with parents because of absence of social smiling, and lack of responses at the sight of parents. Preschoolers may experience difficulty because of inability to see and imitate appropriate social behavior. In middle childhood and adolescence a severe visual restriction delays social perspective-taking skills because the vision-impaired child can not pick up nonlinguistic cues (facial expressions, gestures, stance). They may experience difficulty in self-monitoring social behaviors because they cannot observe the social behaviors of others.

A blind person's self-esteem is affected by the recognition that he is not totally self-sufficient, that s/he is dependent on the sighted to meet some of his needs even with the best adaptive behaviors and coping skills. A vision impairment interferes with acquisition of metacognitive skills and with motivation to explore the environment. Severely vision-impaired children appear to have an external locus of control as do most children who are dependent on adults. The literature on self-concepts of the blind does not reveal overall differences among the self-concepts of visually impaired and sighted individuals. There appears to be a strong relationship between the blind person's ability to travel and his self-esteem.

Chapter Three

COMMUNICATION IMPAIRED STUDENTS

Children who cannot absorb information through listening and reading or who cannot express their thoughts in spoken words are virtually certain to encounter difficulties in their schools and communities (Heward & Orlansky, 1988, 213).

"Speech and language are tools used for purposes of communication" (Hallahan & Kauffman, 1988, 208). Speech is the actual behavior of producing a language code by making appropriate vocal sound patterns (Hubbell, 1985). "Language is the communication of ideas through an arbitrary system of symbols that are used according to certain rules that determine meaning . . ." (Hallahan & Kauffman, 1988, 208). The development of adequate speech and language requires normal hearing, normal organs of speech, appropriate speech models, and adequate articulation, voice, and fluency. The development of adequate language, also, requires normal intelligence.

COGNITIVE AND ACADEMIC FUNCTIONING

While cognitive and academic problems do not appear to be directly related to speech impairments, there is a definite negative relationship between language deficits and cognitive and academic functioning.

Cognitive Learning Problems

Intellectual Functioning

Speech and/or language impairments are associated with numerous other handicapping conditions including hearing impairment, mental retardation, and learning disabilities. Thus, a specific intelligence quotient is not specified, but the child's overall developmental functioning is compared to his/her language functioning to determine if a discrepancy exists. The language deficits of hearing-impaired students especially the deaf significantly reduce and delay the child's acquisition of concepts and a fluent vocabulary which impacts functioning in all language arts and language-based academic tasks.

The more severe the level of mental retardation the greater the child's difficulties in the areas of speech and language. Mildly mentally retarded students often function several years below age-expected functioning. Due to their reduced cognitive and language abilities, mildly mentally retarded children continue to function at the concrete level experiencing difficulty with abstract and symbolic concepts and language even as adults. Moderately retarded children and youth usually learn a functional language, while severely and profoundly retarded students may be unable to use speech and language to communicate.

Some children who are labeled language impaired, also, fall under the category of learning disabled. These children function above the IQ 70 cutoff for mental retardation and experience significant language-related deficits in all language-based academics.

Information Processing Problems

Language-impaired students including those who are learning disabled, mentally retarded, and hearing impaired experience numerous information processing problems in reception, perception, integration, memory processes, retrieval, and behavioral responses (e.g., verbal, fine and gross motor) to learning. Deficits in selective attention and selective intention may impede the entire process by not providing enough or correct information to process. Language is very important at the perception stage as the student labels information and compares it to information in long-term storage.

Deficits in concepts and language may reduce the child's short-term memory capacity, which eventually results in reduced long-term storage, as well. Language-impaired students may be relegated to processing simple literal level information, as complex structures are confusing. Children with language processing deficits make fewer interrelationships among the information they do have in long-term storage.

Language-impaired students may experience difficulty retrieving information from storage for usage. Due to a lack of language-based learning strategies, they may experience "word finding" deficits and problems describing or discussing what they want to relate. Paired with deficits in fine motor skills, language-impaired students may be unable to spontaneously communicate through writing. Language deficits interfere with higher-level cognitive thinking and problem-solving, and social cognition and social skills.

Academic Learning Problems

Most children follow a relatively predictable sequence in their development of speech and language. Heward and Orlansky (1988, 216–218) have described normal language developmental milestones. Before the end of the first year, the baby develops inflection and repeats simple sounds and words. By 18 months of age most children have learned to say several words with appropriate meaning and respond to simple commands. The two-year-old child may understand more than 1,000 words (receptive language). By age 3 years s/he may have an expressive vocabulary of up to 900 different words, averaging three to four words per sentence. The four-year-old child may have an average vocabulary of over 1,500 words and use sentences averaging 5 words in length. The average six-year-old child uses most of the complex forms of adult English.

Speech Disorders

Unusual speech is considered a disorder or a handicap "if it (1) interferes with communication, (2) causes the speaker to be maladjusted, or (3) calls undue attention to itself at the expense of what the speaker is saying" (Gearheart et al., 1988, 229). "Speech disorders are problems associated with the production of oral language" (McCormick, 1990, 335).

Speech disorders involve the faulty production of sounds and the system itself. Disorders are of three kinds: voice, articulation, and fluency. All involve involuntary muscle movements of the speech mechanism—that is, muscular movements that are not under our conscious control as we are speaking (Rice, 1988, 241).

Voice Disorders. Voice disorders occur when the quality, loudness, or pitch of the voice is inappropriate or abnormal in relationship to his/her age, sex, size, and cultural background (Oyer et al., 1987). Voice-quality disorders most frequently found among children of school age are hoarseness (husky and strained sounding), breathiness, and nasality or resonance problems (hypernasality—too much nasality or denasality— too little nasality as with a stuffed up nose) (Heward & Orlansky, 1988).

Loudness or intensity of voice is relative depending on the situation. "A voice too soft or weak can make it difficult or impossible to understand the speaker at a reasonable distance and with a reasonable level of background noise" (Hallahan & Kauffman, 1988, 218).

Pitch refers to the vibration frequency of the human voice concerned with the highness or lowness of tonal quality. "If a person's voice is markedly lower or higher in pitch than is expected, considering age and sex, that person may experience social censure, and communication may be less than optimal" (Hallahan & Kauffman, 1988, 216). Examples of pitch problems include monotone voices, stereotyped inflections or "sing-song voice," voice that constantly cracks or breaks into falsetto, and pitch breaks beyond adolescence in males (Hallahan & Kauffman, 1988; Rice, 1988).

Articulation Disorders. The most prevalent type of speech disorder among school-aged children is articulation disorders. "Articulation disorders are characterized by defective nonstandard speech sounds" (McCormick, 1990, 338). The major types of articulation errors include sound omission, substitution, distortion, and addition (McCormick, 1990). "A severe articulation disorder is present when a child pronounces many sounds so poorly that his speech is unintelligible most of the time. In that case even the child's parents, teachers, and peers cannot easily understand him" (Hallahan & Kauffman, 1988, 224).

"Omission is the failure to pronounce all of the expected sounds in a word. It constitutes the most serious misarticulation because the resultant speech is often unintelligible. "In omission errors, only parts of words are pronounced. For example, [t] may be consistently omitted ("ie my shoes igh" for "tie my shoes tight" . . .) (Hallahan & Kauffman, 1988, 220).

"In substitution errors, the substituted sound is generally somewhat similar to the replaced sound" (McCormick, 1990, 339). "These include such errors as substituting [w] for [r] or [l] (e.g., "wed" for "red" or "wike" for "like"). Common substitutions are [b] for [v] and ("berry" for "very"), [t] for [k] ("tate the rate" for "take the rake" . . .) (Hallahan & Kauffman, 1988, 220). Sound substitution can cause considerable confusion for the listener (Heward & Orlansky, 1988, 224).

Distorted sounds may approximate the phoneme but not produce it precisely. There are many ways of producing an approximation of what an [s] should sound like; children may produce the word *sleep* as "schleep," "zleep," "thleep" (Heward & Orlansky, 1988, 224). "There are many types of distortions, the most common example is the lisp" (McCormick, 1990, 339). "Distortions can cause misunderstanding, though parents and teachers often become accustomed to a child's use of them" (Heward & Orlansky, 1988, 224).

Additions of an extra sound occur most often in the speech of young children, especially in the context of consonant blends (McCormick, 1990). For example, a child may say "He's my fuhriend" for "He's my friend" (Hallahan & Kauffman, 1988, 220).

Fluency Disorders. "Fluency disorders interrupt the natural, smooth flow of speech with inappropriate pauses, hesitations, or repetitions" (Heward & Orlansky, 1988, 226). Fluency disorders affect millions of Americans; about one percent of children and adults are considered stutterers (Hallahan & Kauffman, 1988). Most stutterers are identified by age five years (Andrews et al., 1983).

The two major fluency disorders include stuttering and cluttering. Stuttering is "frequently applied to speech that for some reason is punctuated by irregularities and includes repetitions of sounds or syllables, or prolongation of these basic components" (Oyer et al., 1987, 81); and struggle behaviors, such as contortions of the lips and mouth, facial grimaces, eye blinks, and other extraneous body movements that can accompany the effort to speak (Rice, 1988).

Cluttering is a type of fluency disorder in which "speech is very rapid and clipped, to the point of unintelligibility" (Heward & Orlansky, 1988, 226). "Although the person who clutters may repeat, the distinguishing elements here are excessive speed of verbal output; disorganized sentence structure; and slurring, telescoping, or even omitting syllables or sounds" (Cartwright et al., 1989, 264).

Academic Deficits. Children should be intelligible to strangers by the time they are three to four years old (Shriberg, 1980). "Research has shown that there tends to be a natural developmental sequence to speech sound acquisition and that it is reasonable to expect different sounds to be produced correctly in a child's speech at different ages" (Oyer et al., 1987, 32). Maturity for articulation is usually complete by the third grade or when a child is eight years old. The most frequently misarticulated sounds among children and adults are the "r" and "s" sounds (Shriberg, 1980).

"Considerable research time has been spent examining the relationships among reading, spelling, and articulation. However, the evidence is not clear. In our experience, such problems do not often exist for children with only a few articulatory errors" (Oyer et al., 1987, 47). There does, however, appear to be a relationship between severely delayed or deficit phonological development and learning to read and spell. Phonological deficits may interfere with the acquisition of phonics skills, which may delay acquiring decoding skills, and delay acquisition of a fluent reading vocabulary in children. Many of the spelling words in the first several grades have regular sound-symbol relationships, thus, a phonological deficit or delay could significantly hamper spelling accuracy.

Language Disorders

Language disabilities in children are some of the most common impediments to learning and fulfillment during school years (Wiig & Semel, 1984). "Children and youth who have educational difficulties with language (language disabilities) fall under the broader term *learning disabled*" (Oyer et al., 1987, 55). "The language-disordered child may follow the same sequence of development as most children, but achieve each skill or milestone at a later age" (Hallahan & Kauffman, 1988, 228). This type of information is very important in diagnosing a child as handicapped.

> Language disorders are usually classified as either receptive or expressive . . . a receptive language disorder interferes with the understanding of language. A child, for example, may be unable to comprehend spoken sentences or to follow a sequence of directions. An expressive language disorder interferes with the production of language. The child may have a very limited vocabulary, may use incorrect words and phrases, or may not even speak at all, communicating through gestures (Heward & Orlansky, 1988, 227).

Language is considered to have three major components: form, content, and use. Form includes the surface or structure aspects of language that connect to and express meaning (phonology, morphology, syntax) (McCormick, 1990). Content is the meaning or semantic aspect of language and includes cognitive information (concepts about the physical and social world) and linguistic information (concepts about how to express cognitive knowledge) (McCormick, 1990). Use is the pragmatic or social interaction aspect of language (McCormick, 1990).

Dimensions of Language Disorders. Language disorders can also be categorized according to the major dimensions of language. Language dimensions which may pose problems for a child include the following: (1) phonology, (2) morphology, (3) syntax, (4) semantics, and/or (5) pragmatics. "The child's knowledge and skills in one (or some combination) of these dimensions may be deficient (atypical) or delayed (like that of a younger, normal language learner) (McCormick, 1990, 30).

Problems with phonology include experiencing difficulties learning the sound system of language and the linguistic rules governing how sounds can be combined (McCormick, 1990, 340). "Phonological awareness, or the ability to recognize that words are made up of sound elements, appears to be developmental in normal children" (Lerner, 1989, 321). Many of the children who encounter reading problems have not attained the ability to recognize phonemes or syllables (Lerner, 1989). Since children who have problems with the phonological aspects of receptive language are slow to acquire a sense of sound-symbol association, they also experience difficulty acquiring phonetic analysis (Levine, 1987). Also, children with poor phonological sense may be predisposed to difficulties learning foreign language (Levine, 1987).

Problems with morphology involve children with language disabilities who frequently ignore word endings, such as plural suffixes, comparative and superlative objective suffixes and the -ly endings of adverbs, and low stress words such as prepositions and conjunctions (Wiig, 1986). "Difficulties occur with possessives, the past tense of verbs, and prefixes" (Oyer et. al., 1987, 68). "Younger elementary school-age youngsters may omit inflectional endings altogether. . . . The morphological problems of older students are most often associated with irregular past verb tenses and irregular plurals" (McCormick, 1990, 341).

Problems with syntax include language disorders involving the grammatical rules of language (organizing and ordering words to form sentences). "Syntax difficulties include problems in understanding and producing structurally complex sentences, wh-questions, sentences with demonstrative pronouns (this, that, those), passive sentences, and sentences that express relationships between direct and indirect objects" (McCormick, 1990, 341). The vast majority of language-impaired children are identified by their failure to achieve normal syntactic production with or without accompanying deficits in comprehension (Ludlow, 1980).

"Children with language-related learning problems seem to encounter difficulty with linguistic complexity" (Levine, 1987, 150). A particular problem occurs with the transformation of sentences which involves rearranging, deleting, and substituting words in the base structure of a sentence in order to form new sentences (Oyer et al., 1987). "Sentences in which the usual order of words is changed present problems in expression as well as comprehension" (Oyer et al., 1987, 67). Language-disabled children can be "deficient in understanding the role of word order in affecting the meaning of a sentence. They can have significant difficulties recognizing how a subordinate clause in a sentence relates to and modifies the main one" (Levine, 1987, 150).

Children who have language disabilities may have difficulty with sentences that contain both a direct object and an indirect object; with reflexives (e.g., myself, herself, and themselves), infinitives, irregular past tense verbs, irregular plural nouns, and with auxiliary verbs (Oyer et al., 1987). They may experience significant difficulty answering wh-questions (who, what, when, where, why, which), confused about the types of answers required. Language-disabled children are likely to rely too heavily on the context in which the sentence is heard, on key words (i.e., semantics rather than syntax), and on their own predictions or expectations from prior experience, using a processing style similar to that of preschool children (Levine, 1987). In general, studies of the language abilities of language-impaired children seem to suggest that their linguistic development reveals using structures and strategies similar to those used by younger, normal children (Ratner, 1989).

Problems with semantics consist primarily of deficiencies of vocabulary (Levine, 1987). "Language disordered children may experience problems acquiring their initial lexicon (mental dictionary) and later demonstrate word finding difficulties (problems retrieving an appropriate, known word when that word is required in a particular situation); and problems with figurative language" (McCormick, 1990, 341).

Students may have increasing difficulty dealing with words that have multiple meanings and with content areas that demand a rapid growth in vocabulary (Levine, 1987). Learning-disabled youngsters lack a precise knowledge of familiar words, have a restricted knowledge of less familiar words, and experience difficulty in classifying word categories

(Lovitt, 1989). They also experience difficulty in understanding that sentences that express comparison, or passive, spatial, temporal, familial relationships also express a sequence in time or space (Lovitt, 1989).

Many language-impaired students experience difficulty in processing multiple meaning words, idioms, metaphors; and in understanding implied meanings of fables, myths, parables, and proverbs (Lovitt, 1989, 154). Often, there is evidence that the meanings they have assigned to words and word relationships are much narrower than those of same-age peers (McCormick, 1990).

Problems with pragmatics involve the failure to automatically adjust language to the social context. "Children with pragmatic or language use problems may produce syntactically well-formed and semantically accurate utterances but have problems with communicative interaction strategies such as turn taking and initiating and maintaining dialog" (McCormick, 1990, 341). They may fail to use even the most common nonlinguistic communication devices such as establishing and maintaining eye contact. "They may introduce topics out of context and string together ideas tangentially without regard for the listener's perspective" (McCormick, 1990, 341).

Children who have difficulty with pragmatics demonstrate a tendency to interpret language very literally (Ratner, 1989). They have more difficulty than their normally achieving peers in asking questions, responding to inadequate messages, sustaining a conversation, and disagreeing with and supporting an argument (Bryan et al., 1981). They may have problems comprehending a speaker's intentions which results in difficulties understanding in the classroom, at home and in social situations (Wiig & Semel, 1984). They may produce less appropriate requests or respond less appropriately to the requests of others (Prinz & Ferrier, 1983).

There is also considerable evidence that language-impaired adolescents and adults have poorer language and communication skills than normally achieving peers (Johnson & Blalock, 1987). Learning-disabled youth demonstrate a broad variety of pragmatic impairments including displaying less sensitivity to their conversational partners' needs for information or clarification (Spekman, 1981), experience problems in guiding conversations (Bryan et al., 1981), reveal deficits in narrative abilities (Roth & Spekman, 1986), and experience deficits in persuasive abilities (Donahue, 1987).

There appears to be a relationship among syntactic and pragmatic deficits. At this point it is unclear whether pragmatic and syntactic deficits arise separately in language-impaired children, whether their pragmatic deficits may be attributable to subtle linguistic deficiencies, or whether pragmatic deficiency actually constrains the development or displaying of certain syntactic skills (Donahue, 1987).

Academic Problems. Language-impaired students comprise one category of learning-disabled students. These students specifically manifest the underlying language processing problems that impede progress in most academic subjects requiring reading, writing, and verbal demonstrations of competence. Thus, many academic learning problems, cognitive learning problems, and social learning problems are directly related to the language impairment.

Reading problems, especially decoding and comprehension, are a significant concern for language-impaired students. Decoding words may be hampered by a number of language processing and production deficits including the following: (1) phonological deficits: interferes with word analysis; (2) morphological deficits: result in problems in understanding and using prefixes, suffixes; (3) syntactic deficits: impair understanding of structure and sequence; (4) semantic deficits: impair word and passage comprehension; and (5) metalinguistic awareness deficits: impede word analysis and comprehension (Levine, 1987).

Phonological deficits are likely to cause severe decoding problems for children who have not mastered the basic phonology and morphology of their native language (Levine, 1987). Evidence suggests that poor readers suffer from: (1) a lack of phonological awareness which impairs their ability to segment, analyze, and synthesize the speech stream; (2) a lack of lexical-decision skills which enable readers to decide whether a string of letters form a word; (3) a lack of phonological recoding or the spelling-to-sound regularity of letters (Lovitt, 1989). Phonological awareness deficits include problems with phoneme discrimination, phoneme sequencing, sound blending. Phonological awareness may be particularly difficult for learning-disabled children who experience difficulties in auditory perception (Lovitt, 1989).

Phonological recoding at the word level involves spelling-to-sound regularity of letters; at the sentence level involves the translation of written words into their sounds; and at the passage level, decoding is assumed to be automatized (Lovitt, 1989; Levine, 1987). Recent research indicates that phonological coding is as important for processing syntax as it is for deriving meanings from single words (Levine, 1987). "When reading a sentence, we temporarily store the words as meaningful sounds (phonetic units) in verbal memory, while striving to understand the overall meaning of a sentence" (Levine, 1987, 287). "A child whose phonological memory is deficient, resulting in sparse sight vocabulary, will expend too much effort decoding words, so that little attention, active working memory, and higher-order cognition are likely to be available for more sophisticated comprehension" (Levine, 1987, 293).

Morphological and syntactical deficits appear to be common among poor readers. Deficits in morphology make it difficult for the child to determine appropriate verb tenses in a sentence, and to decode polysyllabic words. Learning-disabled students do not appear to use the structure of the sentences (syntax) to facilitate recall, but depend on consistencies in word and sentence meaning for their recall (Wiig & Roach, 1975). Language-disabled children also reveal syntactical problems with expressive narrative.

> Children with language production problems may be overwhelmed by the need to produce narrative. Since the ultimate product represents a culmination — the combining of effective word finding, morphology, syntax, pragmatics, plus organization — relative weaknesses in one or more of these areas undermine the entire process (Levine, 1987, 159).

Semantics deficits are typified by an impoverished vocabulary, trouble associating words with their meanings, and problems in interpreting metaphors, similes, and other forms of figurative language. Language-impaired students who experience problems with semantic encoding have difficulty storing and retrieving linguistically encoded data which can interfere with the rapid association of written words with their meanings (Levine, 1987).

In addition to any deficiency in syntactic abilities, there is mounting evidence that poor readers are less adept in their use of general comprehension strategies and that this deficit becomes particularly acute in the case of written text (Lovitt, 1989). Many children with learning problems are conspicuously inefficient in their use of cognitive strategies — they lack a problem-solving plan, frequently resorting to trial-and-error methods, and appear unaware of the alternatives available (Levine, 1987). Diminished vocabulary, a poor grasp of syntax, trouble drawing inferences in verbal contexts, weak metalinguistic awareness, and poor verbal pragmatics thwart comprehension (Levine, 1987).

Language-disabled children may exhibit memory deficits that inhibit language comprehension and production (Lovitt, 1989). They may show specific deficits in recalling phoneme sequences, retrieving words within selected categories, and understanding and remembering semantic relations such as verbal analogies, cause and effect relationships, and linguistic concepts (Wiig & Semel, 1984).

"Metalinguistic ability refers to the use of language to describe and think about language. Through metalinguistic skill we can form judgments about the adequacy of grammar, about ambiguity in words or sentences, about metaphor, figurative language, humor, paradox, and irony" (Levine, 1987, 140). Elementary school children become increasingly capable of thinking about language as their metalinguistic skills develop (Van Kleeck, 1984), and enable them to detect errors in their speech and that of others.

Writing Problems are characteristic of students with language disabilities. Youngsters with learning disabilities involving written language are without a doubt the largest group in the learning disabilities population (Myers & Hammill, 1990).

Language-impaired students may experience numerous problems related to their underlying language processing deficits that hinder development of fluency in written communication including the following: (1) word finding problems: which impair ability to use higher-level vocabulary; (2) syntax deficits: which cause problems in formulating sentences, using clauses effectively, and using complex syntax; (3) underdeveloped metalinguistic awareness: impairs one's ability to monitor the accuracy of their written communication; (4) deficits in writing styles: hampers ability to alter writing style to fit the needs of the occasion; (5) poor verbal pragmatics: interfere with the writer's ability to target a specific audience; (6) limited vocabulary: results in immature writing products (Levine, 1987; Cicci, 1980; Wiig & Semel, 1984). It is likely that such disabilities in writing would be accompanied by similar deficits in oral language (Myers & Hammill, 1990).

Children with language disabilities may use a concrete, rigid writing style; be unable to use logic to defend an argument or position; lack sophisticated ideas, abstract language, and persuasive content; lack automaticity in rules regarding punctuation, capitalization, grammar, and spelling (Levine, 1987). Some language-impaired students lack the sound cognitive schema needed to elaborate in writing on a topic. Language-impaired students who experience difficulty with active working memory during writing may keep forgetting what they wanted to write (Levine, 1987).

Mathematics problems, particularly story problems, are typical of students who have difficulty with reading (Levine, 1989). "Mathematics can be regarded as a symbolic language having the practical function of stating spatial and quantitative relationships and the theoretical function of facilitating thinking. As such, mathematics ability is a vital component of an individual's general communication capacity" (Myers & Hammill, 1990, 56).

Mathematics word problems and reasoning problems are almost an impossible task for language-impaired students because of the following: (1) difficulty translating word problems into computational processes; (2) mathematical explanations involve complex sequential processing and memory; (3) difficult multistep explanations and processes; (4) use of complex syntax in explanations; (5) difficulty with problem-solving; (6) expected to operate on a highly abstract symbolic level (Levine, 1987). "There are some particular features of 'story problems' that are especially troublesome for many LD youngsters: extraneous information, numbers that are words (for example, four), aspects of time, converting units of measurement or time, and making change" (Lovitt, 1989, 154).

Content area difficulties are common in children who experience language deficits and delays. By upper intermediate grades, the curriculum places heavier emphasis on social studies, science, and literature; and students are expected to learn to reason, prepare written and oral reports, and to analyze stories in terms of character and plot development (Oyer et al., 1987). Language-impaired students, however, continue to experience difficulty in vocabulary, morphology, syntax, and metalinguistic awareness which interfere with success in reading and writing. Social studies classes prove to be difficult for language-impaired students for numerous reasons: (1) understanding historical events challenges sequential organization and memory, (2) social studies vocabulary is polysyllabic and requires understanding of morphology for decoding, (3) requirements for integrated papers and reports, (4) focusing on "a bit" of history and expecting it to be representative of an era on a timeline, (5) essay tests requiring comparing and contrasting, analysis and synthesis, and (6) time and distances are very abstract.

Science courses are extremely difficult for a language-impaired student because "scientific writing tends to include an unusually large number of passive verbs and complex embedded clauses," and an enormous number of new concepts and definitions introduced during each class or chapter (Levine, 1987, 389). Science is also difficult because it integrates abstract scientific concepts with abstract mathematical concepts, both of which are likely to give the language-impaired student difficulty in isolation. The product required at the conclusion of a period of scientific thinking is a written report written in a scientific style.

Social and Emotional Functioning

Feelings of Personal Control

It is difficult to make generalized statements about the speech and/or language-impaired student's feelings of personal control due to the wide range of handicapped students who carry speech or language impairments as a secondary handicapping condition. The feelings of personal control elements of metacognition, motivation, and attributions also depend in large measure on the intellectual and academic functioning levels of students.

Attributions, metacognition and motivation of mildly speech-impaired students of average ability will be very similar to that of nonhandicapped students. "Within the broad range of normal psychological profiles, personality does not appear to have a causal relationship to speech sound production. However, there are some indications that children with severe speech sound distortions have more adjustment and behavioral problems than other children do" (Oyer et al., 1987, 38). Feelings of personal control of severe speech-impaired students may be very similar to that of hearing-impaired students who experience difficulties communicating and controlling their environment due to speech deficits.

Language-impaired students who are learning disabled will experience similar feelings of personal control as other learning-disabled youngsters. The language deficit and cognitive deficits interfere with automaticity and functioning in academics; with social-cognition, social problem-solving, and social perspective-taking; and with the metacognitive aspects of self-monitoring, self-planning, self-evaluation, and self-control. Language-impaired learning-disabled students experiencing numerous information processing problems, attribute their failures to task difficulty or low ability and successes to luck or the teacher. They see success and failure as beyond their control, thus, tend to be externally motivated. Self-motivation and spontaneous goal-directed activity require good metacognitive skills which language-impaired learning disabled lack.

Therefore, it is not surprising that language-impaired learning-disabled youngsters lack independence and motivation; feel incompetent and negative about their academic and social performance; and feel that they have little control over their environment.

Language-impaired students who are mildly mentally retarded will experience similar feelings of personal control as other mildly mentally retarded students. Retarded students lack spontaneous metacognitive skills which results in the inability to control their social and academic functioning; inability to monitor their academic learning and social behaviors, and inability to generalize learning to new situations. Due to significant cognitive limitations retarded children do not experience any personal control over their environment, and accept no responsibility for their learning, thus, they are externally motivated. Retarded children cease to try after failures, therefore, possess little spontaneous motivation to learn. They are motivated by tangible reinforcers. Language-impaired mentally retarded children would be expected, then, to have little sense of personal control over their environment, little independence and motivation, and little control over academic and social learning.

Self-Concepts of Communication-Impaired Students

Speech-Impaired Students

The majority of speech defective children are physically normal; their speech deficits cannot be directly attributed to the existence of a specific disability (Eisenson, 1972). Speech defectives as a group are not typically seriously maladjusted or neurotic, however, they do have more than their share of adjustment problems. They tend to be less acceptable to their peers.

Goodstein (1958) conducted a survey of the literature from 1932 to 1957 regarding the research on disorders of speech as related to personality and determined that there were no conclusive results regarding a relationship between delayed speech and personality adjustment. The literature revealed considerable research relating to persons who stutter and personality adjustment. "In general, there is little evidence to support the contention that the stuttering child has a particular pattern of personality or is neurotic or severely maladjusted" (Goodstein, 1958, 368).

Peckham (1973) indicated that the personality adjustment of speech defectives was not strikingly different from that of normal speakers. In a study of children with functional articulation disorders, Sherrill (1967) found children with severe disorders revealed more fluctuation of self-acceptance than their peers. Children with the most severe functional articulation disorders appeared to be less well accepted by others and themselves than children with less severe disorders.

Johnson et al. (1967) reported that a speech defect tends to cause decreased confidence, self-esteem, enthusiasm, acceptance, happiness, understanding of themselves, cooperativeness, and feelings of belongingness. The higher the grade level, the greater the difference between self-concept scores of boys with speech problems and those with normal speech patterns for their age (Johnson et al., 1967).

Language-Impaired Students

The self-concepts of language-impaired students depends on the level of functioning and the presence of other handicapping conditions. Severe speech/language impaired students may experience similar self-concepts as hearing-impaired students. Language-impaired students who are learning disabled experience significant failure in school which negatively impacts the general and academic self-concept. Language-impaired mentally retarded students would be expected to have similar self-concepts as other mentally retarded students.

Jones (1985) found that speech-language impaired students had a significantly more negative phenomenal (conscious) self-concept than nonhandicapped students in the areas of self-perceptions of intelligence and school status, and popularity. The mean performance scores indicated that speech-language impaired students experience high levels of anxiety. The scores on the nonphenomenal (unconscious) self-concept measure did not differ significantly from those of nonhandicapped students. The negative self-perceptions of intelligence and school status, popularity, and high anxiety suggest a negative academic self-concept.

SUMMARY

The development of normal speech and language skills requires normal hearing; normal organs of speech; appropriate role models; adequate articulation, voice, and fluency; and adequate intelligence. Speech is the behavior of producing a language code by making appropriate vocal sound patterns, whereas language is concerned with meaning.

Speech disorders are associated with the production of oral language and include three types: voice, articulation, and fluency. A speech disorder or impairment may be organic, attributable to a specific physical cause, or functional cause not attributable to a physical cause. Voice disorders result when the quality, loudness, or pitch of the voice is abnormal. Articulation disorders, the most prevalent type of speech disorder among school-aged children, include four major types of sound errors: omission, substitution, distortion, and addition. Fluency disorders interrupt the natural, smooth flow of speech with inappropriate pauses, hesitations, or repetitions. The two major fluency disorders include stuttering and cluttering.

Language is considered to have three major components: form, content, and use. The form of language is the surface or structure aspects that connect to and express meaning (phonology, morphology, syntax). Content is the meaning or semantic aspect of language. Use is the pragmatic or social use of language. Language disorders are usually classified as either receptive or expressive. A receptive language disorder interferes with the understanding of language, while an expressive language disorder interferes with communication through language. Language disorders are also classified according to the major dimensions of language:(1) *phonological problems:* difficulties learning the sound system of language and the linguistic rules governing combination of sounds; (2) *morphological problems:* difficulties understanding and using word endings, suffixes, prefixes, prepositions, conjunctions, and verb tenses; (3) *syntax problems:* language disorders involving the grammatical rules of language or problems in organizing and ordering words to form sentences; (4) *semantics problems:* deficiencies of vocabulary; and (5) *pragmatics problems:* failure to automatically adjust language to the social context.

Many language-disabled children are included in the category of specific learning disabilities. There appears to be a relationship between severely delayed or deficit phonological development and learning to read and spell. Language-impaired students usually experience deficits in most academic subjects requiring reading, writing, and oral communication. Language-impaired students experience significant deficits in using higher-level vocabulary; forming sentences; monitoring the accuracy of written assignments; in math reasoning problems; and in content area courses.

Speech-defective children are not typically maladjusted or neurotic. Children with severe speech disorders tend to be less acceptable to their peers than are children with normal speech. Language-impaired students are often learning disabled, mentally retarded, or hearing impaired and experience similar feelings of personal control and self-concept. A speech/language deficit may cause decreases in self-confidence, self-esteem, and happiness, and in school status and popularity.

Chapter Four

HEARING IMPAIRED STUDENTS

For the deaf individual, social integration may be extremely difficult because societal views of deafness have reinforced social isolation (Hardman et al., 1990, 295).

Both deaf and hard-of-hearing persons are hearing impaired. "A deaf person is not able to use his hearing to understand speech, although some sounds may be perceived. Even with a hearing aid the hearing loss is too great to allow a deaf person to understand speech through the ears alone" (Heward & Orlansky, 1988, 252). Though a hard-of-hearing person has a significant hearing loss that makes some special adaptations necessary, such as a hearing aid, his/her speech and language skills are developed through the auditory channel (Heward & Orlansky, 1988).

COGNITIVE AND ACADEMIC FUNCTIONING

"In a population as varied as the hearing impaired, it is difficult to generalize about their learning and development" (Lowenbraun, 1988, 329). However, a severe to profound hearing loss may result in specific cognitive, academic, and social problems.

Cognitive Learning Problems

Intellectual Functioning

A history of controversy has existed regarding the impact of a hearing impairment and its language deficits or delays on cognition. "To characterize the intelligence of severely hearing impaired people is difficult because many of the traditional standardized tests require an oral response or rely on verbal directions, which do not provide valid measures of intelligence for hearing-impaired people" (Lowenbraun, 1988, 330). Deaf children score considerably lower than normally hearing children on verbal IQ tests (Lowenbraun & Thompson, 1990), however, most authorities agree that if nonverbal intelligence tests are used and especially if these tests are administered using sign language, hearing-impaired students are not intellectually retarded (Sullivan, 1982). Hearing-impaired students who score in the retarded range on performance IQ tests tend to be among the 20 to 40 percent of deaf individuals who have additional handicaps (e.g., visual impairment) (Meadow, 1984).

Genetically deaf individuals score higher on WISC–R performance subtests than do either deaf children of hearing parents who are not genetically deaf or the normally hearing standardization population (Kusche et al., 1983). Thus, "Hearing loss alone does not appear to affect intelligence as measured by performance intelligence tests" (Lowenbraun & Thompson, 1990).

Information Processing Problems

Information processing problems may occur due to an interruption in (1) attention to stimuli, (2) reception of stimuli, (3) storage and processing of information, and (4) expression of cognitive abilities (Fallen & Umansky, 1985). Children who have severe hearing impairments may experience interruption in cognitive processes due to all four causes. Children with hearing impairments may experience difficulty attending to meaningless sound, may be unable to receive auditory stimuli appropriately, and may receive distorted or garbled information. Hearing-impaired children may experience difficulty processing information sequentially, a skill learned through listening to linguistic information. Deaf and hearing-impaired children may experience significant disabilities in encoding and transferring information.

Memory. Short-term memory differences between hearing and deaf children are not found when items to be remembered are presented simultaneously (visually) (Withrow, 1968). On memory tasks involving visual tracking, motor recall, or location in space, deaf individuals perform as well as or better than hearing subjects (Neville & Bellugi, 1978).

A hearing impairment may interfere with the child's ability to attend to a stimulus long enough to process it into short-term or long-term memory storage (Jones, 1988). Numerous studies have shown that deaf children and adults experience significant deficits in remembering visual or verbal sequentially or temporally presented stimuli of numerous types (e.g., digits, words, pictures, signs) (Kusche, 1984). Visual sequential memory skills appear to be highly related to receptive and expressive language achievement (Greenberg & Kusche, 1989); both are areas of difficulty for deaf students.

Short-term memory and processing speed that are dependent on linguistic performance are problematic areas for deaf children as they generally do not attain automaticity in encoding linguistic information or in utilizing linguistically recoded representations of language. The conceptual knowledge and semantic long-term memory stores of deaf children are deficient as compared to hearing children, due to linguistic and concomitant environmental deprivation (Greenberg & Kusche, 1989).

Piagetian Stages

Hearing-impaired children appear to develop sensorimotor skills in a similar sequence to that of nonhandicapped children. Research involving Piagetian tasks indicates that deaf children first begin to show developmental delays by the end of the preschool years in abstract thinking and concept formation because their experiences are mediated primarily through sensorimotor and visual-spatial processing rather than verbal-sequential means (Greenberg & Kusche, 1989). "Language has a strong effect on concrete and formal operational modes of thinking, while it has relatively less influence on sensorimotor and preoperational thought (largely based on visual-spatial processing)" (Greenberg & Kusche, 1989, 101).

Average hearing children make the transition from reliance on visual perceptual information to understanding conceptual information between the ages of 5 and 7 years, while deaf children do not make this transition until adolescence (Greenberg & Kusche, 1989). As a result, elementary school-aged deaf children think predominantly in a preoperational manner in some areas but process information in a concrete operational way in others (Greenberg & Kusche, 1989). Language deficits delay the acquisition of logical and abstract thinking.

Academic Learning Problems

It has been found repeatedly that although the nonverbal intelligence scores of deaf children are comparable to those of normal-hearing children, achievement scores in academic subjects are quite poor (Meadow, 1980). "Academic achievement among hearing impaired students varies widely; however, according to achievement test results over the past 50 years, there is an approximate lag of 4–6 years relative to normally hearing peers. The area of greatest deficit is language, including reading" (Lowenbraun, 1988, 330).

Language and Speech Problems

"Auditory deficits, particularly during the developmental years, severely impact normal development in the acquisition of receptive and expressive language, in concept development particularly involving problem-solving tasks, in social development and interpersonal relationships, and in school-related activities involving reading and language-based skills" (Jones, 1988, 55).

Speech Problems. The sense of hearing plays a crucial role not only in the understanding of speech but also in providing the cues needed for the acquisition of speech and language in the normal, developing child (Levitt, 1989). Speech intelligibility in hearing impairment appears to be predictable on the basis of the severity and configuration of the child's hearing loss (Calvert, 1982). Obviously, greater hearing losses are more detrimental to language development than lesser losses. Additionally, while amplification may provide the child with the ability to hear some otherwise inaudible sounds, it cannot restore normal hearing function, especially in cases of severe loss (Ratner, 1989).

Most profoundly hearing-impaired children do not develop intelligible speech (Lowenbraun, 1988). "The speech of most severely and profoundly prelingually hearing-impaired children and adults is characterized by multiple articulatory errors, including neutralization of vowels, nasalization of vowels, and omissions, distortions and substitution of consonants" (Lowenbraun, 1988, 331). The most common articulatory error in the speech of hearing-impaired children is that of omission of consonants, particularly consonants in the final position of a word at the end of a phrase or sentence (Levitt, 1989; Ratner, 1989). The next most common set of articulatory errors is that of phoneme substitution; usually consonants are substituted for consonants and vowels for vowels (Levitt, 1989).

"Speech also is characterized by distortion of prosodic elements, including prolongation of syllables, inappropriate fundamental pitch, inappropriate pitch variation, and hypo- or hypernasality" (Lowenbraun, 1988, 331). Individuals with hearing impairments often do not use the rising pitch we expect to hear at the end of a question or the falling pitch that indicates the conclusion of a declarative sentence (Lowenbraun & Thompson, 1990).

Language (Oral Expression) Problems. The extent to which a child is handicapped by hearing loss depends upon the severity of the loss, the utility of hearing aids in restoring some hearing ability, and the age at which the hearing loss occurred (Ratner, 1989). "On the average, the use and comprehension of standard English by hearing-impaired students is below that of their normally hearing peers, and their competence in English is negatively correlated with increased hearing loss" (Lowenbraun, 1988, 330).

At least 80 percent of language development has occurred by 3 years of age (McFarland & Simmons, 1980). Children incurring a profound hearing impairment prior to 2 or 3 years of age (prelingual loss) have been found to perform significantly inferior to those deafened after this age on certain language tasks (Quigley & Paul, 1989). A hearing loss that occurs after a child has learned spoken language (postlingual loss) is less likely to cause as severe an educational problem as a prelingual loss (Lowenbraun & Thompson, 1990). Children who are born with a hearing impairment that limits their perception of sounds to those exceeding 60 decibels (dB) generally will not be able to develop spontaneous oral language that approximates that of normal children (Ratner, 1989). Children born with losses exceeding 90 dB are considered deaf and will not develop speech and language skills spontaneously (Ratner, 1989).

Hearing-impaired children experience problems with language in all areas of form (phonology, syntax, morphology), content (semantics), and use (pragmatics) (Fallen & Umansky, 1985). Deaf children experience difficulty with **syntactic structures** including the verb system, negation, conjunction, and question format (Ratner, 1989). By ten years of age, when most hearing children are using their reading skills to acquire new knowledge, the average hearing-impaired child has yet to acquire the basic syntactic structures (Fallen & Umansky, 1985).

"**Morphological** development is typically delayed in hearing-impaired children because the morphological components of our language are particularly difficult to hear" (Fallen & Umansky, 1985, 310). By 4 years of age, hearing children are using most morphological elements of language, while same-aged hearing-impaired peers have acquired few or none of these morphological components (Blackwell et al., 1978).

Research has consistently shown that deaf children experience significant difficulty with **semantics** especially in the comprehension and use of figurative language including metaphors, similes, proverbs, idioms, and verbal humor (Arnold & Hornett, 1990). In addition to the slang and sarcasm students encounter in their social interactions, research has revealed that one in eight of the utterances made by teachers contains a nonliteral reference (Nippold, 1985). The correct interpretation and use of figurative terms are important in both the academic and personal-social realms (Nippold, 1985; Wiig, 1986).

Deaf students are at a serious disadvantage because instructional texts, particularly in the middle grades, are replete with figurative language (Arnold & Hornett, 1990). Since idioms are idiosyncracies of language that transgress the laws of grammar and the laws of logic, they are not susceptible to grammatical analysis (Arnold & Hornett, 1990). Thus, the deaf child who must interpret each individual word, attempts to apply literal meaning to such expressions.

Additionally, deaf children have fewer experiences with societal language that includes idioms and other figurative speech. They may have fewer opportunities to practice since parents and teachers attempt to communicate in unambiguous language, thus reducing opportunities to practice interpreting idiomatic expressions and other figurative language (Arnold & Hornett, 1990). However, the deaf child's problems in acquiring and using the syntactic and semantic aspects of language and in using such skills to develop proficiency in reading and writing are much more significant factors in the ability to succeed educationally and vocationally than is the typical articulation disability (Ratner, 1989).

Hearing-impaired children are delayed in **pragmatic** skills (Fallen & Umansky, 1985). To be considered mature language users, children must not only acquire conventional phonetic, semantic, and grammatical skills, but also learn how to adjust their linguistic performance in accordance with diverse social and environmental demands (Hymes, 1972). Children with hearing impairments who get a late start in learning language and a cultural system are generally less socially mature than hearing children (Lowenbraun & Thompson, 1990, 375).

Reading Problems

Mastery of reading and writing are inextricably linked to knowledge of the oral language system. The poor reading skills of most deaf students are related to their inadequate primary English language development (Quigley & Paul, 1989). Research indicates that deaf students function four to six years behind same-age peers at age 16 years in reading with a median reading grade level of about 4.5 and an annual growth rate to 0.3 grade level with less than 10 percent of the students reading at or above the eighth-grade level (Trybus & Karchmer, 1979). The reading difficulties of deaf students may be attributed to three specific problem areas— (1) inadequate experiences (world knowledge), (2) deficient cognitive functioning, and (3) inadequate linguistic background (word knowledge) (Quigley & Paul, 1989).

Deficient Cognitive Functioning. Hearing-impaired students appear to experience cognitive functioning deficits related to their lack of linguistic proficiency. Research indicates that good deaf readers predominantly use a speech-based code in mediating print, however, the majority of hearing impaired students develop an internal representation employing a nonspeech-based code (e.g., signs, visual or graphic, fingerspelling) (Conrad, 1979). The relationship of nonspeech-based codes to print is not well understood (Quigley & Paul, 1989). Thus, when deaf children begin to read, they do not shift from visual to phonological processing as do hearing children.

At least two important factors are related to good reading comprehension in hearing children including the following: (1) short-term memory capacities which involve phonetic encoding, and (2) processing speed which includes retrieval from semantic memory (long-term memory), scanning speed of working memory contents, linguistic understanding, and past language experience (Hess & Radtke, 1981). Reading, then, appears to be a language-based skill that ultimately depends upon automatic processing and unconscious awareness (Mattingly, 1972).

Deaf children, however, do not generally use a phonetic encoding system which apparently limits their ability to hold in short-term memory certain temporal-sequential verbal linguistic units necessary for comprehending difficult structures such as relative clauses and passives

(Quigley & Paul, 1989). This ability may also be necessary for a high level of development in written language (Quigley & Paul, 1989). Additionally, deaf children do not seem to develop automaticity for such skills as letter decoding and word recognition (Hung et al., 1981). Deaf students not only comprehend fewer words from print, and experience difficulty with multimeaning words (Paul, 1984) but also their receptive and expressive "memory banks" of words in various classes such as nouns and verbs are small compared to those of hearing students (Quigley & Paul, 1989). The conceptual knowledge and semantic long-term memory stores of deaf children are deficient as compared to hearing children due to linguistic and concomitant environmental deprivation (Quigley & Paul, 1989). Therefore, reading comprehension is an area of weakness for most deaf children due to weaknesses in short-term memory, processing speed, and long-term semantic storage (Cohen, 1983).

Language (Written Expression) Problems

The written language of deaf students revealed that they do not have an adequate command of the numerous aspects of the rules of standard English grammar, particularly in the areas of morphology and syntactic structures (Quigley & Paul, 1989). Severely and profoundly hearing impaired children often display a smaller, more concrete vocabulary than do individuals with normal hearing (Lowenbraun & Thompson, 1990). Deaf individuals tend to write shorter sentences and less complex productions; less flexible, more stereotyped, more fixed repetitive phrases; and less grammatically correct compositions than those of hearing peers (Lowenbraun, 1988).

Hearing-impaired students struggle with grammatical structure, often omitting plurals, tenses, possessives, prepositions, and article adjectives (Lowenbraun & Thompson, 1990). Additionally, they use a greater proportion of nouns and verbs in their writing, with a paucity of pronouns, prepositions, adverbs, adjectives, and conjunctions (Lowenbraun, 1988). "Even as they begin to use longer sentences, these students still tend to use a very simple subject-verb-object order. Thus, their language is not as rich or subtle as that of individuals who hear normally" (Lowenbraun & Thompson, 1990, 376).

The average deaf adolescent leaves school with about a seventh grade spelling ability (Quigley & Kretschmer, 1982). Phonetic spelling errors are made far less often by deaf children than by hearing children (Hanson et al., 1983), as deaf children depend on visual cues rather than auditory cues.

Since the skills of writing and reading are interrelated, it is not surprising that the research on the written language of deaf students reveals the same low level of achievement as that of their reading comprehension ability (Quigley & Paul, 1989). It has been argued that the ability to write is generally contingent on the ability to read which, in turn, depends on the adequate development of a primary language form upon which both reading and writing is based (Quigley & Kretschmer, 1982). In general, the written language productions of most deaf students are stereotypic and on a level similar to young hearing students (Quigley & Paul, 1989).

Mathematics and Science Problems

Mathematics. Hearing-impaired elementary students appear to be functioning about three years behind hearing students in the ability to conserve numbers (Springer, 1976). The average deaf adolescent leaves school with a seventh grade mathematical ability, both in the United States (Karchmer, 1985) and in Great Britain (Wood et al., 1983) indicating functioning three years higher in math than in reading skills. Hearing-impaired students appear to experience difficulties in problem-solving particularly in questioning skills (Pendergrass & Hodges, 1976), and they displayed the lack of a systematic approach during logical discovery tasks (Becker, 1974).

At the secondary level hearing-impaired students 18–20 years old functioned similarly to 14-year-old hearing students (Austin, 1975) on word problems. The syntactically more complex text appeared to present a major stumbling block for student achievement. On Computer-Assisted Instruction in mathematics, however, hearing-impaired students performed as well as hearing students when the cognitive task did not directly involve verbal ability, and the performance of hearing-impaired students was almost always better than that of disadvantaged hearing peers (Suppes, 1974).

Science. Lang (1989) indicates that the quality of schooling in science and social studies in most programs for hearing-impaired students is inadequate, and that hearing-impaired students have not benefited from the curriculum innovations of the past two decades because of being educated in resource rooms or special education environments. Cognitive achievement in science appears to be strongly associated with the language ability of the hearing-impaired student (Fleming & Malone, 1983).

SOCIAL AND EMOTIONAL FUNCTIONING

Social and Emotional Problems

Hearing-impaired children tend to experience more social and emotional adjustment problems than nonhandicapped children. "They are frequently more impulsive, throw more temper tantrums, and use a physical expression of feelings due, in part, to a lack of a functional way to express feelings and emotions, and partly due to social imperceptions from misunderstanding a situation or circumstance" (Jones, 1988, 259). However, once the child has an alternate communication mode, these behaviors are usually reduced in frequency.

Communication and Social Interaction

The ability to communicate plays a major role in any person's social and emotional adjustment. "Social and personality development in the general population depends heavily on communication" (Hallahan & Kauffman, 1988, 276). "Most hearing impaired people are fully capable of developing positive relationships with their hearing peers when a satisfactory method of communication can be used" (Heward & Orlansky, 1988, 274).

Nonlinguistic Cues. "Hearing impaired persons have a greatly reduced amount of information due to inability to hear and utilize the intonation system of pragmatics" (Jones, 1988, 259). Frequently, they are unable to discriminate tonal differences. "Although tonal differences are usually accompanied by body language, which would seem to compensate for an inability to hear, hearing impaired children take longer than other children to learn to read body language because a critical cue in reading body language comes from hearing an accompanying vocal tone" (McCoy & Prehms, 1987, 95). Deaf children, also, appear to experience difficulty in reading facial expressions to interpret emotions of others (Odom et al., 1973), therefore, may react inappropriately.

Social Interactions. The hearing-impaired child has fewer means at his/her disposal to initiate social interactions, maintain interactions, and sustain interactions with other children and adults. "Many hearing impaired children function at a developmentally younger stage than their normal hearing peers. Some of this behavior may be attributed to a reduced sensitivity to subtle social nuances" (McCoy & Prehms, 1987, 95). Children who are delayed in social skills or who lack social maturity often display their immaturity in impulsivity, lack of responsibility, and lack of independence (Lowenbraun & Thompson, 1990). They typically exhibit a higher than usual degree of egocentricity and a low tolerance for frustration which causes them to be demanding and to act inappropriately if their demands are not met (Meadow, 1980).

Communication deficits of young hearing-impaired children interfere with normal play development (Higginbotham et al., 1980). Delayed verbal ability may restrict the emergence of cooperative make-believe play involving the symbolic use of objects and sophisticated peer interactions because verbal exchange appears necessary to sustain such play (Higginbotham & Baker, 1983). Thus, hearing-impaired children tend to engage in less complex and less social play than nonhandicapped peers. Research also indicates the amount of interaction among hearing and deaf children was related to the deaf child's oral communication skills (Brackett & Hennings, 1976), and the familiarity of the hearing children with the deaf children (Lederberg, 1989). Hearing children were more responsive and used more visual communication when communicating with a deaf friend versus an unfamiliar deaf child (Lederberg, 1989).

Role-Taking. Normally young children learn appropriate social interaction skills, such as turn taking, sharing, and the use of *please* and *thank you* through language (Lowenbraun & Thompson, 1990). These skills require some understanding of how another person feels or perspective-taking. "Until a child is able to view a situation from another's perspective, it is impossible for her to exhibit the qualities that comprise prosocial behavior. Sharing, cooperation, turn-taking, empathy, and helpfulness require an understanding of another person's needs and feelings" (Fallen & Umansky, 1985, 336).

Hearing impaired children seem to disregard feelings and misunderstand the actions of others, thus, often experience more difficulty interacting with others and establishing friendships (Davis et al., 1986). Research indicates that young school-age deaf children have poorer perspective-taking skills than hearing children especially in situations where the cues to another's need are subtle or when the deaf child does not have the social and emotional understanding to evaluate correctly the other child's internal state (Blaesing, 1978). Deaf children fail to predict accurately other's feelings, revealing a deficit in psychological insight (Coady, 1984). Prelingually severely deaf children, ages 9–14 years, appear to experience a 4–5-year delay in role-taking ability as compared to nonhandicapped peers, thus showing greater egocentrism in their behavior (Bachara et al., 1980).

Social and Emotional Adjustment. Deaf children of deaf parents are thought to have higher levels of social maturity, adjustment to deafness, and behavioral self-control than do children of hearing parents, largely because of the early use of manual communication between parent and child that is usually found in homes with deaf parents (Heward & Orlansky, 1988). Feelings of depression, withdrawal, and isolation are frequently expressed by hearing-impaired persons, particularly those who experience adventitious loss of hearing (Meadow-Orlans, 1987). A number of deaf children do have serious behavior disorders that require treatment (Heward & Orlansky, 1988). However, "severe emotional disturbance is no more prevalent in deaf individuals than in those with hearing. Rather, deaf people have more problems of living including high arrest rates, and more marital, social and vocational problems" (Hallahan & Kauffman, 1988).

The "hearing status of parents, type of school, and other potential variables interact in complex and possibly bidirectional ways to predict social maturity of deaf children" (Greenberg & Reische, 1989, 110). Whether a hearing-impaired child will develop behavioral problems depends on how well those in the child's environment accept the disability (Moores, 1982).

Hearing-impaired children can grow up in relative isolation because they are cut off from communicating with the population at large (Hallahan & Kauffman, 1988). They sometimes have difficulty making friends even from preschool ages because their attempts to interact are likely to be rejected by hearing students (Vandell & George, 1981). Teachers often perceive hearing-impaired students as excessively shy (Loeb & Sarigiani, 1986). This tendency toward withdrawn behavior can be even more pronounced if they do not have hearing-impaired parents or peers with whom they can interact nonverbally (Hallahan & Kauffman, 1988).

It is probably the need for social interaction and acceptance that is most influential in leading many hearing-impaired individuals to associate primarily with hearing-impaired persons. Hard-of-hearing, and especially deaf individuals, more than any other handicapped group, tend to mix socially with people who have the same handicap (Hallahan & Kauffman, 1988, 376).

Feelings of Personal Control

Deaf children may experience significant difficulty in gaining a sense of personal control over their lives. Severe auditory deficits paired with language deficits may leave them feeling helpless in terms of understanding what is occurring in various situations and make them dependent on others to interpret "the world."

Metacognitive Deficits

Deaf children and adolescents are underachievers academically and frequently experience problems in social, emotional, and cognitive skills that interfere with adequate functioning. Due to language deficits, deaf children experience delays in the acquisition of logical, abstract, and higher-level thinking and problem-solving skills. Similarly as their handicapped peers who are learning disabled, educable mentally retarded, language disordered, and behavior disordered, deaf youngsters experience difficulty with the metacognitive aspect that regulates and controls the use of strategies during cognition and gives one control over their learning. Automaticity in the metacognitive skills of planning, organizing, and monitoring learning is delayed due to language deficits which may keep the deaf youngster functioning at a concrete level for an extended period of time.

Deaf children may experience deficits and disabilities in all areas of information processing. Initially deficits in attention due to reduced auditory input may make it difficult for the child to focus attention and sustain attention. Deaf children frequently lack functional cognitive strategies to control and direct their thinking, learning, and remembering; and lack monitoring skills to determine accuracy of their perceptions or reactions. They may have a reduced long-term memory store of concepts with which to identify and interrelate new perceptions. Reduced language facility interferes with rehearsal in short-term memory, and semantically storing information in long-term memory. Additionally, the means to express learning verbally may be significantly reduced if the youngster can not use speech and oral language fluently.

The lack of metacognitive abilities in social areas may significantly interfere with social acceptability of the deaf youngster. The lack of social perspective-taking interferes with the deaf child's ability to form and maintain friendships as s/he is unaware of how the friend or prospective friend feels emotionally. Deaf children are, thus, frequently described as being egocentric and immature as they only understand their own point of view.

Deficits in social perspective-taking, social problem-solving, and self-monitoring make it difficult for the deaf child to know when his/her behavior is socially appropriate. S/he may be unable to note subtle social cues that indicate a change in behavior is necessary and expected. Language deficits severely impact the child's ability in terms of pragmatics— socially acceptable topics of conversation, changing conversation for various audiences, and monitoring the reactions of others to their behavior.

Deaf children and adolescents frequently function in ways that make them appear behavior disordered. Unless provided a means of communicating effectively, they may experience enormous frustration and tantrum. They may not understand concepts of sharing and turn-taking, so appear disobedient to teachers and hostile to peers. Inability to hear adequately and to read facial expressions and body language may result in social imperceptions and misunderstanding the actual dynamics of a social situation. Thus, their delayed ability to use metacognitive skills for independence in academic learning is a severe deficit, but deficits in social skills may have far greater ramifications in terms of life adaptability.

Motivation/Attribution Deficits

Deficits in language, attention, concept understanding, academic and social problem-solving, social perspective-taking, metacognition, and independence may severely impact a child's motivation to continue to try to succeed in academic and social learning situations. Many handicapped students experience difficulty in maintaining motivation because they attribute success to conditions beyond their control such as their perceived ability or lack of ability, their handicapping condition, the difficulty level of the test. Thus, many underachievers including handicapped children attribute success or failure to external causes rather than to their own effort or the amount they studied.

Kusche et al. (1983) found that lack of ability was poorly understood by deaf adolescents as a reason for academic or social failure, and was often confused with lack of effort as a cause of failure. In understanding causes, emotions, and cause-effect in social situations, deaf adolescents (mean age 17 years) performed comparable to 1st grade hearing students.

Dowaliby et al. (1983) found that external locus of control was related to poor study habits and a lack of acceptance of self-responsibility. Thus, it appears that deaf youngsters experience difficulty with accepting responsibility for outcomes of academic and social situations.

Self-Concepts of Hearing-Impaired Students

The personality of the child who suffers sensory deprivation in early life is also subject to disastrous developmental effects (McConnell, 1973). The deaf child's main tie to the world is impaired. He must remain in a world where his self is the major concern (Levine, 1960). Accordingly, "the limitations and constraints imposed by inadequate language development, thus, modify and restrict the self-identification of the young child" (McConnell, 1973, 382).

General Self-Concept: Deaf Students

The degree of hearing loss will always be a relevant factor in the personality development of hearing-impaired children (McConnell, 1973). The demands made upon the hearing-impaired child are incomprehensible to him and may appear inconsistent and unreasonable. The deaf child is prone to meet these demands with resistance.

The hearing impairment interferes with the groundwork laid in early relationships. The personality features associated with normal deaf persons include emotional immaturity, personality constriction, and deficient emotional adaptability. In disordered deaf these personality features are exaggerated and reveal lack of understanding or regard for the feelings of others, egocentricity, little thoughtful introspection, considerable impulsive behavior (Levine and Wagner, 1974).

Personality investigations of the deaf have yielded divergent findings. The majority of self-concept measures utilized with the deaf rely on self-report measures for global feelings of self-worth which have been developed and normed on hearing populations. The groups available have practically always been selected populations—students in special schools, special classes, or patients referred to clinics (Levine, 1960).

The Social-Emotional Assessment Inventory for Deaf Students (SEAI) (Meadow, 1980), standardized on deaf students, was used to compare the maturity, self-esteem, and adjustment of 200 deaf and hard-of-hearing 10- to 15-year-old students in residential schools and day schools with hearing students in the public schools (Farrugia & Austin, 1980). Results indicated that deaf students attending residential schools and hearing controls were similar in all areas; however, hard-of-hearing and deaf students in public schools had lower levels of social and emotional adjustment and maturity than those in residential and day schools (Farrugia & Austin, 1980).

Warren & Hasenstab (1986) studied 5- to 11-year-old severely to profoundly hearing-impaired children and found a strong relationship between self-concept and parental indulgence, parental rejection, parental protection, parental discipline, and extent of language development at the onset of the hearing impairment.

The barriers of deafness and limited language increase the total incidence of frustration, loneliness, helplessness and despair. One of the consistent research findings is the deaf are less mature than the hearing (Meadow, 1980). In general, the deaf have more difficulty adjusting and are somewhat more egocentric, more emotionally unstable, and have more feelings of depression and suspicion than the normal hearing population (Meyer, 1953).

General Self-Concept: Hard-of-Hearing Students

The hard-of-hearing children, unlike deaf children, can develop a symbol system. They do, however, miss important things and misunderstand others. They may be labeled as uncooperative, mentally defective, or emotionally disturbed. They are allowed to stay in a normal environment but cannot fully understand it (O'Neill, 1964). Though the hard-of-hearing child lives in a world of partial confusions he usually will not totally withdraw but will try to maintain contact. The development of an uncertain self-image usually results in one of two courses of behavior. The child may become passive and inhibited or he may become ambivalent and attempt to compensate by developing a dominating self-image (O'Neill, 1964). Hoben et al.'s (1979) study of sensorially impaired students revealed although the hearing-impaired students generally scored lower than the comparison group students, the general pattern of response remained the same.

Loeb & Sarigiani (1986) studied 250 children, ages 8 to 15 years old, with varying degrees of hearing impairment and found that compared to visually impaired and nonsensory impaired, the hearing-impaired children had lower self-esteem and related problems in self-confidence, peer and family relations, and academics. Communication problems appeared to cause significant difficulty.

Language deficits appear to impact deaf children's internal milieu (e.g., self-esteem, verbal-mediational skills, hemispheric processing strategies), as well as their relationships with the external environment (e.g., interactions with parents, teachers, peers) (Greenberg & Kusche, 1989). Communication with family during development, and positive identification with one's deaf identity and deaf culture appear to be critical to a sense of self-confidence, self-control, and social understanding (Seiler, 1982).

Self-Concept of Academic Achievement

Investigations of personality development in the deaf and hard-of-hearing are greatly hampered by impaired reading ability (Greenberg & Kusche, 1989). Research using paper and pencil tests of personality have revealed generally that deaf children are less well-adjusted than normal hearing children, especially in school and social adjustment (Wiley, 1971).

Personality profiles appear highly related to language ability (Levine & Wagner, 1974); those with advanced language skills (high school level) were similar to hearing persons, while those with very low skills (second-grade level) showed pathological signs of immaturity, impulsivity, and rigidity that fit the familiar, but over-generalized deaf stereotype.

SUMMARY

Hearing loss alone does not appear to affect intelligence as measured by performance IQ tests. Children with severe hearing impairments experience interruption in attention to stimuli, reception of stimuli, storage and processing of information, and expression of cognitive abilities. They may experience difficulty processing information sequentially. They generally do not attain automaticity in encoding linguistic information or in using linguistically recoded representations of language. Deaf children frequently experience difficulty with abstract thinking and concept development. Research consistently indicates that deaf students experience difficulty in the language arts areas especially those requiring reading. Speech problems are a special concern of hearing-impaired students; and most profoundly hearing-impaired students do not develop intelligible speech. Hearing-impaired students experience difficulty in all areas of language, especially the meaning of complex abstract figurative language.

Hearing-impaired and deaf students experience metacognitive deficits in academic and social areas due to language deficits. They experience delays in the acquisition of logical, abstract, and higher-level thinking and problem-solving skills. Deaf youngsters experience difficulty with planning, organizing and monitoring academic and social situations. They demonstrate a lack of social perspective-taking, social problem-solving, and social monitoring which may interfere with their social acceptability.

Deaf children and youth experience deficits in motivation and attribution. Due to language deficits and delays, they may not understand the difference between lack of ability and/or lack of effort, and causation in failure. Deaf children, as with other handicapped youngsters, tend to have an external locus of control.

The degree of hearing loss and facility with language and communication greatly effect the self-concept and personality development of the hearing-impaired youngster. In general, deaf youngsters have more difficulty adjusting. Research suggests that deaf and hard-of-hearing youngsters educated in schools for the deaf have higher self-concepts than those educated in the public schools without deaf peers.

Chapter Five

MENTALLY RETARDED STUDENTS

One of the major problems in individuals with intellectual deficits is a parallel deficit in social behavior (Kramer et. al., 1988, 48).

"Mental retardation generally refers to delayed intellectual growth and is manifested in inappropriate or immature reactions to one's environment and below average performance in the academic, psychological, physical, linguistic, and social domains" (Patton et al., 1990, 33).

COGNITIVE AND ACADEMIC FUNCTIONING

Cognitive Learning Problems

Intellectual Functioning

The 1973 American Association on Mental Deficiency's definition of mental retardation was implemented into P.L. 94-142, the Education for All Handicapped Children Act. This definition required three components for a diagnosis of mental retardation: significant subaverage general intellectual functioning, significant adaptive behavior deficits, and manifested during the developmental period (Morrison, 1988). Subaverage general intellectual functioning was defined as "two or more deviations below the mean" (Patton et al., 1990, 46) or measured IQ below 70 on the Wechsler scales. Adaptive behavior includes age and situation appropriate behaviors such as social skills, self-care, communication skills, and functional academics. The developmental period is considered to be from conception to age 18 years.

Mentally retarded persons are often classified according to cognitive functioning. The classification system cited most often is the AAMR system which uses the terms **mild** (IQ 56–70), **moderate** (IQ 41–55), **severe** (IQ 26–40), and **profound** (IQ 25 and below) (Patton & Polloway, 1990, 202).

"Historically, terms such as **educable** and **trainable** (corresponding to **mild** and **moderate**, respectively) have often been used in school environments and in the literature" (Patton & Polloway, 1990, 202). The educator's classification scheme contains three subgroups: (1) educable mentally retarded (EMR) with IQs from 50 or 55 to 70; (2) trainable mentally retarded (TMR) with IQs from 30 or 35 to 55; and (3) severely and profoundly mentally handicapped (SPH) with IQs of about 30 or lower (Cartwright et al., 1989).

Mild Mental Retardation

Most students classified as mildly mentally retarded obtain IQ scores between 50–55 and 70–75; thus, they progress intellectually at one-half to three-fourths the rate of average nonhandicapped children. It is a common assumption that individuals who are mildly mentally retarded will not reach Piaget's level of formal thought and even as adults will engage in thought consistent with the concrete operations stage (Patton & Polloway, 1990). Therefore, mildly mentally retarded individuals will have limited ability to engage in symbolic and abstract thought. Studies reveal that a critical difference between retarded and nonretarded learners is the ability to reason (e.g., plan ahead, exhibit foresight, and understand relations); and that mentally retarded individuals are behind not only their chronological-age, nonretarded peers but also their mental-age nonretarded peers (Spitz, 1979).

Information Processing Deficits. Research studies of the information processes of the mentally retarded reveal that these individuals are deficient in most aspects of information processing. This deficit is due partly to sensory input limitations in the visual cortex which processes less visual information and at a slower rate than nonhandicapped students (Saccuzzo & Michael, 1984).

Attention deficits are common among retarded students. Mildly mentally retarded students have deficits in selective attention and selective intention. They have short attention spans, and attend to task for only brief periods before being distracted by extraneous stimuli. Frequently, they are unable to determine what they should pay attention to—teacher talking to another group, their neighbors whispering, or their partners in a collaboration activity (Jones, 1992). Mentally retarded individuals are deficient in the number of dimensions that can be attended to at any one time (Morrison, 1988). For example, a primary grade mildly mentally retarded child may categorize by two dimensions simultaneously—color (red and blue) and shape (blocks)—but be unable to categorize by several examples of size, shape, and color simultaneously (Jones, 1992).

Short-term memory problems appear to be characteristic of retarded individuals and primarily result from their inability to automatically use strategies that facilitate transfer of information through the memory systems such as verbal rehearsal, mneumonics, and image rehearsal (Morrison, 1988). The capacity of the short-term or working memory is smaller among retarded persons than among normal persons (Brown, 1974); thus, the amount of information placed in long-term memory storage is reduced, also.

Long-term memory deficits among the retarded have been observed in capacity and in access to long-term storage. "Differences in knowledge (contained in long-term memory) clearly influence what will be attended to, what will be perceived, and the likelihood of passing new information into long-term memory" (Kramer et al., 1988, 45). Mentally retarded children appear to have less information stored in long-term memory and, therefore, have fewer concepts that can be related to and integrated with new information (Jones, 1992). However, most researchers contend that once learned, information is retained over the long term about as well as by those with retardation as those without (Patton & Polloway, 1990).

Inefficiency in learning is a characteristic more than any other that distinguishes retarded learners from their nonretarded peers (Kramer et al., 1988). Mentally retarded learners are generally characterized as passive learners who do not spontaneously use appropriate strategies (Loper, 1980). They do not acquire information incidentally, but only that information which is directly relevant to the task being learned (Cartwright et al., 1989). "Students who are retarded tend to show deficiencies in the ability to apply knowledge or skills to new tasks, problems, or stimulus situations" (Patton & Polloway, 1990, 210). "The ability to profit from experiences and to generalize is poor for individuals who are retarded. Therefore, it takes more time for them to form a learning set (a systematic method of solving problems)" (Cartwright et al., 1989, 236).

Moderate Mental Retardation

Individuals with moderate retardation are those who display significant deficits in adaptive behavior and are functioning intellectually within the 30–35 to 50–55 IQ range (Grossman, 1973). Cognitively, the moderately mentally retarded child develops from one-third to one-half the rate of an average child. This developmental delay becomes obvious during the infancy and preschool years.

Information Processing Deficits. Moderately mentally retarded individuals possess all of the information processing deficits of mildly mentally retarded, but to a much greater extent. A large portion of the children labeled moderately mentally retarded experience some form of brain damage, a specific syndrome, physical abnormalities, and sensory deficits which all negatively impact information processing. Therefore, moderately mentally retarded youngsters experience deficits in all aspects of information processing—attention, reception, perception, memory, and behavioral responses to learning.

Severely Handicapped

Students with severe mental retardation function 3–4 standard deviations below the mean both on tests of adaptive behavior and on standardized intelligence tests (Wolery & Haring, 1990). Youngsters functioning within the severely and profoundly retarded ranges demonstrate IQs of approximately 30 or less (Cartwright et al., 1989).

> The population described by the term severely handicapped is quite broad. It includes diverse subpopulations such as children with autism; people with moderate, severe, or profound mental retardation; children who are deaf-blind; and students with moderate to profound retardation who also have physical or sensory impairments (Wolery & Haring, 1990, 244).

Information Processing Deficits. "Severely multihandicapped individuals are frequently fixated within the sensorimotor stage of cognitive thinking for a lifetime" (Jones, 1988, 214). "Students with severe disabilities develop and learn at much slower rates than do their nondisabled peers (or even other populations of exceptional children). Typically, they demonstrate severe lags in social, intellectual, and physical development" (Guess & Siegel-Causey, 1988, 301).

Academic Learning Problems

Mentally retarded children and youth experience academic failure in the regular public school classroom on materials designed for average nonhandicapped peers. Frequently, mildly retarded students have been retained one or more times prior to being formally diagnosed (Reschly, 1987). Moderately retarded children exhibit developmental delays that are usually diagnosed during infancy and preschool years, whereas severely handicapped are usually identified at birth or during infancy.

Communication Problems

Mild Mental Retardation. The development of speech and language is closely associated with intellectual development, therefore, it is not surprising that mentally retarded individuals display more problems in these areas than nonhandicapped students (Patton & Polloway, 1990). Research indicates that nearly 90 percent of students labeled mildly retarded have speech and language disorders (Epstein et al., 1989).

> Mentally retarded students experience a higher prevalence of speech problems especially in articulation areas of substitution and omission of sounds which decrease the intelligibility of speech. Articulation and voice problems are probably a result of marked delays in motor development (Edwards & Edwards, 1970).

Delayed language development is associated with mental retardation and is similar to the language development found in younger children who are of the equivalent mental age (Morrison, 1988). This delayed language development has been documented in a number of language areas including the following: restricted vocabulary development, auditory discrimination, incorrect grammatical structure and usage, and sentence length; pragmatic language; and delayed oral language development. These language difficulties are manifested in both receptive and expressive language deficits including the following:

1. Problems understanding verbal language.
2. Inability to determine main idea of orally presented information.
3. Problems with tasks requiring listening.
4. Problems understanding abstract information and directions.

5. Experiences difficulty maintaining a conversation (pragmatics).
6. Difficulty retelling a story read orally.
7. Responds inappropriately to verbal questions.
8. Difficulty understanding pronoun antecedents.
9. Omits common prefixes and suffixes (Patton & Polloway, 1990; Wallace et al., 1989; Cohen & Plaskon, 1980).

"Academic or intellectual tasks that are dependent on language or verbal learning will often be difficult for children who are retarded. . . . Due to the high correlation between cognitive and language abilities, severe language delays may be a sign that a child is not progressing at a satisfactory rate" (Cartwright et al., 1989, 237). Language skills deficits may be one of the greatest obstacles that individuals with mild mental retardation must overcome if they are to be integrated fully into society (Polloway & Smith, 1982).

Severely Handicapped. One of the most striking characteristics of persons with severe disabilities is the extent of their deficiency in communication (Falvey, 1986). "This population is highly diverse in communication skills. Some students speak, some do not. Those who speak may do so in single words, short phrases, whole sentences, or rather complex conversations. Many who can speak have articulation difficulties that make inexperienced listeners unable to comprehend" (Nietupski & Robinson, 1990, 237).

"Without exception, students with severe disabilities show some type of speech and language deficiency" (Guess & Siegel-Causey, 1988, 305). The communication deficits of severely multihandicapped students could be categorized as follows: (1) speech and language delay, (2) speech clarity deficits, and (3) deviant speech patterns. "Almost all children with severe handicaps are greatly limited in their ability to express themselves and to understand others. Many cannot talk or gesture meaningfully; they do not respond when communication is attempted" (Heward & Orlansky, 1988, 371). "A small number may never be able to talk because their speech mechanisms are impaired. The impairment is often associated with brain damage" (Guess & Siegel-Causey, 1988, 305).

Some severely handicapped students exhibit deviant speech patterns including the following: (1) responses may be out of context or inappropriate to the situation; (2) repetitiously recite nursery rhymes or TV commercials; (3) clear articulation with meaningless content; (4) repeating or echoing what is said—echolalia (Guess & Siegel-Causey, 1988).

"A fundamental and pervasive problem in working with deaf-blind children is achieving adequate communication" (Sternberg, 1979, 36).

The communication problems of deaf-blind severely multihandicapped children are extremely severe. Deaf-blind severely multihandicapped children frequently continue to function communicatively at the prelinguistic stage due to auditory deficits that severely impact development in receptive and expressive language, to vision deficits that severely restrict exploration and concept development, to severe cognitive deficits that delay representational thought, to oral motor skill deficits that may preclude intelligible expressive language, to motor skill deficits that delay exploration, to fine and gross motor skill deficits that preclude natural gestures, and to social/emotional developmental deficits that reduce or eliminate the need for pragmatics or social language (Jones, 1988, 215).

"Thus, the combined deficits in expressive language prerequisite skills . . . result in no automatic linguistic learning. Prerequisite skills in hearing, vision, cognition and memory, oral motor, and attention areas must be consciously, consistently taught and integrated before the child can become communicative" (Jones, 1988, 221–222).

Academic Achievement Deficits

Mentally retarded children and youth experience academic and developmental deficits in all areas compared to their same-age peers due to their various cognitive and information processing deficits.

Mild Mental Retardation. Mildly mentally retarded children enrolled in the primary grades (1st–3rd) will be functioning at preschool and readiness levels; intermediate age students will be functioning at the primary grade level just beginning real academics; and Jr. High age students will focus on functional academic rather than academic skills foundations.

Reading, especially comprehension other than literal level, is very difficult for mildly retarded students. The majority of these students read at a lower level than would be expected for their mental age (Carter, 1975). Since retarded students appear to have a higher "forget" rate than nonhandicapped students, they may spend years learning, forgetting, and relearning the same sight vocabulary words; thus, progress to successively higher levels of academic achievement may proceed very slowly. Many mildly mentally retarded students learn some phonics basics and "word families" that assist them in decoding unfamiliar words.

The difficulties retarded children have in understanding and using language severely impact reading comprehension. Additionally, their cognitive functioning at the concrete operational level restricts their ability to understand inferences, cause-effect, evaluation, and other higher-level comprehension skills.

"In **mathematics** the majority of students with mild retardation can learn the basic computations" (Thomas & Patton, 1990, 218). The performance of mildly retarded students in computation tasks is more consistent with their mental age (Whorton & Algozzine, 1978). However, they must be taught using concrete and practical experiences due to deficits in cognition. Mildly retarded students experience significant difficulties in mathematics reasoning and "word" problems. Since generalization is difficult for them, mildly retarded students will need to be taught functional use of mathematics.

While the mildly retarded may learn functional **writing skills,** they will probably experience significant difficulty in creative writing or writing a report because they do not possess automaticity in the underlying skills of penmanship, language processing, creative thinking, grammar, punctuation and capitalization, paragraph organization, paragraph transition, and mechanics of paper writing. Programs for mildly retarded students will usually focus on functional writing skills such as letters and applications.

"**Adaptive behavior** deficiencies in school settings are associated with coping behavior, social skills, language development, emotional development, self-care, and applied cognitive and academic skills" (Drew et al., 1988, 252). Adaptive behavior involves several major perspectives depending on age ranges including the following: (1) Infancy and Early childhood: sensory-motor skills, self-help skills, communication skills, and socialization; (2) Childhood and Early Adolescence: application of basic academic skills in daily life, and application of reasoning and judgment in mastery of the environment, and social skills; (3) Late Adolescence and Adult Life: vocational and social responsibilities and performances (Grossman, 1983, 13).

Moderately and Severely Handicapped. The school program of moderately mentally retarded children and youth deviates markedly from the regular school program due to the significant cognitive deficits and developmental delays. During their school years moderately retarded children and youth are usually taught in self-contained classrooms with highly structured curriculums in communication, self-help and daily living skills, prevocational skills, and limited or functional academics

(Heward & Orlansky, 1988). Many moderately retarded adults live in group homes and work in sheltered workshops.

> "Students with severe disabilities typically do not read, write, or perform academic skills. Frequently, they cannot successfully perform many of the skills necessary for reading and writing. For example, many cannot recognize or match colors, shapes, or objects. They may not be able to follow simple directions, such as "come here" or "sit down." Many cannot hold a pencil, draw a straight line, or fit puzzle pieces together. They may be unable to sort objects, point out pictures, or recognize names or pictures of familiar persons. Again, variability in cognitive skills exists among students with severe disabilities. Some can successfully perform preacademic tasks, and some (with early and intensive education) can learn to read, write, and perform other academic skills (Guess & Siegel-Causey, 1988, 305).

"Most severely handicapped children have limited physical mobility" (Heward & Orlansky, 1988, 372). "The most frequent cause of motor handicaps is cerebral palsy, a nonprogressive disorder resulting from damage to the brain and resulting in abnormal posture or movement" (Nietupski & Robinson, 1990, 340). "Children with severe forms of cerebral palsy are commonly seen in classrooms that serve students with severe and multiply disabling conditions" (Guess & Siegel-Causey, 1988, 300).

The severity of the physical involvement varies greatly. "Many children cannot walk or even sit up by themselves. They are slow to perform such basic tasks as rolling over, grasping objects, or holding their heads up. Physical deformities are common and may be worsened by lack of therapy and lengthy stays in bed" (Heward & Orlansky, 1988, 372).

SOCIAL AND EMOTIONAL FUNCTIONING

Social and emotional deficits are extreme problems for all levels of mentally retarded individuals. Social-cognition requires higher-level thinking ability than that possessed by mentally retarded children and youth.

Social and Emotional Problems

Mild Mental Retardation

Research clearly indicates that children and adolescents who are mildly mentally retarded display more social and behavioral problems than their nonhandicapped counterparts (Epstein et al., 1989). Mildly retarded individuals often develop patterns of behavior that further distinguish them from nonretarded peers because they may not fully comprehend what is expected of them and may respond inappropriately not so much because they lack the particular response required as because they have misinterpreted the situation" (Cartwright et al., 1989). Mildly retarded students experience difficulties in social imperceptiveness (social sensitivity and insight), social communication, self-concept and self-esteem, and social interactions (Greenspan, 1981; Patton & Polloway, 1990).

Social Imperceptiveness. Social and cognitive skills are interrelated in that the development of such skills as self-awareness, interpersonal skills, role-taking, social communication skills reflect both social and cognitive development (Kramer et al., 1988). Research clearly indicates that mentally retarded children display a significant delay in social perspective-taking and in perceiving others in several ways; and they view others in more egocentric terms and demonstrate limited insight into the motives and characteristics of others (Kramer et al., 1988).

Mentally retarded individuals from infancy through adulthood have demonstrated reduced abilities to interpret and express emotions through nonverbal cues such as facial expressions. Retarded infants and children were less able to express facial emotions and less able to identify facial emotional expressions in photographs than nonhandicapped infants and children (Maurer & Newborough, 1987). The ability to interpret and express facial emotions does not appear to develop automatically. Wilczenski (1991) studied mentally retarded adults (mean IQ, 34.9; mean MA, 56) and found that happiness and sadness were easier for them to express than emotions such as anger and fear. Strong, negative feelings were especially difficult for adults with mental retardation to express (Wilczenski, 1991). In social situations, nonverbal facial emotional expressions influence the responses of others. Thus, it should not be surprising that an inaccurate interpretation of nonverbal affective cues such as facial expressions may result in inaccurate expressions or behavior in responses. Singh (1990) suggested that inability to recognize and produce facial expressions contributes to behavior problems in mentally retarded persons.

During middle childhood intermediate grades, 4th–6th, ages 9–12 years, nonhandicapped children make significant growth in the area of social perspective-taking (role-taking). Since mildly mentally retarded same-aged peers would be cognitively functioning more like children of 6–8 years old or 1st–3rd graders, their social development would also reflect delayed development. Social comprehension and moral judg-ment are two areas of social ability that depend to a great extent on the cognitive functioning level, thus, are areas of difficulty for mildly retarded children and youth.

Social Communication and Problem-Solving. "Referential communica-tion requires skills in taking the perspective of the potential learner (role-playing) as well as communication and language skills" (Kramer et al., 1988, 51). Mildly mentally retarded individuals experience deficits in both cognition and language which significantly reduces their func-tioning level and rate of acquisition of social skills and problem-solving skills. They appear to have limited interpersonal problem solving strate-gies and fail to see sequential relationships among a series of interactions (Asher & Renshaw, 1981). Thus, mildly retarded individuals experience difficulty in most aspects of social functioning including social imper-ceptiveness, social sensitivity (role-taking & social inference), social insight (social comparison & moral judgment), and social communication (referential communication & social problem-solving) due to reduced cognitive and language capacities.

Social Interaction. Individuals who are mildly retarded frequently have poor interpersonal relationships and are more often rejected than accepted by their peers (Polloway et al., 1986). The reasons for this reduced social status seem to reside in a complex interaction of the characteristics exhibited by the mentally retarded children (MacMillan & Morrison, 1980) including reduced cognitive competence, lack of social competencies, and inappropriate communication and behavior.

"The differences between young children who are retarded and their normal peers seem to be related to behavior; that is, children with mild retardation act like normal children who are younger in chronological age" (Cartwright et al., 1989, 238). Although mildly mentally retarded children demonstrate a higher frequency and quality of interactions than moderately and severely retarded, levels of solitary play and lim-ited exchanges are the predominant behaviors observed (Morrison, 1988). Thus, at a very early age, limited social interchange is apparent in mentally retarded children.

These social differences among retarded and nonhandicapped chil-dren and youth appear to escalate with age as social appropriateness becomes more important. "Mildly mentally retarded students as adults have serious adjustment problems, often related to the specific domains of behavior that led to the initial referral, classification, and placement.

These domains of behavior have to do with abstract thought, application of concepts of time and number, and literacy skills" (Reschly, 1988, 31). Thus, mildly mentally retarded persons do not magically disappear as normal adults into the community (Edgerton, 1984).

Severely Handicapped

"A severe handicapping condition significantly impacts a child's social, emotional, and play skill development, resulting in deficits in interactions with adults, with other children, with the environment, and with the development of self-awareness" (Jones, 1988, 257–258).

Social Interaction. "Often, persons with severe disabilities appear to be oblivious to others. They neither initiate interaction nor respond. This type of behavior may be associated either with profound mental retardation or with a withdrawal pattern, as is frequently found in cases of severe emotional disturbance" (Guess & Siegel-Causey, 1988, 302). By virtue of the label, the mentally handicapped child experiences deficits in cognitive behaviors and progresses more slowly through the developmental skills.

The mentally retarded child often has difficulty giving the cues to the caregiver that elicit nurturance and reinforce the attachment process. Interactions with adults may be delayed if the child does not react motorically, visually, vocally, or affectively to adult interactions. It may take considerable time for the severely mentally handicapped child to be responsive to adults, children, and the environment.

Due to short attention span the severely retarded child has little interest or motivation to sustain activity of any kind and demonstrates no spontaneous play. The severely handicapped child must be taught to play with a toy because initial toy play will involve banging the toy repeatedly on the floor or on the child's own head. Since severely mentally retarded children progress at a delayed rate in all areas (e.g., fine and gross motor skills, communication, cognition), they remain socially immature, which frequently makes their behavior socially inappropriate. They spontaneously engage in little social interaction which, in turn, delays social conversation abilities. Severely mentally retarded children engage in limited cooperative play.

Severely handicapped persons who do interact socially often do so inappropriately. Their interactions range from antisocial behaviors such as undressing in public, to an inability to recognize situations in which certain behaviors should or should not occur. Hugging and kissing strangers, laughing at the

misfortune of others, and playing in the toilet bowl are examples of inappropriate social behaviors. . . . Many of these behaviors are directly related to overall
delayed development and would not be considered deviant in very young
children. Essentially, students with severe disabilities have not learned social
behaviors appropriate to their age level (Guess & Siegel-Causey, 1988, 302).

Most children with severe handicaps do not play with other children,
interact with adults, or seek out information about their surroundings.
"They may appear to be completely out of touch with reality and may
not show normal human emotions. It may be difficult to capture a
severely handicapped child's attention or to evoke any observable response"
(Heward & Orlansky, 1988, 372).

Frequent Inappropriate Behavior. "People with severe disabilities sometimes engage in behaviors that appear deviant. The most common of these
are termed stereotyped behaviors—seemingly purposeless motor responses or unusual body posturing" (Guess & Siegel-Causey, 1988, 302).
These purposeless activities include the following behaviors: (1) ritualistic behavior: rocking back and forth, waving fingers in front of the face,
twirling the body or objects; (2) self-stimulatory behaviors: masturbating,
grinding the teeth, patting the body; (3) self-injurious behaviors: head
banging, hair pulling, eye poking, hitting or scratching, biting oneself
(Guess & Siegel-Causey, 1988; Heward & Orlansky, 1988). These behaviors are common among children with severe emotional disturbances,
children with profound retardation, and children with retardation who
are partially or totally blind as well (Guess & Siegel-Causey, 1988).

Stereotyped behaviors are not unique to individuals with severe
disabilities; such behavior is common among normally developing infants
(Whelan, 1988). "Although some of these behaviors may not be considered abnormal in and of themselves, the high frequency with which
some children perform these activities is a serious concern, because these
behaviors interfere with teaching and social acceptance" (Heward &
Orlansky, 1988, 372). "Numerous factors are recognized as potential
causes of self-injurious behavior in children with severe disabilities. As
in the case of stereotyped and other behaviors, brief episodes of self-
injurious behavior are not uncommon in normal infants" (Guess &
Siegel-Causey, 1988, 304).

Severely handicapped children often look noticeably different from
nonhandicapped children because of their severe and multiple impairments, and their behavior may be considered deviant or extreme, par-

ticularly by people who are not familiar with them (Heward & Orlansky, 1988).

> Since the educational process for deaf-blind/severely multihandicapped children requires consistent, one-to-one teaching, these children may continue to be very self-centered for a considerable time, exhibiting inappropriate behaviors. The vision deficit reduces the signal information gained from body language and facial expressions. The deficit in auditory reception reduces the emotional cues from voice intonation. Cognitive deficits may preclude understanding and interpreting the social and emotional cues perceived (Jones, 1988, 269).

Deficits in Self-Help Skills. "Severely handicapped children are often unable to care for their most basic needs, such as dressing, eating, exercising bowel and bladder control, and maintaining personal hygiene. Such children usually require special training to learn these basic skills" (Heward & Orlansky, 1988, 372). These deficits significantly (negatively) impact their social acceptability, especially for the severely handicapped youth and adult.

Feelings of Personal Control

Due to significant cognitive deficits, academic deficits, developmental delays, social and emotional deficits, mentally retarded children and adults are under almost constant supervision. It is extremely difficult under those circumstances to feel any personal control over their daily behaviors or over their destiny.

Metacognitive Deficits

Metacognition involves two processes: (1) cognitive self-awareness or knowledge about one's own cognitions, and (2) the ability to regulate and control one's own cognitions (Mann & Sabatino, 1985, 220). Actual application of metacognition during learning situations involves using strategies to facilitate learning and using self-regulation to determine appropriateness, accuracy and goals during academics and social situations.

Mild Mental Retardation. The literature has long indicated the failures of mentally retarded individuals to spontaneously use cognitive strategies such as mneumonics (Ellis, 1970) or to select, modify, and sequence strategies (Campione & Brown, 1977). The accumulated evidence from numerous early training efforts indicates that mildly mentally retarded students can learn task-specific cognitive strategies such as verbal elaboration, repetitive rehearsal, visual imagery, and self-instruction (Kramer et al., 1980).

However, numerous studies revealed that mildly retarded learners have failed to generalize the use of trained task-specific cognitive strategies to new situations (Kramer & Engel, 1981). The difficulty that retarded individuals have in generalizing new information is well documented (MacMillan, 1982). Recent studies aimed at improving the intellectual abilities of mildly retarded students have also failed to result in generalization (Kramer et al., 1988, 53). Attempts to train mildly retarded individuals to use cognitive strategies to improve social skills, (Kneeder, 1980), academic skills (Lloyd, 1980), or general problem-solving skills (Pray et al., 1984) have also revealed failure to generalize.

Thus, "retarded students can be trained to use task-specific cognitive strategies and they will continue to use these strategies when presented with the training task. Attempts to modify more general memory monitoring or problem-solving skills have met with little success" (Kramer et al., 1988, 53). It appears that for generalization to occur, students must demonstrate the effective use of the executive skills (metacognition) such as strategy selection and monitoring (Borkowski and Varnhagen, 1984). The literature clearly indicates that mildly retarded individuals are unable to use metacognitive skills effectively in strategy selection, in monitoring their learning, and in generalizing learning to new situations.

Severely Handicapped. In general, severely handicapped students functioning at significantly lower levels than mildly retarded students do not reach the cognitive developmental level to use metacognitive skills. They do not learn spontaneously nor incidentally. Severely handicapped children and youth do not generalize learning to new situations, thus, are inefficient learners.

Attribution Deficits

Attributions involve the reasons children and youth give for their success or failure in academic situations, and the amount of personal control they perceive as having over their successes or failures. "Research has shown that many retarded individuals do not believe they are in control of their own destinies; they believe they are controlled by external or outside forces. They tend to think that things happen to them by chance and that they can do little to change anything" (Hallahan & Kauffman, 1988, 69). External control is considered to be a debilitating orientation, as it keeps the child/youth from accepting responsibility for his/her own successes and failures and impedes the development of self-reliance (Thomas & Patton, 1990, 204).

"Popular belief indicates that mentally retarded students are more likely to expect to fail because of the belief that they encounter a higher rate of failure in their natural environments and a lower rate of success than normal children of the same age" (Kramer et al., 1988, 49). Mentally retarded individuals react to failure by decreasing their efforts on tasks following failure experiences (Logan & Rose, 1982). When given negative feedback on cognitive tasks they were performing, retarded children stopped looking for effective strategies (Weiss, 1984). In contrast, successful experiences lead to increases in performance and expectations of success (Ollendick et al., 1971). Thus, it appears that motivation to learn and positive expectancies for success can be enhanced by minimizing the failure experiences of mentally retarded children and maximizing the successes.

Severely handicapped children and youth functioning within the sensorimotor stage of development are constantly supervised. Their developmental functioning is so low that external control is required for their own safety. Most severely handicapped children, being trained using various behavior management strategies, have little concept of success or failure.

Motivation Deficits

"Given that experiential factors for mentally retarded children differ substantially from that of normal children, it is not surprising that a retarded individual's motivation differs from that of a nonretarded individual of the same mental and chronological age" (Kramer et al., 1988, 49). Little research has been conducted regarding the motivations of mildly retarded youngsters. However, considering the results of attribution research that mentally retarded individuals tend to be outer-directed, it is not surprising that tangible reinforcers such as candy, stickers, toys, etc. are more effective in motivating mentally retarded students than verbal reinforcers or grades.

Severely handicapped children are not spontaneous learners. Their motivation to learn is externally orchestrated. They often are unaware of their environment, and have no concept of school and learning.

Self-Concepts of Mentally Retarded Students

General Self-Concepts

Mild Mental Retardation. Research concerning the self-concepts of mildly retarded students may have conflicting results due to the populations of students used in the studies. Research conducted prior to 1973 utilized subjects whose IQs were approximately 70–85. However, the definitional change in 1973 resulted in studies of mildly mentally retarded students using IQs 50–70. Thus, the results of studies during those periods are not comparable. The research after 1973 refers to the "New EMRs."

Robinson and Robinson (1976) found the retarded as a group tended to be more anxious than nonretarded children, and their self-concepts more negative and more defensive than those of nonretarded children. Cline (1975) reported primary level educable mentally retarded students had significantly higher self-concept scores than Junior High level retarded students, but normal children had higher self-concept scores than retarded students at all levels. Stangvik's (1979) results indicated that pupils of low ability have lower self-concepts than average pupils, but the low ability pupils generally indicated higher ideal self-concepts than pupils of average ability.

Jones's (1985) results indicated that educable mentally retarded students possess significantly more negative phenomenal (conscious) and nonphenomenal (unconscious) self-concepts than emotionally disturbed (ED), learning disabled (LD), speech/language impaired (S/L), and nonhandicapped students (NH). "The mean performance scores of the EMR students were significantly lower than the NH students on five of the six cluster scores and on the total score of the Piers-Harris Scale, indicating high anxiety levels and negative feelings regarding their intelligence and school status, popularity, happiness, and behavior" (35).

A number of studies were conducted to determine if placement impacted on the self-concept of mildly mentally retarded students, the "new" EMRs. Walthall (1976), using intermediate level educable mentally retarded students, found no significant differences between the self-concept of the retarded students in the integrated classroom and normals. According to Strang et al. (1978) partially integrated mildly handicapped students had higher self-esteem than totally integrated students because they could refer to other mildly handicapped students in special classes for social comparison. Luftig (1980) reviewed research on the effects of placement on the self-concept of the "new" EMRs, and concluded that they maintain higher levels of self-concept in special classes. It can be concluded that students who are mildly retarded do not hold strong, positive feelings about their own abilities and potential. Obviously, there is considerable correlation between negative self-concept and chronic failure (Patton & Polloway, 1990).

Severely Handicapped. For the most part, severely handicapped students are functioning at the pre-self-concept stage of self-awareness. They are developing body awareness; beginning to recognize when someone is paying attention to them; and beginning the concept of body image. Thus, a discussion of the "self-concept" of severely handicapped children and youth is premature.

Self-Concept of Academic Achievement

The self-image of the retarded child is intricately linked to his academic success. In evaluating self-concept differences between low and high achieving mildly retarded adolescents, Lawrence and Winschel (1973) found a positive relationship between adequate self-concept and high achievement of retarded children.

Research revealed retarded children tended to be more anxious than nonretarded children (Jones, 1985). Many retarded children expect failure and learn to defend themselves against it; as a result, their self-concepts are more negative and defensive than those of nonretarded children (Robinson & Robinson, 1976). Low-ability pupils are met by more negative attitudes from others both in school and society (Guskin & Jones, 1982). Due to a history of failure and of dependency-oriented treatment, mentally retarded individuals have become especially sensitive to others' evaluations of them (Stangvik, 1979).

Jones's (1985) results indicated that educable mentally retarded students viewed their intelligence negatively, perceived their school status to be low; experienced high anxiety, low popularity, and low happiness levels. Thus, the results suggested that educable mentally retarded students exhibited a negative "school-related self-concept" or negative academic achievement self-concept.

SUMMARY

Mild Mental Retardation

Mildly retarded students experience deficits and delays in cognition in the areas of attention, information processing, learning efficiency, transfer generalization, and level of learning. Reduced and/or unfocused attention, restriction to the cognitive operational developmental level, inability to learn automatically and incidentally, and inability to generalize significantly reduces the child's functioning level in academics as well as language acquisition and usage.

In general mildly mentally retarded children enrolled in the primary grades (1st–3rd) will be functioning at preschool and readiness levels; intermediate age students will be functioning at the primary grade level just beginning real academics. The majority of mildly retarded students read at a lower level than would be expected for their mental age, experiencing deficits in comprehension. They can learn mathematics computation, but experience significant difficulty in math reasoning. Adaptive behavior deficiencies in school settings are associated with coping skills, social skills, language development, emotional development, self-care, and social interaction.

Mildly retarded students are unable to use metacognitive skills effectively in strategy selection, in monitoring their learning, and in generalizing learning to new situations. They are controlled by external or outside forces, and feel that things happen to them by chance and that they can do little to change anything. Mildly retarded individuals react to failure by decreasing their efforts on tasks following failure experiences.

Most of the literature on self-concept of mildly retarded students indicates that they do not hold strong, positive feelings about their abilities and potential. Retarded students appear to have a low self-concept of academic achievement including negative feelings about their intelligence, school status, and popularity. They appear to experience significant anxiety about school-related situations and activities.

Severely Handicapped

General characteristics of severely handicapped children and youth include the following: (1) moderate to severe/profound mental retardation; (2) little or no communication; (3) almost total dependence regarding dressing, toileting, feeding, and hygiene; (4) deficits in visual and auditory functioning; (5) severe psychomotor retardation often accompanied by cerebral palsy; (6) medical concerns such as epilepsy, scoliosis, respiratory health concerns, (7) no spontaneous interpersonal interactions; (8) severe social and adaptive behavior deficits; (9) frequent inappropriate behavior (e.g. self-stimulatory, self-injurious behaviors, ritualistic behaviors).

Chapter Six

BEHAVIOR DISORDERED STUDENTS

"The emotionally disturbed child and adolescent (as well as the adult) is likely to differ from peers in terms of greater egocentricity and lack of decentration in cognitive and social tasks" (Monson & Simeonsson, 1987, 67).

Students who experience behavioral and emotional problems are referred to by a variety of terms including emotionally disturbed, socially maladjusted, psychologically disordered, emotionally handicapped, behavior disordered, behaviorally impaired, socially/emotionally handicapped, etc. (Heward & Orlansky, 1988). There is general agreement among professionals that these disorders refer to behavior that is extremely different from usual, the problem is a long standing chronic condition, and the behavior is unacceptable because of social or cultural expectations (Hallahan & Kauffman, 1988).

COGNITIVE AND ACADEMIC FUNCTIONING

Discussions of cognitive and academic functioning are frequently omitted from texts on behavior disordered children and youth due to the significant focus on the inappropriate behavior. The deviant behavior must be brought under control as a prerequisite to adequate academic functioning and to age-appropriate cognitive advances.

Cognitive Learning Problems

Intellectual Functioning

A significant proportion of mild-moderate behavior disordered children fall into the slow learner and mildly retarded categories with average IQs of about 90 or dull normal range (Hallahan & Kauffman, 1988). The low normal IQs for mild-moderate disturbed children and adolescents indicate delays in learning to perform academic tasks that nonhandicapped peers can perform successfully, and the failure to gain adequately from their environmental experiences (Jones, 1992). These children and youth are usually educated in self-contained classrooms, and are gradually mainstreamed into regular education classrooms as they learn to control their inappropriate behaviors.

Severe-profound behavior disordered children are frequently untestable, however, those who can be tested usually perform within the severely retarded range (Cullinan & Epstein, 1990). Children who are severely and profoundly disturbed are described as having pervasive developmental disorders including (1) infantile autism and (2) pervasive developmental disorder (childhood onset) (Keith, 1987). "Most children with pervasive developmental disorder have been diagnosed by age three, because the signs and symptoms are so striking and devastating for the child and the parents" (Keith, 1987, 216). Many of these children are educated in special self-contained schools or hospitals.

Information Processing

Information processing skills of mild-moderate behavior disordered youngsters reveal significant deficits. "These problems involve distortions in the whole range of psychological functions during childhood development including attention, perception, learning abilities, language, social skills, reality contact, and motor skills" (Rizzo & Zabel, 1988, 146).

Their initial problem is not paying enough attention to lessons to even get the process started. Attention deficits, also, reduce the amount of information processed in the short-term memory and stored in the long-term memory. Information that is stored may be composed of only partially accurate information due to lack of attention to detail. The use of working memory may be very minimal due to lack of metacognitive skills to manage the organization and use of information. Information may be difficult to retrieve because of lack of labeling and integrating with the long-term memory store. Some behavior-disordered youngsters may be capable of processing information appropriately, but their extreme anxiety "short-circuits" the whole process and significantly reduces learning (Jones, 1992).

Selective attention and selective intention deficits severely affect the behavior disordered child's progress in the classroom. Aggressive mild-moderate disturbed youngsters frequently demonstrate characteristics of attention deficit hyperactive disorder (AD/HD) including impulsivity, overactivity, not persisting on tasks, easily distracted, inadequate decision-making skills, interrupting others, and aggression (American Psychiatric Association, 1987). Mild-moderate disturbed children with selective attention problems also experience selective intention deficits such as failure to monitor what they say; poorly planned and inappropriate action; inconsistent performance on tasks they do complete shows sacrifice of accuracy for speed; and failure to learn from experience (Levine, 1987). They are constantly at odds with authority figures and have no friends among peers due to their hostile actions.

The seriously withdrawn or depressed behavior disordered child or youth also possesses selective attention and selective intention deficits. Their overriding anxiety and depression, avoidance of possible failure in academics, daydreaming or "existing in another time and space" severely impairs their ability to focus attention on classroom tasks at hand. Children who are schizophrenic experience cognitive and academic deficits due to delusions, hallucinations, incoherence in thought and language (Rizzo & Zabel, 1988).

Behavior-disordered children who are also learning disabled may experience perceptual difficulties producing inaccurate information, experience deficits or delays in understanding complexities of language, or may experience significant fine motor skill deficits that limit the child's ability to demonstrate learning through written responses (Jones, 1992).

Learning efficiency among behavior disordered children and adolescents may be almost nonexistent. Those youngsters who are also learning disabled may not spontaneously use strategies, such as verbal rehearsal and clustering, to help themselves remember. Since behavior-disordered students, both aggressive and withdrawn, fail to use metacognitive skills to monitor and adjust their behavior, it is unlikely that they will be able to use metacognition to monitor their memory processes and academic functioning (Jones, 1992).

Automatization is a skill very important to effective and efficient learning. Mild-moderate behavior disordered youth, both aggressive and withdrawn, are so involved with themselves and the deviant behaviors that rule their lives that they may have little time, inclination, or patience and concentration to develop prerequisite academic skills to a level required for automaticity. Behavior-disordered children may lack a fluent automatic reading vocabulary which is a prerequisite to reading comprehension. They may lack automaticity with basic math facts which impairs their ability to perform math processes (addition, subtraction, multiplication, division). The frustration of attempting to perform a task for which they do not possess the basic prerequisites may increase the aggressive or withdrawn behaviors of these children, thus, interfering with skill acquisition (Jones, 1992).

Severe-profound behavior disordered youngsters may function as infants and preschoolers in their abilities in cognition, language, and developmental skills. Their overriding behavioral and emotional concerns (aggressive or withdrawn) prevent acquiring the developmental prerequisites to learning. They may process little or no information and often engage in self-stimulatory behaviors that significantly interfere with learning.

Academic Learning Problems

Mild-Moderate Behavior Disordered

Mild-moderate behavior-disordered students are underachievers when considering both chronological age and mental age. Their behavior at school interferes with attending to task and completing the required academic assignments. For some children, the pattern of failure in academic situations is so severe and long-standing that they do not have the skills to handle academic situations (Cartwright et al., 1989).

Mild-moderate behavior-disordered students perform behind non-handicapped peers in reading, arithmetic, and spelling (Kauffman et al., 1987). They frequently experience difficulty in written composition assignments due to interference from attention deficits, and lack of automaticity in the prerequisite skills necessary to produce a written assignment (Jones, 1992). Of significant concern is the fact that academic retardation increases with age or grade level, and increased failure in academics produces even more deviant behavior (Whelan, 1988). Research (Epstein & Cullinan, 1983), however, indicates that behavior disordered students function at higher academic levels in reading, math, and other academics than learning disabled peers.

Schloss (1985) indicates that major concerns regarding behavior disordered children and youth include the following: (1) Skill deficits: the absence of a response in the student's repertoire; (2) Motivational deficits: the student's failing to perform a behavior even though the prerequisite skills are present in his repertoire; and (3) Discrimination deficits: result when an individual has the skill and motivation necessary to engage in the desired behavior, but is not aware of appropriate conditions for performing it.

The aggressive "child who is refusing to work, swearing at teachers, knocking materials off other children's desks, and performing all sorts of inappropriate behaviors obviously is not a participant in instruction" (Cartwright et al., 1989, 290). The significantly withdrawn child who retreats into fantasy and depression, refuses to talk in class or complete assignments, experiences "illnesses" and phobic reactions at school, appears extremely anxious and nervous when asked to perform, also, is not an active learner.

Severe-Profound Behavior Disordered

Severe-profound behavior-disordered children may totally lack academic skills, displaying severe deficits in skills such as language, communication, self-help, and play (Cartwright et al., 1989). Seriously behavior-disordered youngsters experience an inability to communicate or they may "use language as a noncommunicating self-stimulatory behavior" (Gelfand et al., 1988, 292). The majority of autistic children never develop useful speech; however, those who develop language engage in echolalic behaviors or in unusual nonspeech sounds such as tongue clicking, repetition of nonsense syllables, screeches, and screams (Rizzo & Zabel, 1988). Schizophrenic children may evidence peculiarities of voice including peculiar intonations, strange and repeated noises and sounds, echolalic speech; and occasionally a child with language will carry on both parts of a conversation in different voices (Rizzo & Zabel, 1988).

Severe-profound behavior-disordered children often experience perceptual deviations and deficits. "The may seem deaf or blind to the casual observer because at first they appear to be oblivious of what is going on around them: They ignore people and do not seem to be affected by conversation or loud noises or bright lights" (Hallahan & Kauffman, 1988, 184).

SOCIAL AND EMOTIONAL FUNCTIONING

In normal development there is a close relationship among cognitive and social/emotional development. As a normal child or youth develops cognitively, s/he acquires more mature ability in social developmental skills including the following: social perspective-taking, social regulation, moral development, social problem-solving, and social relationships. The normal child and youth, also, matures emotionally in terms of self-knowledge (beliefs, commitments, attitudes, values), self-competence, and self-evaluation as s/he develops cognitively. These complex social and emotional skills depend on abstract thinking, the use of logic, and automaticity in self-monitoring.

Social and Emotional Problems

The behavior disordered child and adolescent is likely to differ from peers in terms of greater egocentricity and lack of decentration in cognitive and social tasks (Monson & Simeonsson, 1987). Thus, the behavior-disordered youngster is more self-centered, less able to engage in social perspective-taking, and less able to empathize with others. These weaknesses severely hamper abilities to form satisfying interpersonal relationships, engage in socially appropriate behavior, and understand his/her role in the success or failure of social situations.

Inappropriate Behavior

Mild-Moderate Behavior Disordered. Aggressive children and adolescents with conduct disorders tend to be disruptive, impulsive, angry, destructive, and aggressive (Rizzo & Zabel, 1988). Aggressive behavior is probably the most common presenting problem among youngsters classified as emotionally and behaviorally disturbed (Epanchin, 1987). Aggressive conduct disorders involve repeated episodes of violent confrontation with others, including acts of physical assault, robbery or theft involving physical confrontation, or sexually assaultive behavior (Rizzo & Zabel, 1988).

Within the school setting disorders of aggression may involve cruelty, bullying peers, threats, petty extortion, fighting on the playground, screaming, tantrums, hostile resistance; disrespect, disobedience, and threatening teachers (Cullinan & Epstein, 1990). Unpredictable outbursts and threats disrupt the class and interfere with other children's concentration, frequently all day long (Epanchin, 1987).

"From a social learning perspective, conduct disorders in children and adolescents result either from a failure to learn appropriate social skills, or from learning inappropriate social behaviors or both" (Rizzo & Zabel, 1988, 130). Many behavior-disordered children have problems determining when and where certain behaviors are appropriate (Heward & Orlansky, 1988). Additionally, aggressive children learn many aggressive responses through observation and imitation of family members. Children are more likely to be aggressive when they are victims of physical assault, verbal threats, taunts, insults, and/or when positive reinforcement decreases or ends (Epanchin, 1987). It is the conduct-disordered (hyperaggressive) child or youth whose adulthood is most likely to be characterized by socially intolerable behavior (Kazdin, 1987).

Results of studies indicate that aggressive youth are different in childhood than their behavior-disordered peers (Griffin, 1987). As a group, they exhibit a significantly greater number of conduct-disordered behaviors, developmentally related organic factors, and academic problems prior to age nine than the comparison subjects in the other two groups (Griffin, 1987).

Personality disorders involving extreme cases of worry, self-consciousness, insecurity, fears, depression, and anxiety often result in inappropriate and deviant behaviors. "Periods of withdrawal may alternate with angry outbursts, tantrums, crying, or running away" (Rizzo & Zabel, 1988, 90). Withdrawn behavior-disordered youngsters often retreat into their own daydreams and fantasies; some regress to earlier developmental stages and demand constant help and attention (Heward & Orlansky, 1988).

A major concern regarding withdrawn behavior-disordered adolescents is depression—a condition that may include mood disturbances, inability to think or concentrate, lack of motivation, sadness, apathy, poor self-esteem and pervasive pessimism (Hallahan & Kauffman, 1987). Depression has frequently been linked to suicide among teens. "Obviously, these behavior patterns limit the child's chances to take part in and learn from the school and leisure activities that normal children participate in" (Heward and Orlansky, 1988, 187). Social incompetence reduces the youth's chances for profiting from classroom and informal learning activities and opportunities for friendships (Cullinan & Epstein, 1990).

"For the child with personality problems, disappointment, self-blame, and hopelessness are constant life companions" (Rizzo & Zabel, 1988, 91). A pattern of immature and withdrawn behavior together with school failure is predictive of poor adjustment in adulthood for girls" (Cartwright et al., 1989, 292).

Severe-Profound Behavior Disorders. "Children who are severely disturbed may be qualitatively different from other children because they frequently exhibit bizarre and inappropriate behaviors, such as repetitive motor behaviors, self-mutilation, and complete lack of eye contact" (Cartwright et al., 1989, 292). Behavior that is stereotyped, repetitive, and useful only for obtaining sensory stimulation (such as swishing saliva, twirling an object, flapping one's hands, staring at lights) is common in severely disturbed children (Hallahan & Kauffman, 1987). Some severely disturbed children injure themselves purposely and repeatedly to such an extent that they must be kept in restraints so they will not mutilate and/or slowly kill themselves. They seem totally unaware of the self-inflicted pain.

Interpersonal Relationships

Mild-Moderate Behavior Disordered. Children and youth exhibiting mild-moderate behavior disorders in interpersonal relationships frequently engage in aggressive behaviors against peers or completely withdraw from them. "These children cannot develop normal social interactions and are deprived of normal kinds of approval and satisfaction from others" (Lerner et al., 1989, 35).

> Behavior-disordered children are seldom really liked by anyone—their peers, teachers, brothers or sisters, even parents. Sadder still, they often do not even like themselves. They are difficult to be around, and attempts to befriend them may lead only to rejection, verbal abuse, or even physical attack (Heward & Orlansky, 1988, 169).

Aggressive behavior includes physical assaults such as hitting, kicking, biting, shoving, and destruction of others' property; and verbal assaults such as making threats, hurling insults, and name-calling (Epanchin, 1987). The behaviors occur often and with great intensity repeatedly violating the rights of other persons and socially accepted norms for appropriate ways of behaving (Whelan, 1988). It is not surprising, then, that aggressive children in the regular elementary and secondary classrooms are seldom socially accepted by peers. They are seldom allowed to participate very long in community activities such as Little League ballgames, scouting, etc. due to the aggressive and hostile behavior toward other children (Jones, 1992). "It appears that aggressive behavior patterns have already become a major component of the child's behavioral repertoire by the age of 10 years" (Griffin, 1987, 251).

Withdrawn behavior involves too little social interaction, "children are unusually quiet, having few emotional highs or lows. Preferring to be alone, they will avoid group activities . . . These children will not spontaneously initiate conversation. Often they will try to avoid verbal contacts" (Lerner et al., 1987, 34). "They are social isolates who have few friends, seldom play with other children their own age, and lack the social skills necessary to have fun. Some retreat into fantasy or daydreaming; some develop fears that are completely out of proportion to the circumstances" (Hallahan & Kauffman, 1988, 183).

Obviously, neither the mild-moderate aggressive behavior-disordered youth nor the mild-moderate withdrawn behavior-disordered youth experience appropriate, satisfying interactions with peers. Many children who experience difficulty with peer interactions lack insight into the reciprocal nature of interactions or lack critical social-cognitive developmental skills (Youniss, 1978). The behavior-disordered youngster may not see the relationship between their behavior and the social rejection they receive.

Studies have revealed that behavior-disordered children lack social-evaluation ability (Jurkovic & Selman, 1980). Mild-moderate behavior-disordered youth frequently made errors in interpreting peers behavior toward them in that they perceived peers to be hostile whenever the peers' intentions were ambiguous, and they reacted aggressively to the perceived hostile behavior (Dodge & Frame, 1982). Behavior-disordered youngsters were found to be less knowledgeable about appropriate ways to be helpful to peers in situations of need (Ladd & Oden, 1979).

Nonverbal communication skills deficits negatively influence the quality of an individual's interpersonal functioning. Emotionally disturbed adolescent males have shown decreased abilities to interpret nonverbal facial emotions (Feldman et al., 1982). Depressed patients displayed significant impairment in the production of facial emotional expressions, particularly for positive facial expressions (Jaeger et al., 1986). Thus, the inability to accurately interpret and express facial emotions seems to contribute to personal adjustment problems in emotionally disturbed students.

Severe-Profound Behavior Disordered. "Childhood onset pervasive developmental disorders are characterized most importantly by extensive, severe, and ongoing defects in interpersonal relationships" (Rizzo & Zabel, 1988, 161). These severely behavior-disordered youngsters fail to develop interactive human relatedness and/or social communication (Epanchin, 1987).

> One of the most disconcerting aspects of severely disturbed children's behavior is that they tend to react to other people, including their parents and siblings, as physical objects. Often these children ignore or resist their parents and others when they try to show love and affection. They do not adapt their posture to their parents' when they are being held and they do not develop an anticipatory posture when being picked up. There is no exchange of warmth and gratification between adults and such children (Hallahan & Kauffman, 1988, 185).

Feelings of Personal Control

"Many behavior-disordered children think they have little control over their lives. Things just seem to happen to them, and being disruptive is their means of reacting to a world that is inconsistent and frustrating" (Heward & Orlansky, 1988, 200).

Metacognitive Deficits

Youngsters who have mild-moderate behavior disorders experience difficulty with both academic and social problem-solving because they are deficient in the metacognitive operations to direct the learning process, and to monitor and control their behavior. These youngsters lack cognitive strategies to control and direct thinking, remembering, and learning; and lack monitoring skills to determine if their responses (academic and social) are correct or appropriate. They frequently lack automaticity in the prerequisite skills to fluently perform academic tasks, which paired with the lack of metacognitive skills relegates them to focusing on the subskills unable to understand the process. Severe-profound behavior-disordered youngsters have not developed any metacognitive skills, do not possess any insight into or understand their behavior, thus, are unable to evaluate or modify their behaviors.

The lack of metacognitive abilities in social areas significantly interferes with the social acceptability of the behavior-disordered student. The lack of social perspective-taking interferes with the youngster's ability to form mutually satisfying social relationships as s/he can not understand the other person's reasoning, cannot empathize, cannot feel happy at the friend's good fortune, and thus is relegated to immature egocentric behaviors (Jones, 1992). The lack of self-monitoring and social evaluation in social situations renders the behaviorally disordered youth unable to determine when his/her behaviors are socially appropriate or inappropriate; thus, s/he can not monitor accuracy or effect and change the behaviors when social responses indicate that the behavior is inappropriate. Since they cannot understand behaviors from the perspective of the other person, they will not understand why they are ignored, not asked to parties, not included in "the group" activities, nor why they are no longer friends. The lack of metacognitive skills means that the behavior-disordered youth will be unable to engage in social problem-solving, will be socially incompetent, and will continue to function at an immature moral development stage.

The lack of metacognitive abilities renders the child unable to control his/her behavior. This deficit means that the hostile, aggressive child continues to rampage until his energy is spent; and the withdrawn, anxiety-inferiority obsessed child will be unable to halt the destructive emotions of depression and fear. This lack of self-control is far more devastating than just academic deficits or just behavioral deficits, for the lack of self-control interferes with independence and appropriateness in all functioning areas: social, emotional, cognitive, and academic (Jones, 1992).

Attribution Deficits

Academic Attributions. "Students with long histories of academic failure and a weak need for achievement typically attribute their success to easy questions or luck and their failures to lack of ability" (Biehler & Snowman, 1986, 482). Luchow et al. (1985) studied learned helplessness and perceived effects of ability and effort on academic performance among emotionally handicapped and learning disabled/emotionally handicapped children. Results indicated that EH children took significantly more personal responsibility for academic failure than did LD/EH, although the two groups did not differ significantly in taking responsibility for academic success. LD/EH children attributed success to effort and failure to a lack of effort; EH children attributed success to ability, but failure to both a lack of ability and a lack of effort. Among EH children, significant positive correlations were found between report card grades and perceived internality for success. Among

LD/EH children, significant negative correlations were found between report card grades and perceived lack of effort as the cause of failure.

> Because low achieving students attribute failure to low ability, future failure is seen as more likely than future success. Consequently, satisfactory achievement and reward may have little effect on the failure avoiding strategies that poor students have developed over the years. . . . It may be, then, that rewards will not motivate low-need achievers to work harder so long as they attribute success to factors that are unstable and beyond their control (Biehler & Snowman, 1986, 482).

Research indicates that emotionally disordered adolescent boys with a higher degree of internal locus of control made greater gains in academic achievement; and that chronological ages and IQ scores did not effect their degree of internal locus of control (Perna et al., 1983). Children labeled learning disabled were found to be significantly more internally controlled than children labeled behaviorally disordered or than children labeled learning disabled with behavioral disorders (Morgan, 1986).

Severely anxious and withdrawn children often display learned helplessness, a belief that nothing they do can change the bad situations in their lives. Learned helplessness results in severe deterioration in performance after failure because the failure just serves to reinforce in them that there is nothing they can do to change things (Kirk & Gallagher, 1989). The inability to change the bad situations in their lives and to gain love and respect from parents, who frequently are themselves disturbed, adds to feelings of helplessness and reinforces low self-image and low self-worth (Jones, 1992).

Social/Emotional Attributions. Similarly, research regarding children's beliefs about failure in social situations revealed that low-accepted children tended to attribute rejection to their own personal incompetence rather than to peer compatibility or rejection traits (Goetz & Dweck, 1980). Depressed children report significantly more hopelessness, more negative self-perceptions, and more dysfunctional attributional styles than nondepressed students (Asarnow & Bates, 1988). Depressed children often have a depressed parent; receive harsh, power-assertive discipline from their parents; have a rigidly adaptive family style; have a more internal locus of control; and tend to internalize aggression more than do non-depressed conduct-disordered children (King et al., 1986).

Research shows that emotionally disordered and nondisturbed subjects ages 9–11 years old possess an external locus of control and poorer performance in decoding voice tone and facial expression (Nowicki & DiGirolamo, 1989). They frequently are unable to determine the emotions of their peers and adults; thus, they react inappropriately due to lack of comprehension of the social situation.

The portrait of a typical emotionally disturbed child or youth reveals unsuccessful academic performance in combination with inadequate social coping behaviors (Whelan, 1988). All major facets of emotionally disturbed children's lives (internal and external) are chaotic. "The ways that children cope with internal and external chaos are as varied as the children who display them. . . . Deficit and excessive behaviors are ways of avoiding circumstances associated with pain and failure, of coping with problems from within and without . . . " (Whelan, 1988, 204).

Self-Concepts of Behavior Disordered Students

General Self-Concept

Much of the research regarding the general self-concept of emotionally disturbed youngsters indicates an over-evaluated delusional self-concept or a significantly lower self-concept than that of nonhandicapped youth. Farnham-Diggory (1966) pointed out one of the psychotic child's chief limitations was a lack of a sense of competence which is necessary for the child to obtain before he can even develop a realistic self-concept. Goldfarb (1963) found schizophrenic children possess both defective self-concepts and marked anxiety states.

Delusional Self-Concepts. A number of researchers found that some emotionally disturbed children tend to over-evaluate their abilities to a delusional degree. The children were in an almost constant state of anxiety and panic whenever they were forced to go to school because of fear of failure which was incompatible with their over-evaluated self-image (Levanthal & Sills, 1964). Additionally, the behavior of emotionally disturbed students appears more affected by interpersonal distortions which are irrelevant to, or are misperceptions of, the classroom situation than are normal students (Grossman, 1965).

Anxiety appears to contribute both to the disorganization in a child and to a blurring of his consciousness or reality testing (Levitt, 1980). Knoblock (1971) indicated that a compartmentalized view of self was characteristic of many disturbed children and approaches to tasks often revealed an inability to conceptualize and look at the total situation.

Low Self-Concept. Numerous research studies of the self-concept of emotionally disturbed students indicated lower self-concepts than normal students (Clark, 1975; Wood & Johnson, 1972; Politino, 1980). Jones (1985) found that emotionally disturbed students, in public school settings mainstreamed for at least part of the day, possessed significantly more negative phenomenal (conscious) and nonphenomenal (unconscious) self-concepts than nonhandicapped students ages 10–13 years old. Also, the emotionally disturbed students indicated experiencing high anxiety levels.

Sweeney & Zionts (1989) examined the differences between regular education and emotionally disturbed early adolescents with respect to self-concept, body image, and selected uses of clothing. Their findings revealed that emotionally impaired were less likely to use clothing to influence mood than were regular education students.

Self-Concept of Academic Achievement

Although the intelligence quotient is generally agreed to be an excellent predictor of school success and achievement, caution must be used in predicting the achievement level of emotionally disturbed students. Achievement is a significant factor in emotional disturbance, however, the precise cause-and-effect relationship has not been determined (Shea, 1978). It appears that the more years an emotionally disturbed child stayed in school, the further educationally he was behind his nonhandicapped peers (Stennett, 1966), perhaps because being in the classroom was a threatening experience for students with emotional problems (Grossman, 1965).

Many behavior-disordered students have not acquired the educational skills necessary to meet the educational demands imposed upon them. Their emotional problems interfered with their ability to use even those skills they had developed. Even when their lower-than-normal IQ scores are taken into account, most disturbed children are underachievers, as measured by standardized tests (Hallahan & Kauffman, 1988). The poor self-concept of emotionally disturbed children manifests itself as a lack of self-confidence, fear of the unfamiliar, feelings of inferiority, hypersensitivity to criticism, resistance to independent functioning, and reluctance to attempt many activities (Shea, 1978). These behaviors lead to inadequate academic functioning.

Jones (1985) found that emotionally disturbed students perceived their behavior to be significantly less acceptable to adults and peers than nonhandicapped students. They, also, perceived their intellectual ability, school status, and popularity more negatively than did nonhandicapped students.

Anxiety-withdrawn behavior-disordered children have such low self-concepts that failure in a school task or a social setting only confirms for them their worthlessness and helpless in the face of an unfriendly environment (Seligman & Peterson, 1986). Their performance in the classroom may be much worse than they are capable of doing simply because they are so pessimistic about themselves and their ability. "Low self-esteem seems to be at the heart of much of the underachievement of anxious-withdrawn children" (Kirk & Gallagher, 1989, 406).

Hardt (1988) indicates that passive-aggressive behavior in an emotionally disturbed child affects the child's progress and affects peer interactions in classroom settings. Passive-aggressive personalities are typically helpless, dependent, impulsive, overly anxious, poorly oriented to reality, and .procrastinating. They use numerous tactics to control the classroom environment, such as selective vision, selective hearing, slow-down tactics, losing objects, and the destructive volunteer tactic. The passive-aggressive child fails to develop satisfying interpersonal relationships and possesses a negative self-esteem.

Therefore, the research indicates that the general self-concepts and academic self-concepts of behavior-disordered children are significantly negative and interfere with their functioning in all aspects of life. Their external locus of control and expectancy for failure perpetuates a severely negative cycle.

SUMMARY

Behavior-disordered students, both aggressive and withdrawn, are a significant concern of the public school system in terms of their social, emotional, cognitive, and academic progress but, also, on the effects they have on other children in the classroom. The inappropriate and maladaptive behaviors exhibited by behavior-disordered children and adolescents are evident in deficits in academic learning, cognitive development, and social interactions. Disturbed behaviors are frequently categorized as mild-moderate behavior disorders (aggressive behaviors, withdrawn behaviors) and severe-profound behavior disorders.

Mild-moderate behavior-disordered children are usually educated in the public school systems in self-contained classrooms, gradually mainstreamed to the regular classroom as they learn to control their behaviors. Though most mild-moderate behavior-disordered students possess normal-range IQ (around 90), they experience many cognitive delays including metacognitive skills, attention deficits, information processing deficits, inefficiency in learning, and lack automatization. These deficits interact to prevent higher-level cognitive functioning, academic success, and age-appropriate social interactions. These children, also, experience significant deficits in terms of self-concept and have expectancies for failure in academic and social situations.

Severe-profound behavior-disordered students are frequently educated in special schools or hospitals. Many severe-profound behavior-disordered children and youth are untestable; those who are testable generally function as severely retarded individuals. They experience distortions in most psychological functions including attention, perception, learning abilities, social skills, reality contact, and motor skills.

Chapter Seven

LEARNING DISABLED STUDENTS

Children with learning disabilities often have social and emotional behavior problems (Mercer & Mercer, 1989, 146).

A student is considered to have a specific learning disability if s/he does not achieve at the proper age and ability levels when provided appropriate learning experiences, and demonstrates a severe discrepancy between intellectual ability and achievement in one or more academic areas (Lerner, 1989). Social and emotional deficits are seldom considered in making a diagnosis of learning disabled.

COGNITIVE AND ACADEMIC FUNCTIONING

Cognitive deficits in higher level intellectual processes impede learning disabled students in attaining logical thinking abilities, academic skills, and age-appropriate social skills.

Cognitive Learning Problems

Intellectual Functioning

By definition, learning disabled students must have at least average range intellectual functioning. At the lower end of the spectrum, learning disabled youngsters attain IQs of at least 70–75 on the Weschler

117

Scales and learn at approximately ¾ the rate of average nonhandicapped students.

A recent focus in the field is on students who are learning disabled with gifted potential in some areas. Thus, the IQ range of learning disabled students varies from functioning just above the mental retardation cutoff through gifted levels. Nevertheless, a student is not diagnosed on basis of cognitive functioning alone, but must demonstrate a significant potential-achievement discrepancy.

Information Processing Deficits

Information processing problems have long been associated with learning disabilities and are included in the P.L. 94-142 definition as psychological processing problems. These major cognitive problems include attention, reception, perception; memory processes (short-term, working, and long-term) and retrieval; and, usage or behavioral responses to learning (verbal, fine and gross motor) (Jones, 1992).

Attention Problems. Learning-disabled students experience difficulty with both attention deficit areas of selective attention and selective intention. Selective attention deficit is the inability to attend to relevant information in the presence of irrelevant information and includes the following characteristics which interfere with academic and social functioning: (1) erratic concentration, (2) distractability (auditory and visual), (3) reduced responses to feedback (academic and social), (4) inability to delay gratification, (5) deficit self-monitoring skills (academic and social) (Levine, 1987). Academically, deficits in selective intention include (1) poorly planned academic responses, (2) sacrifice of accuracy for speed, (3) inconsistent academic performance and unpredictable test scores, (4) impersistence on tasks and seldom completes projects or assignments, and (5) numerous errors due to reduced response to feedback (Levine, 1987). Socially, selective intention deficits results in (1) verbal disinhibition (failure to monitor what they say), (2) inappropriate actions, (3) inconsistent behavior, (4) failure to learn from mistakes (Levine, 1987).

Perceptual and Motor Disabilities. Deficits in perceptual and motor skills have consistently been listed among the characteristics of learning disabled students. The major areas of concern include auditory and visual perception, tactile and kinesthetic perception, and perceptual-motor integration. Visual perceptual deficits in spatial relationships, discrimination, figure-ground discrimination, and memory may significantly hamper the acquisition of basic skills in reading and mathematics calculation. Auditory perception deficits in discrimination, blending, memory, and sequencing interfere with learning phonics and acquiring reading decoding skills, language acquisition (adequate vocabulary, following directions), and spelling.

Perceptual-motor deficits involve coordinating visual or auditory behaviors with motor responses (fine or gross motor). Visual-fine motor problems include difficulty in cutting and handwriting. Lack of automaticity in handwriting interferes with progress in all academic areas requiring written responses. Perceptual-gross motor deficits are also common among learning disabled students and may interfere with developmental skills as skipping, jumping; and, later with sports (e.g., kickball, soccer, baseball) which may interfere with socialization.

Memory Problems. Learning-disabled students often experience difficulty with various aspects of memory including short-term, working, and long-term memory. Deficits in sustained attention, language, and high levels of anxiety often make it difficult for learning-disabled students to hold information in short-term memory long enough to process it to long-term memory. Learning-disabled youngsters experience difficulty using their working memory efficiently due to a lack of metacognitive skills. They, also, experience numerous long-term memory problems including difficulty in consolidating and integrating new information with information already in storage. As a result, they frequently exhibit a smaller fund of knowledge in long-term storage.

Retrieval problems, the inability to quickly access information or difficulty finding the correct words to use in making a response, may become significant problems to intermediate grade and older learning-disabled students as the stress on rapid retrieval increases. By intermediate grades much academic work is dependent on automatization (rapid and unconscious retrieval memory) of lower-level skills or prerequisites.

A major concern is that learning-disabled students do not automatically use strategies that help them remember and learn. Many strategies require the effective and efficient use of language, another major deficit area of many learning-disabled students. Thus, memory deficits in reception, perception, storage, retrieval, and use of strategies negatively impact all academic areas.

Problem-Solving Deficits. Many of the cognitive deficits of learning-disabled students are related to language processing deficits and inadequate language skills. Especially difficult are problem-solving tasks requiring higher-level more complex uses of language and cognition such as understanding verbal analogies, cause and effect, inferences, analysis and synthesis, and evaluation. Thus, language deficits and cognitive deficits combine to make problem-solving a very difficult task for learning-disabled students. These same deficits negatively impact the student's abilities in social-cognition and social problem-solving.

Academic Learning Problems

"Academic problems are the most widely accepted characteristics of learning disabled individuals" (Mercer, 1987, 40). The major academic deficits of learning-disabled students are in the areas of reading (basic skills and comprehension), listening comprehension, mathematics (calculation and reasoning), oral expression (receptive and expressive), written expression (handwriting, spelling, composition skills, written composition), and preacademics. However, it is usually the interrelationship of academic deficits, cognitive deficits, and social/emotional developmental problems that results in severe learning problems in learning-disabled students.

Preacademics

The area of preacademics is primarily concerned with young developmentally delayed youngsters of at least borderline cognitive ability who are "at-risk" for academic problems. During kindergarten and first grade "at-risk" students frequently experience difficulty in the following areas: (1) Academic Readiness Skills: alphabet knowledge, quantitative concepts, directional concepts; (2) Language Skills: receptive and expressive; (3) Perception: visual, auditory, and motor integration; (4) Fine and Gross Motor Skills; (5) Attention; (6) Hyperactivity; and (7) Social Skills (Mercer, 1987).

Oral Expression

Language problems are the underlying causes for many learning disabilities, both academic and social. Oral expression problems include receptive language problems (e.g., poor understanding of oral language, problems following directions) and expressive language deficits (e.g., delayed speech/language, inadequate vocabulary fund; disorders of syntax, semantics, and pragmatics).

Learning-disabled children and youth experience delays in language acquisition, often by as much as three to four years or more. They experience significant problems with semantics including interpreting ambiguous sentences, figurative language, words with multiple meanings, synonyms, verbal opposites, and verbal analogies (Wiig & Semel, 1984). Learning-disabled students have underdeveloped meaning systems and poorer comprehension of language than their nondisabled peers (Robinson & Deshler, 1988). "Language disorders may also take the form of written language disabilities in reading, writing, or spelling. Many students with severe reading problems have underlying disabilities in oral language" (Lerner, 1989, 320).

Research indicates that learning-disabled adolescents have poorer language and communication skills than their counterparts who are achieving normally (Johnson & Blalock, 1987). Thus, language deficits continue to be a major concern as students move into secondary levels where the cognitive and language demands escalate in terms of amount (numerous content subject areas) and degree (higher level cognitive and metacognitive requirements).

Reading: Basic Skills and Comprehension

The most common academic disability of learning-disabled students is a pervasive reading disability which adversely affects performance in all subject areas. Difficulties learning to read are caused by a multiplicity of problems, many of which stem directly from oral language disorders and information processing problems. Poor receptive language and poor auditory and visual perception skills hamper the acquisition of adequate sight vocabulary and the development of decoding skills such as phonics.

Reading comprehension is extremely difficult for many learning-disabled students. Students who must expend a great amount of effort in decoding words may have little processing capacity for simultaneous comprehension. Reading comprehension can be hindered by language processing deficits, lack of an adequate conceptual background, and deficient experiences. Students who experience difficulties in oral language and reading comprehension, also, experience difficulties with similar skills in listening comprehension. The lack of higher-level content vocabulary impedes progress in content-area subjects.

Learning-disabled students who have not mastered the "learning to read" skills by the end of third grade find themselves being expected to "read to learn" in content areas of science and social studies without an adequate vocabulary base and comprehension skills needed to be successful. Research (Deshler et al., 1980) indicates that many learning-disabled adolescents reach a plateau at 4th or 5th grade academic achievement during 10th grade and fail to progress.

Written Expression

Most learning-disabled students experience significant disabilities in written composition often due to a lack of automaticity in prerequisite skills (e.g., handwriting, spelling, composition skills). Poor handwriting due to inadequate fine motor control and poor eye-hand coordination interfere with automaticity of letter formation, size, slant, etc. resulting in deficits in written language production (amount and quality). Poor information processing skills (auditory and visual perception, memory, attention) in combination with poor handwriting skills, difficulty with visualization, and poor phonics skills significantly interfere with spelling accuracy. The lack of automaticity in handwriting, spelling, composition skills (e.g., grammar, capitalization and punctuation, paragraph structure) paired with oral language deficits, and cognitive deficits make functional and creative writing very difficult and nearly impossible for many learning-disabled students.

Mathematics Calculation and Reasoning

Many learning-disabled youngsters experience difficulty in math calculation and/or math reasoning. A lack of automaticity in math prerequisites including classification, ordering and seriation, one-to-one correspondence, conservation, information processing, spatial relationships, basic facts, steps in computing the basic arithmetic processes interferes with attaining the new skill.

Intermediate grade learning-disabled students frequently experience difficulty understanding place value, regrouping, fractions, multiplication, and especially division because it requires the integrated use of several math processes (Mercer, 1987). The lack of mastery of basic facts and other math prerequisites continue to interfere with calculation.

Mathematics reasoning, especially word problems, are difficult for most children but may be nearly impossible for learning-disabled students. Word problems not only require the ability to read but to read and interpret mathematical language and concepts. Math reasoning requires automatization of math calculation prerequisites and skills. Auditory and visual preceptual processing deficits, and poor spatial relationships significantly hinder the acquisition of math reasoning skills. Learning-disabled students frequently lack the cognitive functioning required to interpret math reasoning problems.

SOCIAL AND EMOTIONAL FUNCTIONING

"Since a deficit in social skills implies a lack of sensitivity to people and a poor perception of social situations, the deficit affects almost every aspect of the student's life and is probably one of the most crippling disabilities a student can have" (Lerner, 1989, 468–469).

Social and Emotional Problems

The interactions of learning-disabled students with peers, teachers, parents, and siblings are often characterized by inappropriate behaviors. Research indicates that learning-disabled students have less acceptable behaviors than their handicapped peers as follows: (1) less ability to predict the consequences of their behaviors, (2) more frequently misinterpret social cues, (3) more difficulty adapting their behaviors to their listeners, and (4) more frequent performance of inappropriate social behaviors (Schumaker & Hazel, 1984). Appropriate social interactions are predicated upon numerous abilities that are areas of difficulty for learning-disabled students including communication, higher-order cognitive abilities including metacognition, motivation, attribution, and self-concepts.

Communication Deficits

"The learning-disabled child's tendency to have trouble communicating with others, both as a listener and as a speaker, put that child at risk to have social difficulties" (Hallahan & Kauffman, 1988, 124).

Intonation System. By two years of age, most children have mastered the adult intonation system. Thus, they can listen to subtle tone changes and can predict if adults and other children feel angry, happy, sad, etc. even if they cannot understand the words they may say. Many learning-disabled youngsters lack mastery of the intonation system and experience difficulty interpreting emotions by listening to the intonation of someone's voice.

These "children may have difficulty adjusting language and tone of voice to a specific social situation. They may fail at integrating either accurate or adaptive feelings or emotions with expressive language. Their intonation and word choice, for example, might suggest anger and hostility when this is not actually the case, leading to misunderstanding and sometimes rejection by peers" (Levine, 1987, 158).

Pragmatics Deficits. Related to deficits in the intonation system are deficits in pragmatics, the social use of language. Numerous studies indicate that learning-disabled persons (adults and children) have difficulty in pragmatics in the following areas which negatively affects social interactions: (1) fail to consider the listener's ability to follow the conversation (Oyer et al., 1987); (2) fail to use polite speech or show consideration for others in their language usage (Oyer et al., 1987); (3) more frequently make nasty remarks to peers (Bryan & Bryan, 1978); (4) receive more statements of rejection from peers (Bryan & Bryan, 1978); (5) experience problems conveying intentions to listeners (Levine, 1987); (6) experience difficulty initiating and sustaining a conversation (Levine, 1987).

Learning-disabled boys appear to experience significant difficulty in adapting messages to the needs of the listener and in interpreting and responding to subtle nonverbal feedback (Knight-Arest, 1984). Learning-disabled children appear to be less conversationally persuasive than non-LD peers, and more conversationally compliant, and thus do not regulate the flow of dialogue (Lovitt, 1989). In addition to being widely misunderstood or misinterpreted, they unintentionally commit many faux pas (Levine, 1987).

Language disabilities cause significant problems for adolescents as they attempt to meet increased social demands by adults and peers. Language deficits may prevent learning-disabled adolescents from appropriately using slang and engaging in flirting behaviors with the opposite sex. Learning-disabled students do not exhibit the increase in understanding humor and interpreting implied information and sarcasm that non-learning-disabled students show at intermediate and middle-school ages (Bruno et al., 1987).

Research indicates that LD adolescents and adults experience difficulty in situations requiring extensive language interactions and in maintaining a conversation (Johnson & Blalock, 1987). Overall, there are numerous aspects of the communicative process which place LD students "at-risk" for social and emotional problems. LD students experience problems in both receptive and expressive language; and, syntax, semantics, intonation, pragmatics, as well as metalinguistic and communicative competence.

Social Skills Deficits

Learning-disabled children and youth experience numerous social skills deficits including social imperceptiveness, social disability, lack of empathy, and role-taking ability, and problems with interpersonal relationships. Social skills deficits are directly related to deficits in cognition and information processing (e.g., inability to self-monitor, lack of generalization ability, concrete level thinking) and language deficits. Learning-disabled students, also, experience attention deficits, hyperactivity, and impulsiveness which result in problems drawing social inferences in social metacognitive deficits.

Social Imperceptiveness. Many learning-disabled students experience social and emotional problems due to their social imperceptions or their lack of skill in perceiving accurately the feelings and subtle responses of others (Bryan, 1977). Problems with attention, impulsivity, and hyperactivity interfere with socialization efforts and the ability to read the social scene (Levine, 1987). Learning-disabled students are at high risk for social rejection because they experience difficulty predicting social consequences, generating appropriate interactional strategies, and controlling aggressive outbursts (Levine, 1987).

The inability of learning-disabled youngsters to interpret nonverbal and verbal communication interferes with understanding the affective states of others (Bryan & Pflam, 1978). Learning-disabled students may experience difficulty reacting appropriately to others' facial expressions, hand and arm gestures, posture, tone of voice, or general moods (Mercer, 1987).

Learning-disabled children who are unable to infer emotions from verbal and nonverbal communication also have difficulty taking the perspective of others. They lack the ability to understand the emotions, motives, and intentions of other people (Mercer, 1987). "Children who are overly preoccupied with their own needs and appetites may have real trouble sharing, compromising, and in particular, taking the perspective of another child. This can seriously thwart any efforts at sustained interaction" (Levine, 1987, 261).

Learning-disabled students with social disabilities appear less attuned than their peers to the feelings of others. Due to misinterpretation, they may react with inapropriate behavior or language (Lerner, 1989). Learning-disabled students may behave inappropriately because of social cognition problems or social interaction problems which involve a wide variety of cognitive processes such as perspective-taking, empathy, and knowledge of social conventions of behavior. It is their knowledge base that helps direct children's social behavior or tactics" (Pullis, 1988, 86).

Social Disability. There is increasing evidence that learning-disabled children experience problems in social relationships whether interacting with parents, teachers, peers, or strangers (Bryan & Bryan, 1986). Many learning-disabled students are said to have a social disability. Such students have been described in general as performing poorly in age-appropriate social activities, inept in judging moods and attitudes of people, insensitive to the atmosphere of a social situation, displaying inappropriate behaviors, and making inappropriate remarks (Lerner, 1989).

The **peer relationships** and social life of LD youngsters is different from that of other students (Bryan, 1986). Learning-disabled children tend to be either rejected or ignored by peers when attempting to initiate a social interaction. The socially different behavior of learning-disabled youngsters is even noted by strangers, who are able to detect differences between learning-disabled and non-learning-disabled youngsters after viewing interactions for only a few minutes. Several authorities believe that learning-disabled children elicit negative reactions from others because they lack social comprehension skills (Weiss, 1984).

Learning-disabled girls are even more at risk for social rejection and isolation than are learning-disabled boys (Hallahan & Kauffman, 1988). When working with a partner, they tend to resist the partner's initiatives for cooperative work. Some of the negativeness emitted toward learning-disabled youngsters may be due to not making appropriate eye contact with other people during conversations (Bryan, et al., 1980). Learning-disabled youngsters have been described as both deferential and hostile (Lerner, 1989).

Learning-disabled adolescents tend to engage in fewer activities related to extracurricular events and go out with friends less frequently than non-learning-disabled adolescents (Deshler & Schumaker, 1983). Even adolescents who have had opportunities for peer interactions and modeling as children may have failed to learn social skills. Many learning-handicapped youngsters have as much difficulty learning social skills as they have with reading, writing, and arithmetic. They reach adolescence with inadequate social tools to choose the right clothes to wear, the right things to say, the right things to do (Silverman et al., 1983).

Learning-disabled adolescents do not develop a broad enough repertoire of social behaviors to react differently to different situations; thus, their behavior is often inappropriate (Zigmond, 1978). They also lack social judgment and do not seem to understand the role they play in influencing the consequences that accrue to them so are continuously getting themselves and their peers into trouble, both in school and in the community. Learning-disabled adolescents do not appear to have the skills of social metacognition which would allow them to analyze and reflect consciously on personal social ability: analyze themselves, the social scene, and its requirements (Flavell, 1985). They often use egocentric reasoning strategies and are less able than their peers to make moral decisions based on group norms and expectations (Derr, 1986). Research indicates that even though learning-disabled students are aware of social norms, they admit that they are more willing than nonhandicapped peers to violate social norms by committing antisocial acts (Bryan et al., 1982).

Parents and teachers view learning-disabled students more negatively than their non-learning-disabled children (Lerner, 1989). Research indicated that teachers, parents, and peers rated mainstreamed LD students as deficient in task-related, interpersonal, and self-related social skills (e.g., accepting authority, helping others, expressing feelings, and having positive attitudes); and that LD children were more poorly accepted by peers in play and work situations (Gresham & Reschly, 1986). LD youngsters are likely to be rejected by parents, teachers, and peers because of their numerous problems in social behavior, language, and temperament (Bryan, 1986).

Feelings of Personal Control

Learning-disabled and nonhandicapped learners appear to be significantly different in motivation, attention, social skills, and locus of control (Reschly, 1987). They lack the metacognitive skills to control their academic and social behaviors. Teachers and parents often report that learning-disabled students do not have the inner motivation needed for learning academic tasks (Lerner, 1989).

Metacognitive Deficits

A characteristic of learning-disabled students is that they lack functional cognitive strategies. They do not know how to control and direct their thinking to learn how to gain more knowledge or how to remember what they learn (Mercer, 1987). In other words, they lack age-appropriate metacognitive skills.

Metacognition can be divided into categories according to specific cognitive processes including metamemory, metalistening, meta-attention, and metacomprehension (Hallahan et al., 1985). These specific categories of metacognitive skills continue to involve the student's specific knowledge of his/her abilities in that area and the strategies necessary for organizing, planning, and learning the specific skills involved in memory, listening, reading comprehension, etc. and controlling one's attention for better task focus. Learning-disabled children frequently experience difficulty in all areas of metacognition.

Learning-disabled children do not develop a schema that promotes active, independent learning (Beckman & Weller, 1990). Due to lack of automaticity in metacognitive skills, learning-disabled children are frequently unable to plan and organize for task completion whether a daily assignment or a term paper (Jones, 1992). They lack the ability to monitor their progress toward task completion and plan needed time allotments. They frequently are unable to monitor their own errors and to evaluate the accuracy of task performance once the assignment is completed. This lack of metacognitive skills often results in a student who is dependent on others to plan and organize academic tasks and to depend on others to determine if the finished product is accurate. However, it may appear that learning-disabled individuals lack the motivation needed to complete tasks and reach goals independently when the problem is much more complex than just a lack of motivation.

Motivation Deficits

Learning-disabled students do not appear to have the motivation needed for learning academic tasks (Lerner, 1989). They frequently experience difficulties in consistently maintaining motivation and often experience a loss of motivation. Like all humans, children with deficits of attention and intention have little difficulty performing under conditions of high motivation (Levine, 1987). "The real issue is how effectively a child concentrates and produces under moderately motivating conditions.

This is indeed what separates children with intention problems from those without such problems" (Levine, 1987, 32). Inconsistent performance may relate to variations in levels of motivation (Douglas, 1983).

Negative feelings about the self in the student role are often manifested in two areas—lack of motivation on tasks and classroom misbehavior (Pullis, 1988). Lack of motivation appears to be a consequence of chronic failure and negative feelings about their intellectual abilities (Lerner, 1989). Children who have developed negative feelings about their academic performance often will not be very task oriented because their school experiences cause them to anticipate failure, feelings of incompetence, and embarrassment (Pullis, 1988).

Learning-disabled students who lack motivation may engage in numerous avoidance behaviors as follows to prevent failure and feelings of incompetence: (1) not starting tasks without several reminders, (2) asking many questions about the quality of their work (Is this right?), (3) looking busy without actually finishing any academic tasks, (4) withdrawal into excessive daydreaming, (5) excessive talking during work periods, (6) excessive out-of-seat behavior, (7) aggression towards peers, (8) conflicts with teachers concerning compliance with rules or assignments, (9) distracting self by playing with strings and toys brought to school, (10) distracting others by tapping pencils, tearing up papers, muttering to self, etc.

Personal and family priorities may effect a student's motivation. If completing academic tasks in school is a low priority of the student and his/her family, the learning-disabled student will lack persistence and task focus to complete assignments. Some children may be motivated to strive for success in one subject area or situation and not in others, which may also be a coping strategy to avoid failure. "If a particular goal requires too much effort or too much delay of gratification, or if it greatly exceeds the capacity of a child's attention, it may be abandoned" (Levine, 1987, 424). Thus, it is not unusual for children who have experienced continual frustration in the classroom to merely "give up" trying to meet the demands of the school situation.

Children rapidly lose motivation when they perceive the likelihood of success as minimal. Children have little tolerance for failure and are commonly drained of motivation when they are least likely to succeed. They have a common, innate sense that is better not to try at all than to make an effort and fail. This is true in the classroom, on the playing field, and in social settings (Levine, 1987).

Attribution Deficits

Locus of control is developmental in nature and appears to be external for both success and failure at the age of 4 to 5 years, becomes internal for success by age 6 to 7 years, and finally becomes internal for both success and failure by the age of 10 to 11 years (Lawrence & Winschel, 1975). Learning-disabled children do not follow this typical pattern and are more external in their orientation than nondisabled children of the same age (e.g., Rogers, 1983). When internality does develop for learning-disabled children, it is internality for failure and not for success (Dudley-Marling et al., 1982). Learning-disabled children take significantly less responsibility for their academic successes and failures than normal achievers (Rogers & Saklofske, 1985).

"There is considerable evidence that children's causal attributions (personal analyses of reasons) for failure are good predictors of their responses to difficulties in achievement situations" (Levine, 1987, 425). Learning-disabled "students often attribute their successes and failures to factors outside of their control (reflecting an external locus of control). They attribute success to luck or to the teacher, and they blame failures on their lack of ability or the difficulty of the task" (Lerner, 1989, 475). Children "who believe somehow that uncontrollable forces, such as their innate inability, caused them to fail are likely to respond in a helpless fashion. This is typically accompanied by a loss of motivation, a sense of diminished expectancy from goals" (Levine, 1987, 425). LD children and youth have been labeled "at risk for developing learned helplessness" (Hallahan & Kauffman, 1988, 125), a belief "that one simply does not have the ability to succeed and therefore any intensification of effort would be doomed to failure" (Levine, 1987, 425).

Learning-disabled children appear to have low self-perceptions of ability, reflecting relatively negative academic self-concept, along with tendencies toward learned helplessness and lower expectations for future success in school (Chapman, 1988). LD children therefore have relatively little confidence in their ability and expect to achieve at lower levels, but when success does occur, they see it as being caused by a teacher's assistance or easy work (Chapman, 1988). In essence, the attribution studies indicate that learning-disabled children differ from their more successful peers on many personality variables considered important for school learning.

Self-Concepts of Learning-Disabled Students

General Self-Concept

"In general, the investigation of self-concept differences between learning disabled and normally achieving children has yielded inconsistent results" (Gresham, 1988, 294). Numerous researchers have reported that learning-disabled students have significantly lower or more negative self-concept scores than nonhandicapped or normally achieving peers (e.g., Jones, 1985; Margalit & Zak, 1984; Rogers, 1983). Other researchers, however, reported no significant differences between the general self-concepts of the learning-disabled and normative populations (Silverman & Zigmond, 1981; Vallecorsa, 1980).

These inconsistent results may be due in part to the fact that the self-concept is currently viewed as complex and multifaceted. A number of factors are considered relevant to the development of the student's self-concept including athletic skills, personal physical attractiveness, social attractiveness, special aptitudes, intelligence, academic performance, peer acceptance, moral code, and leadership qualities. Thus, individuals may simultaneously have positive and negative perceptions regarding various aspects of their personality and their abilities to function in their world. More consistent research results may be achieved by analyzing the separate factors of self-concept rather than trying to determine a generalized self-concept.

Self-Concept of Academic Achievement

Research has suggested that the academic self-concept was formed before the end of the third grade and that it quickly stabilized as patterns of school success and failure were established (Battle, 1981). Studies with learning-disabled children suggest that decrements in academic self-concept occur by age 8 or 9 (around Grade 3) and remain relatively stable through at least Grade 10 (Chapman, 1988). The cognitive-motivational characteristics of learning-disabled children including academic self-concept, locus of control, and achievement expectations appear to be significantly related to success and failure in school (Chapman, 1988). Numerous studies indicate that learning-disabled children tend to report significantly lower academic self-concepts than do non-learning-disabled or normally achieving peers (e.g., Chapman, 1987; Bryan & Bryan, 1986).

Learning-disabled children have been portrayed as lacking confidence in their ability to positively influence learning outcomes (Bryan, 1986), as having more negative perceptions of their ability (Chapman, 1988), and as having relatively low expectations for future successful achievement outcomes (Chapman, 1988). It would "seem likely that negative self-concepts, external locus of control beliefs and low academic performance expectations should have a detrimental effect on persistence and effort in learning situations, leading to failure experiences" (Rogers & Saklofske, 1985, 276). The relationship between academic failure experiences and negative academic self-concept reinforce continued poor academic performance.

Deficits in academic self-concept usually co-exist with peer rejection, deficits in social behaviors, and excessive negative social interaction patterns (Gresham, 1988). "LD children's social interaction problems may exacerbate their academic problems. If they are not able to interact effectively with their classmates or teachers, their school experiences (which may already be marked by severe academic failure) can become even more negative" (Pullis, 1988, 86).

Learning-disabled children experienced higher levels of anxiety than nondisabled peers related to their feelings that events beyond their control happen to them (Margalit & Zak, 1984). Additionally, the learning-disabled children expressed lower levels of self-concept related to their feelings of self-dissatisfaction, and they tended to attribute to themselves negative self-reference items.

Jones (1985) found that learning-disabled students experienced significantly negative self-concepts in intelligence and school status, and physical characteristics and attributes in comparison to other handicapped and nonhandicapped children, and high anxiety levels.

"Success is essential for normal development. Children who are achieving mastery in no area, those with no recent triumphs, are very much at risk" (Levine, 1987, 426). Various studies of learning-disabled children have suggested that a loss of self-esteem, high levels of performance anxiety, and clinical depression are further complications of learning disabilities (Levine, 1987). Childhood depression is a common psychiatric complication of developmental dysfunction as between 10 percent and 20 percent of children with learning disabilities have been found to have significant depression (Stevenson & Romney, 1984).

SUMMARY

A student is considered to have a specific learning disability if s/he does not achieve at the proper age and ability levels when provided appropriate learning experiences, and demonstrates a severe discrepancy between intellectual ability and achievement in one or more of the following areas: Oral expression, listening comprehension, written expression, basic reading skills, reading comprehension, mathematics calculation, mathematics reasoning, and/or preacademic skills. The major characteristics of elementary and secondary learning-disabled students can be categorized into three areas: (1) academic deficits, (2) cognitive deficits (attention, perceptual, motor, memory, problem-solving, metacognition), (3) social and emotional problems (hyperactivity, self-concept, learned helplessness, social imperception, distractability, motivation).

The social-emotional problems of learning-disabled students may be their most serious weakness. The social behaviors of many learning-disabled students are less acceptable than their nonhandicapped peers as they evidence (1) less ability to predict the consequences for their behaviors, (2) greater misinterpretation of social cues, (3) more difficulty adapting their behaviors to the characteristics of their listeners, and (4) more frequent performance of inappropriate social behaviors. Numerous explanations for the social skills problems of learning-disabled students have been postulated including the following: (1) cognitive and social cognition deficits, (2) communication deficits, (3) social imperceptiveness, (4) lack of empathy and role-taking ability. Learning-disabled adolescents do not seem to develop a broad enough repertoire of social behaviors to react differently to different situations.

Research indicates that learning-disabled youngsters demonstrate a reduced sense of personal control in all aspects of their lives as compared to nonhandicapped peers. Metacognitive deficits render them less aware of their own cognitive abilities, and unable to regulate and control strategic aspects of their cognition. Learning-disabled youngsters frequently experience difficulties in consistently maintaining motivation and often experience loss of motivation. They often attribute their successes and failures to factors outside of their control (reflecting an external locus of control); thus, they do not believe in their own abilities and do not understand the role of their effort in the success or failure. Learning-disabled children report significantly lower academic self-concepts, significantly less responsibility for their academic successes and failures, and (3) significantly lower expectations for future successful achievement outcomes.

Chapter Eight

PHYSICALLY AND OTHER
HEALTH IMPAIRED STUDENTS

"Many individuals with physical handicaps also have problems of social and emotional adjustment. Crippling physical conditions frequently give rise to anxiety, frustration, and resentment" (Best et al., 1990, 330).

"The population of children with physical disabilities is very heterogeneous; it includes youngsters with many different conditions. Most of these conditions are unrelated, but for convenience they are often grouped into two categories: physical disabilities [orthopedic impairments] and other health impairments" (Kirk & Gallagher, 1989, 494). Orthopedic impairments affect the neurological system (the brain, spinal cord, and nerves) or the musculoskeletal system (the muscles, bones, and joints) (Kirk & Gallagher, 1989).

Physical or orthopedic impairments are caused by congenital anomaly (e.g., clubfoot), disease (e.g. poliomyelitis), and impairments from other causes (e.g., cerebral palsy, spina bifida, spinal cord injury, head trauma, amputations, burns which cause contractures, scoliosis, arthritis, etc.) (Cartwright et al., 1989; Federal Register, 1977). Other health-impaired conditions include acute health problems such as cancer (leukemia, malignant tumors), diabetes, hemophilia, asthma, sickle cell anemia, cardiac disorders, cystic fibrosis, epilepsy, AIDS, lead poisoning, etc. (Kirk & Gallagher, 1989; Federal Register, 1977).

COGNITIVE AND ACADEMIC FUNCTIONING

There is no universally accepted definition of physical and health impairments; thus, it is difficult to generalize cognitive, learning, and social characteristics to all students labeled as such. Frequently, these handicapping conditions occur with other handicapping conditions such as mental retardation, vision impairment, and/or hearing impairment (Heward & Orlansky, 1988).

Cognitive Learning Problems

Intellectual Functioning

The intellectual abilities of physically and other health-impaired children and youth range from severe/profound retardation to gifted. A long-standing health impairment can greatly limit a child's range of experiences, negatively impacting cognitive concept development (Heward & Orlansky, 1988). Most physically and health-impaired students experience restricted mobility and reduced levels of independence. Their orthopedic and/or chronic health problems may delay progress in all developmental areas and result in reduced functioning compared to nonhandicapped children and youth.

Physical impairments that are the result of neurological damage may result in reduced intellectual functioning. The intelligence levels of children with cerebral palsy range from profoundly retarded to gifted (Cartwright et al., 1989). Children with spina bifida occulta exhibit the normal range of intelligence; but those with myelomeningocele generally have IQs in the low-average to mildly retarded ranges (Cartwright et al., 1989). "Spina bifida is generally accompanied by hydrocephalus, the accumulation of cerebrospinal fluid in tissues surrounding the brain. If left untreated, this condition can lead to head enlargement and severe brain damage" (Heward & Orlansky, 1988, 339). In spinal cord injuries a number of important functions are left intact including eye function and hearing, speech, facial muscles and therefore facial expression, and intelligence (Mullins, 1979).

Other health impairments such as asthma, cancer, diabetes, cardiac disorder, and epilepsy (seizure disorders) are not directly related to cognitive functioning. However, "children with cerebral palsy or moderate to severe mental retardation are much more likely to have seizure disorders than their normal counterparts" (Hardman et al., 1990, 355–356).

Information Processing

Information processing requires adequate skills in reception, attention, perception, perceptual-motor integration, language, memory storage and retrieval, and behaviors that demonstrate that information processing has occurred (e.g., speech/language, fine and gross motor skills). Any condition that interferes with the reception, processing, storage, retrieval, and usage of the information processed reduces the efficiency and effectiveness of the entire information processing system.

Physically handicapped children with impairments to the musculo-skeletal system experience problems involving legs, arms, joints, or spine, making it difficult or impossible for the child to walk, stand, sit, or use his hands (Hallahan & Kauffman, 1988). Thus, learning during the sensorimotor stage when the child learns through sensory input and motor output may be significantly delayed. Any learning requiring motor input or a motor output as a demonstration that learning took place will be delayed—all fine and gross motor skills and spatial relationships.

Physically handicapped children with impairments to the neurological system generally experience some deficits or delays in information processing. **Cerebral palsy** is frequently considered a multihandicapping condition due to brain damage also involving speech and language disorders, mental retardation, visual deficits, hearing loss, convulsive seizures, and oral-dental disorders (Cartwright et al., 1989). In spastic cerebral palsy, the most common form of cerebral palsy, "the spasticity is related to injury in the higher centers of the brain, the brain damage may also extend to centers of perception, reasoning, hearing, vision, and speech" (Mullins, 1979, 156). Cerebral palsy, then, may interfere with numerous aspects of information processing including reception, storage, retrieval, and usage.

Head trauma, common to children and adolescents, occurs during accidents such as automobile, trampoline, diving, bicycle, motorcycle, assaults, and child abuse. "Temporary or lasting symptoms may include cognitive and language deficits, memory loss, seizures, and perceptual disorders. Inappropriate or exaggerated behaviors may be displayed, ranging from extreme aggressiveness to apathy" (Heward & Orlansky, 1988, 341). Head trauma obviously interferes with all aspects of information processing.

Other health impairments such as epilepsy may hault information processing altogether during a seizure when there are disturbances of movement, sensation, behavior, and/or consciousness caused by abnormal electrical activity in the brain. Other health impairments such as asthma, diabetes, AIDS, hemophilia, and cardiac disorders may have little effect on information processing unless the child or youth is experiencing an attack, seizure, or critical condition.

Academic Learning Problems

It is impossible to make many valid generalizations about the academic achievement of physically and other health-impaired children because they vary so widely in nature and severity of their conditions (Hallahan & Kauffman, 1988). Frequent interruptions in school attendance due to hospitalization and/or illness cause some physically and other health-impaired youngsters to fall behind their peers even though they have normal intelligence. Some academic learning problems are disease or handicapping condition specific.

Cerebral Palsy

"A severely crippled cerebral-palsied child cannot take part in most outdoor play activities and travel experiences and may not be able to hold and turn pages in books, write, explore objects manually, or use a typewriter without special equipment" (Hallahan & Kauffman, 1988, 392). Since children who have cerebral palsy do not possess voluntary motor control, they experience difficulty with all fine and gross motor skills. Children who have spastic cerebral palsy experience extreme difficulty in oral language (Heward & Orlansky, 1988). "A number of secondary disabilities are associated with cerebral palsy, including sensory impairments, and behavioral and social-emotional problems" (Best et al., 1990, 290). Some children with cerebral palsy who have severe visual disability may not be able to gain benefit from wearing glasses because they cannot hold their head still enough to focus well; thus, they cannot read print. Vision-impaired children with cerebral palsy may not be able to read braille either because they cannot control the gross movement of their hands or they do not have fine sensory discrimination in their fingertips (Best et al., 1990).

Spina Bifida

"Most children with spina bifida who have no signs of hydrocephalus have normal intelligence. Like other children, they may be average, below-average, or above average in their intellectual performance. Consequently, they receive their education in a normal school environment" (Hardman et al., 1990, 360). Many children with spina bifida experience perceptual-motor weaknesses which interfere with learning to read and write. Children with spina bifida experience a number of personal self-care problems due to lower-body paralysis including bowel and bladder control, and mobility (walking) problems (Heward & Orlansky, 1988). Young students with the severe forms of spina bifida are often absent from school for significant periods of time for surgery, therapy, and related medical appointments (Hardman et al., 1990).

Hemophilia

Children who have hemophilia "should not be involved in any form of contact sport or any noncontact sport where they may be hurt by an object (e.g., baseball). However, exercise is important, and normal physical activities such as calisthenics, swimming, and hiking should be encouraged" (Cartwright et al., 1989, 199). Thus, the normal physical education program will need to be modified. Although learning problems are not directly related to hemophilia, frequent short absences from school because of internal bleeding may retard academic progress (Best et al., 1990).

Arthritis

Children who have arthritis may miss a considerable amount of school. They may not be able to participate fully in many of the activities pursued by others during recesses or physical education periods (Hardman et al., 1990). "The physical education program will have to be modified for the arthritic students because they must avoid severe twisting or jarring, such as that encountered in body contact sports" (Mullins, 1979, 84). Writing may be extremely difficult for arthritic children. Extended sitting in one position may cause significant difficulties when the student decides to move to another location.

Muscular Dystrophy

Students with muscular dystrophy "progressively lose their ability to walk and to use their arms and hands" (Hardman et al., 1990, 372). All fine and gross motor skills deteriorate and become nonfunctional, requiring a significantly modified educational program in terms of responding and demonstrating that learning has occurred.

Epilepsy

That epilepsy is "the alteration in brain function associated with seizures does not imply learning problems or mental retardation. Academic ability varies among individuals with epilepsy as it does among nonhandicapped persons" (Best et al., 1990, 294). Side effects of medication can interfere with academic performance. Many physically impaired youngsters whose handicapping condition is a result of brain injury also experience epilepsy as well as severe mental retardation. Thus, the programming should be modified to meet the specific needs of the student.

Diabetes

Controlled diabetes will have very little impact on classroom functioning unless there is significant change in routine related to physical exercise or excessive amounts of food containing sugar (Best et al., 1990, 295). Diabetic youth can often participate in strenuous or demanding physical activities with other children but may require a sugar snack prior to or after the activities. Peers need to be aware of the health-impaired child's condition so they will be prepared to provide appropriate assistance if needed.

Sickle Cell Anemia, etc.

Frequent hospitalization due to physical and other health impairments (e.g., osteogenesis imperfecta, sickle cell anemia, cystic fibrosis) may cause the child to fall behind in academic progress. A significant concern with osteogenesis imperfecta is the possible development of severe hearing impairment. Academic ability is not affected if hearing ability remains intact. However, absence due to hospitalization for treatment of multiple fractures may affect performance. Again, the physical educational program will need to be modified. Although learning potential is not directly affected by sickle cell anemia, frequent absence from school may affect academic performance. In cystic fibrosis, "learning potential is not directly affected by the disease, although psychological adjustment may periodically interrupt attention to academic performance" (Harvey, 1980).

Asthma

"Asthma is the primary reason cited for school absence by children. . . . If the episodes are extremely serious or frequent, hospitalization may be required" (Hardman et al., 1990, 393). Absence from friends, school activities, and family due to hospitalization can be extremely upsetting to juvenile asthmatics. Extended school absences without appropriate homebound or hospital teaching/tutoring make it difficult for the asthmatic student to function on grade level.

In general, then, children with physical and health impairments experience difficulty with fine and gross motor skills and communication problems. Skills in communication range from just a few words to body movement or signals, to the use of communication boards or electronic communication devices or typing or handwriting, to highly intelligible speech. The educational goals of physically handicapped children should ordinarily be the same as for nondisabled with additional instruction in mobility, daily living, and adolescent transitional/occupational skills (Hallahan & Kauffman, 1988). Students with other health impairments may experience delays in academic progress due to frequent absences from school. As previously mentioned, the intellectual abilities of physically and other health-impaired children and youth range from profoundly mentally retarded through gifted; thus, their academic progress should reveal a similar range.

SOCIAL AND EMOTIONAL FUNCTIONING

The physically impaired child, by virtue of his/her handicapping condition, experiences fine and gross motor skill delays or abnormalities. Their limited abilities in movement and/or poor control of voluntary motor acts interferes with acquisition of social skills. "The prevalence of social and psychological problems in children who have serious health disorders is somewhat higher than that in normal children. A serious health problem seems to heighten an individual's chances for experiencing personal adjustment difficulties" (Hardman et al., 1990, 381).

Social and Emotional Problems

A range of social, psychological, and environmental factors may affect the psychosocial development of individuals with physical and other health impairments. Some may have developed coping mechanisms and strategies for acceptance of their disability and adjustment; others may have had such negative experiences that they are seriously affected by their disability (Wright, 1983). Youth who were born disabled may experience a different psychological acceptance process than youth who have suddenly become physically disabled as a result of an accident. Regardless of the time or circumstances of acquiring the physical or other health impairment satisfying interpersonal relationships cannot be built until the handicapped youth accepts the situation and shifts constant focus of attention from himself to others.

"People with physical disabilities have the same social and emotional needs as do their nondisabled peers. Primarily and specifically, they need to communicate with and relate to others" (Sirvis, 1988, 400). Many individuals with physical handicaps also have problems with social and emotional adjustment because crippling physical conditions precipitate anxiety, frustration, and resentment" (Best et al., 1990).

Interactions with Adults

The physically handicapped child may experience problems responding to adults if/when attempts to respond by smiling may look like a grimace and attempts to respond motorically may result in different responses than intended. Interactions with adults may be particularly unrewarding in situations where the adult attempts to manipulate the child through action songs and simple games if the muscles of the child with cerebral palsy react the opposite of expectations. Imitation of simple adult activities may be particularly difficult for the physically handicapped child. The gross motor disabilities will interfere with the child's ability to seek an adult for play. Additionally, involuntary muscle responses may severely reduce the enjoyment experienced by the adult and child during cooperative play activities.

Children with physical and other health impairments may experience difficulty in bonding with parents and siblings due to frequent hospitalizations and absences from home, and to fragile medical conditions which may not allow for early bonding in the normal fashion (e.g., gastrointestinal feeding vs breast feeding). Parents may be afraid to care for their young handicapped child or experience guilt or revulsion which inhibits bonding. Parents may experience significant financial hardships due to the expensive medical care required by the physically or other health-impaired child. The high level of physical care required may not end with early childhood as with most children but continues indefinitely if the handicapped individual cannot perform basic self-care functions. The physical and health needs of the handicapped child may dominate the family life. Parents may resent the handicapped child and the loss of a "normal" life.

Another concern regarding the parent-child relationship deals with over-protection. Parents must constantly guard against making the physically and other health-impaired child and youth more dependent on them than necessary. They must constantly emphasize having the child become as independent in self-care as possible even if it takes longer for her to do the task. For the physically handicapped numerous types of adapted equipment have been designed to foster independence.

Adolescence is generally a difficult period for adults and "emerging adults" as the parent-child roles must be redefined. Parents and other adults must allow and assist the young adult in assuming responsibility, and independence, and in making some life choices, and forging new relationships. This is very difficult if the adolescent remains physically and emotionally dependent on adults.

Interactions with Peers

A physical handicap significantly interferes with a young child's ability to play with other young children who may not understand the disabilities of the handicapped child. Attempts to offer a toy may result in hitting the other child with the toy. Attempts to reach and grasp may result in inability to grasp or, once grasped, may result in inability to voluntarily release the toy. The young physically handicapped child may experience reduced opportunities for exploratory and practice play. His/her experiences in attempting to apply learned movements to new situations may fail because muscular movements are unpredictable. Games and activities requiring squeezing and other fine motor activities may be painful. The physically handicapped child may be very frustrated and upset at attempts to play.

Children with physical and other health impairments may spend considerable time in the hospital. Hospitalization often hampers the development of satisfying social relationships with siblings and peers, complicating the process of building and maintaining friendships. Activity limitations often do not allow the physically and other health-impaired child to be actively engaged in team sports such as football.

Many physically handicapped individuals experience difficulty eating (e.g., drooling, spillage, eating with mouth open) which can significantly affect social acceptance. Problems with self-care may make slumber parties, camping out, and other peer activities very difficult if not impossible, thus reducing participation in activities which encourage peer interaction and friendship building.

Physically and health-impaired children and youth need to develop healthy coping strategies. Nonhandicapped youngsters, also, need to deal with stress in life situations. These skills can be learned and practiced in classroom situations. Since asthma may be triggered by stress, it may be helpful for classmates and peers to learn stress-reduction techniques and to assist the asthmatic child in reducing anxiety. Practicing stress-reduction techniques may encourage friendship building and empathy among handicapped and nonhandicapped children.

Other health-impaired children especially those with terminal conditions think about death and dying more than other children do. However, death and dying are concerns that affect everyone. All children may benefit from looking at the normal life cycle from birth to death. At certain stages in childhood, many healthy children become concerned with death and dying. Realistic dealing with this issue may significantly help not only the handicapped child but also the nonhandicapped child in assisting them in developing empathy and reducing egocentrism.

It may be helpful for peers of arthritic children to understand that they frequently display mood swings, anger, and depression which have nothing to do with their friendship. "It would seem natural that a child suffering in pain, helplessness, and uncertainty about the condition would feel angry and depressed. Further, arthritic children have few ways to vent their anger and fear" (Mullins, 1979, 85).

Cystic fibrosis may significantly interfere with social relationships due to chronic coughing, small stature, delayed onset of secondary sex characteristics, and offensive digestive conditions (e.g., odors and gas) (Hardman et al., 1990). Depression is common among teenagers with cystic fibrosis, and the quality of life for such adolescents declines immensely (Hardman et al., 1990).

Children with sickle cell anemia may experience difficulty with peer relationships because they have less energy and tire easily; thus, they are not able to participate in active, rough-and-tumble activities. Peers and teachers need to be alert to the signs of anemia that may indicate a crisis situation. These children may spend considerable amount of time in the hospital which does not help the development of close personal relationships with peers.

Many physically and other health-impaired youngsters and the adults in their lives have spent so much time dealing with the medical that they "have neither the socialization experiences nor the information about social and sexual development they need to interact with their peers in school" (Sirvis, 1988, 402). Because of their medical condition, physically and health-impaired children and youth may remain at the egocentric stage of development far longer than peers, which interferes with the development of satisfying peer relationships. Handicapped teenagers must face difficult situations as they learn to live with the physical and health conditions that affect their lives and the life-styles and choices that are available to them. Concerns about dating and sexuality need to be addressed for the physically and health-impaired youth to understand appropriate behavior in numerous situations.

Feelings of Personal Control

Physically and health-impaired children may feel that they have very little personal control over their lives. For orthopedically handicapped children and youth, the environment may seem hostile as they attempt to use braces, wheelchairs, and adaptive aids to accomplish basic tasks of locomotion and self-care. They may spend considerable time in the hospital or in one-to-one situations with adults in therapy (e.g., speech, physical, occupational). It may seem to physically handicapped children that they are always being monitored or assisted by someone. Health-impaired children may feel at the mercy of the disease that may hospitalize them, require them to have special diets and medication, and limit their physical activities.

Metacognitive Deficits

It is difficult to specify the social, emotional, and cognitive deficits of physically and other health-impaired children and youth due to the variances in functioning levels. The metacognitive or self-planning, self-monitoring, and self-evaluative aspect of cognition may be difficult to achieve even for physically and other health-impaired students with normal ability. Physical skill deficiencies may limit the child's ability in gaining independence, in planning and executing tasks, in engaging in social interactions, in exploring the environment, and in acquiring the automaticity in these areas necessary for automatic metacognitive functioning.

Physically and other health-impaired children and youth may experience significant social skills deficits in the area of social-perspective taking. Due to their obvious physical or health condition they may have always been on the receiving end of empathy but not provided any experiences in understanding the feelings and emotions of others. A child who is continually served by adults, and whose inappropriate behaviors are ignored by adults because of his/her illness or condition may experience difficulty learning peer-group socially appropriate behaviors. The physically and other health-impaired child or youth who is unable to empathize, may be unable to engage in social problem-solving, and may continue to function at an immature level. With reduced opportunities to practice self-regulatory and interaction skills, the physically and other health-impaired child may remain egocentric.

Motivation/Attribution Deficits

The functioning level of the physically and other health-impaired child or youth will depend on the intellectual level and the severity of his/her handicapping condition. Thus, it is difficult to make definitive statements about the motivation and attributional skills of physically and other health-impaired youngsters. Logically, the physically and other health-impaired child is "at-risk" for deficits in these areas because of dependence on adults for even basic self-care needs. It would be difficult to remain at a high motivation level in learning to walk, for example, if one constantly fell and got hurt. It may be difficult to maintain academic motivation if frequent hospitalizations and handicapping conditions (e.g., cerebral palsy) limits expressing the learning that has occurred or the written product is substandard compared to that of peers, and the student continually falls behind peers academically. Underachieving or nonachieving physically handicapped students may experience similar negative attitudes and anxiety as other handicapped and nonhandicapped students who are not academically successful.

Additionally, the handicapped child may feel a sense of power in having a number of adults in his/her service, coaxing them to try to do various tasks. The child may enjoy being "center stage." Children whose lives are controlled so significantly by adults generally have an outer-directed locus or external locus of control despite comparable intellectual ability (Lee & Mak, 1984).

Peter et al. (1984) studied 36 physically handicapped children (10–14 years old) by assigning them to internal and external groups based on scores on the Norwicki-Strickland Locus of Control Scale. The data revealed that, despite comparable intellectual ability, students exhibiting an internal locus of control received higher teacher ratings on task performance and in arithmetic performance than externally motivated students.

Gregory et al. (1987) found that orthopedically handicapped 12th graders with similar academic functioning as nonhandicapped controls expressed significantly more external loci of control and lower estimates of their own physical attractiveness than did normal controls. These 12th graders also rated their schools significantly more negatively than did their nonhandicapped peers.

Self-Concepts of Physically and Other Health Impaired Students

"A physically handicapped child may face special difficulties in psychological adjustment because of the nature of his disability and the responses of others to him" (Calhoun & Hawisher, 1979, 53). The physically handicapped child is different by reason of his disability. He may suffer pain, fatigue from undue exertion, accidents, and fear of injury or social rejection. These factors make it difficult for him/her to form realistic perceptions of his inadequacies and limitations (Telford & Sawrey, 1977).

General Self-Concepts

Physically handicapped children have more difficulty with psychological adjustment than do nonhandicapped for reasons that are related both to the physical disability itself and to the way in which others view the disability (Calhoun & Hawisher, 1979). The way in which children think about themselves and the degree to which they are accepted by others often is affected by the visibility of the condition (Heward & Orlansky, 1988). Physically handicapped children and youth are often quite visible and different from nondisabled peers because of orthopedic appliances (e.g., wheelchairs, braces, crutches, adaptive tables, helmets) and the assistance they need in completing basic self-help tasks (e.g., feeding, toileting) (Heward & Orlansky, 1988).

Harvey & Greenway (1984) indicated that the presence of a congenital physical handicap is associated with an adverse effect upon the measured self-concept of both the affected child and, though to a lesser degree, the sibling nearest in age. They concluded that the "presence of the physical handicap was associated with a lower sense of self-worth, greater anxiety, and a less integrated view of self" (p. 280).

Calhoun and Howisher (1979) summarized studies indicating that health-impaired children (e.g., cystic fibrosis, diabetes, juvenile rheumatoid arthritis, muscular dystrophy) experience more emotional difficulties and psychological stress even in the best of circumstances due to recurrent hospitalizations, pain, dependency, medication, physical restrictions, and threat or fear of death.

Adolescent Self-Concept. Adolescence at best is a very precarious time which bridges childhood and adulthood. During adolescence important mental, emotional, social, biological, and physical changes interact to change the child into a young adult. Accompanying these many changes is a redefinition of the self-concept to include the "new aspects" of self. In our society, great emphasis (e.g., via TV commercials, magazines) is placed on the physically trim athletic body. Adolescence may be a particularly difficult time for physically impaired who deviate so significantly from this ideal that they are unable to date and form close relationships with the opposite sex. It is a very difficult time for adolescents who want and need to reduce the emotional and physical dependence on parents but are unable to do so because they are unable to perform self-care tasks. Reduced self-concept is often a result of being unable to participate in age appropriate social activities and to assume at least some measure of independence.

In general, the research on the general self-concept of physically and health-impaired youngsters indicates lower self-concept than that of nonhandicapped peers. Because our body parts and the connotations they assume are an important part of our perceptions, it is reasonable to suppose that defects in physical development may have detrimental effects upon the self-esteem of the individual, particularly where the defect is congenital in origin (Harvey & Greenway, 1984).

Self-Concepts of Academic Achievement

Little research appears to have been conducted regarding the self-concept of academic achievement of physically impaired students due to the wide variety of handicapping conditions and intellectual functioning levels. The primary concerns have regarded the impact of the handicapping condition on the overall self-concept.

SUMMARY

Physically and other health-impaired students include a very heterogeneous population, including orthopedically and neurologically impaired children. Physical impairments include congenital conditions such as clubfoot or absence of a limb, impairments caused by diseases such as poliomyelitis, and impairments from other causes (e.g., cerebral palsy, burns). Neurological impairments, such as cerebral palsy and spina bifida, are caused by damage to the central nervous system (brain and spinal cord). Children and youth with chronic health problems such as asthma, sickle cell anemia, cardiac disorders, cystic fibrosis, and AIDS often spend considerable time in the hospital. Asthma is the most common childhood pulmonary disease, often triggered by severe allergies.

The intellectual abilities of physically and other health-impaired children and youth range from severe/profound retardation to gifted; therefore, a generalized statement about cognitive or academic learning problems of these children cannot be made. However, frequent interruptions in school attendance due to hospitalization and/or illness cause some students to fall behind peers in academic performance. Physical activities may be delayed or significantly affected depending on the specific handicapping condition. In general, children with physical impairments experience fine and gross motor problems. Serious physical and health problems interfere with the development of social and interactional skills, bonding, parent-child relationships, and peer relationships due to the physical or health condition.

Physically and other health-impaired children often experience a reduced self-concept compared to nonhandicapped children. Due to their illnesses and/or physical handicapping condition and the adult influences and control in their lives, they also tend to be externally motivated.

Chapter Nine

GIFTED AND TALENTED STUDENTS

Intelligence can be a trap. It can lead a young person to expect that success will come easily. It almost never does . . . (Feldman, 1985, 5).

Suzanne Jessup

To adopt a particular definition for gifted and talented is to select from a wide variety of definitions reflecting various theoretical bases. The choice of definition results in the selection for special programs from 3 to 5 percent of the student population based on measurement of intelligence (Terman & Oden, 1951) to as many as 15 to 29 percent of the student population based on multiple measures of intellectual competency (Gardner, 1983).

DEFINITIONS OF GIFTED AND TALENTED STUDENTS

Although the terms *gifted* and *talented* are often used interchangeably to describe achieving students, identification processes for placement in special programs usually delineate categories of superior functioning in academic settings. Thus, the 1972 U.S. Office of Education definition of gifted, widely adopted and adapted by states and school districts for developing programs for the gifted, reflects aspects of giftedness observed in educational settings:

Gifted and talented children are those identified by professionally qualified persons who by virtue of outstanding abilities are capable of high performance. These are children who require differentiated educational programs and services beyond those normally provided by the regular school program in order to realize their contribution to self and society.

Children capable of high performance include those with demonstrated achievement and/or potential in any of the following areas:

1. General intellectual ability
2. Specific academic aptitude
3. Creative or productive thinking
4. Leadership ability
5. Visual and performing arts
6. Psychomotor ability (Marland, 1972).

Gardner (1983) has restated the concept of multiple intelligences suggested by the federal definition by separating intelligence into linguistic, logical/mathematical, spatial, musical, bodily-kinesthetic, interpersonal and intrapersonal competencies.

The U.S. Congress (Educational Amendment of 1978) revised Marland's definition to exclude psychomotor ability, but American public education has traditionally supported the gifted athlete. Other legislation, such as the 1984 funding for grants to strengthen teacher skills in mathematics, science, foreign languages and computer learning, focuses on the *gifted* student with specific proficiencies, but emphasizes underserved populations:

...a student, identified by various measures, who demonstrates actual or potential high performance capability in the fields of mathematics, science, foreign languages, or computer learning...[including students from] historically underrepresented and underserved groups, including females, minorities, handicapped persons, persons of limited English-speaking proficiency and migrants (Regulations for the Education for Economic Security Act, 1984).

Both the 1972 and the 1984 statements specify potential and/or demonstrated giftedness, as well as the value of giftedness to society, without excluding the underachieving gifted who may require services.

Gagne (1985) suggests that an underachiever may possess "giftedness" (ability) but not "talent" (performance). Other theorists, such as Renzulli (1986), emphasize that the individual must demonstrate productivity and that:

research on creative/productive people has consistently shown that although no single criterion should be used to identify giftedness, persons who have achieved recognition because of their unique accomplishments and creative contributions possess a relatively well-defined set of three interlocking clusters of traits: above average ability, task commitment, and creativity.

More importantly, Renzulli states that it is not superior ability but the interaction between these traits or "clusters which contribute to giftedness (Renzulli, 1978). Similarly, Sternberg's (1985) "triarchic" theory of intelligence emphasizes the importance of intelligent behavior. He defines intelligence in terms of the ability to adapt to real-world environments (contextual subtheory), the ability to respond to novelty or automatic processing (experiential subtheory), and the individual's efficiency in information processing (componential subtheory).

In summary, both the 1972 and 1978 U.S.O.E. definitions and definitional challenges of the 1980's continue to lend support to the observation that "a child is gifted whose performance, in a potentially valuable line of human activity, is consistently remarkable" (Witty, 1985).

COGNITIVE AND ACADEMIC FUNCTIONING

Research focusing on characteristics of the gifted includes studies which describe superior traits and gender differences in academic performance (Benbow & Stanley, 1983), in cognitive functioning (Clark, 1988), and in social relationships (Clark, 1988).

Cognitive Learning Characteristics

Frequently listed cognitive characteristics of gifted include advanced comprehension, the ability to manipulate abstract symbol systems, a longer attention span, retentive memory, intellectual curiosity, preference for individual work or persistent, goal-directed work, multiple interests, intuitiveness, the ability to generate original ideas, and the ability to evaluate self and others (Clark, 1988; Baska, 1989).

Learning-Disabled Gifted Students

Deficits in cognitive ability, as evidenced by discrepancies between higher-level thinking skills and academic performance, are characteristic of underachieving or learning-disabled gifted. While underachievement may be encouraged by unrealistic expectations on the part of teachers or parents, as well as the student's motivation, interest, or specific aptitude for a particular task, below grade-level achievement signals the possibility of learning deficits. These deficits may include visual or auditory processing difficulties, long- and short-term memory problems, and poor motor skills (Whitmore, 1980). Often, learning-disabled gifted students' severe deficits are matched by extraordinary strengths in abstract reasoning and creative thinking, masking the disability and at times supporting average achievement (Suter & Wolf, 1987), with the result that the student is not provided available services because he or she is not failing. Gifted students with subtle learning disabilities may succeed initially because of verbal strengths or the ability to compensate, but often find it increasingly difficult to achieve in middle school or junior high, where their problems with independent projects and longer written assignments are met with adult reactions that their failure is due to lack of initiative.

Academic Learning Characteristics

A fifty-year study of the academic characteristics of over 1500 white, middle-class gifted students (Terman & Odin, 1951; Terman, 1981) confirmed:

> ... the superiority of gifted over unselected children in reading, language usage, arithmetical reasoning, science, literature and the arts. In arithmetical computation, spelling and factual information about history and civics, the superiority of the gifted was somewhat less marked. . . .

Since selection for the Terman study was based on teacher nomination, students may well represent academically conforming gifted, "well behaved, pleasant, attractive and high achieving" (Davis & Rimm, 1989, 20).

Goertzel & Goertzel (1962) report that 60 percent of four hundred eminent men and women studied had serious school problems, and subsequent studies of 317 eminent men and women indicate learning per se was not the problem but inflexible teachers and curricula not designed to meet the individual needs (Goertzel et al., 1978). However, the population in this study was limited to those who had demonstrated achievement as adults, and their educational profiles suggest that many might not have met current criteria as gifted, an ongoing concern in identification for gifted services.

Although not all gifted children display the same academic characteristics, verbal precociousness is often "the overriding trait—indeed, the definition—of very bright students is that they are developmentally advanced in language and thought" (Davis & Rimm, 1989, 20), as evidenced in a study of one thousand gifted children, with the average performance of gifted kindergarten children comparable to that of second grade students (Martinson, 1981). However, recent studies have suggested that precocious reading ability is only moderately associated with general intelligence (Jackson, 1988) and "the early reader has become less of an anomaly in our society in recent years for a number of reasons. . . . Thus, this characteristic alone may be less predictive of gifted behavior than it once was" (Baska, 1989, 19).

Other researchers have defined giftedness in terms of academic mastery in domain specific areas, such as the ability to perform above grade-level in mathematic courses (Stanley, 1984), which is often objectively measured by content mastery and not by the original contributions (products) often valued by society (Renzulli & Delcourt, 1986). Research on gender differences in mathematics has found that mathematically talented males bring to accelerated course work extensive mathematical knowledge gained by working informally with math puzzles and games as well as by independently pursuing advanced mathematics through a more structured approach, while mathematically talented girls, who often value interpersonal relationships over competitive activities, are less likely to pursue these interests (Landau & Olszewski-Kubilius, 1988).

SOCIAL LEARNING CHARACTERISTICS

Although Terman (1925) initiated studies of the social and emotional characteristics of gifted when attitudes viewed advanced behaviors with suspicion as signs of neurotic deviance from the norm, the results of these studies, as well as later studies, suggest that the gifted generally proceed better in social-emotional development than same-age peers (Terman & Odin, 1947).

The most frequently cited social characteristics of gifted are independence and leadership skills, competitiveness and the need for self-actualization, and what Clark (1988, 132) refers to as "involvement with the metaneeds of society (e.g., justice, beauty, truth)" or an emotional responsiveness or sensitivity to societal pressures, often displayed in awareness of injustices at the personal or worldwide levels, criticism of self and others, or in self-deprecating humor (Ziv & Gadish, 1990).

These characteristics may play an important role in gender differences found in academic achievement as well problems related to development during adolescence. Social relationships and the attitudes of teachers may inhibit creativity and risk taking in gifted females (Hollinger, 1988), encourage independence and specialized skills such as mathematics in boys (Sherman, 1982), or produce internal conflicts when the behaviors of others are compared with personal values as adolescent gifted seek identity (Loeb & Jay, 1987).

Feelings of Personal Control

Metacognition

In order to enhance productivity in gifted and talented students, it is appropriate that these students are aware of their distinctive metacognition: an understanding of individual cognitive abilities and skill in using the variables which influence thinking. Metacognitive strategies improve decision-making and monitoring of task performance (Bjorklund, 1989), skills which underachieving gifted may lack. This "cognition about cognition" includes knowledge of person: awareness of one's own and others' abilities in thinking, such as differences between auditory or visual learners; knowledge of task: understanding the requirements to complete the process, such as needed information or resources; and knowledge of strategy: cognitive techniques available and appropriate to complete the task, such as concentrated study, outlining, or merely skimming contents (Flavell, 1985).

Sternberg's (1985) triarchic theory of intelligence underscores the differences between the intellectually gifted and other individuals:

> First, the gifted will, in most cases, show superior performance to others on standard kinds of intelligence tests. According to the present view, such superiority is attributable to better metacomponential, performance-componential, and knowledge-acquisition-componential skills. . . . Second, the gifted can be expected to be superior in dealing with novel kinds of tasks and situations in general. Third, the gifted are likely to have automatized highly practiced performances to a greater extent than the nongifted, as well as being more adept at automatization than are others. Fourth and finally, the gifted are individuals who are particularly adept at applying their intellectual skills to the task or situational environment in which they display their gifts (291).

Shore and Dover (1987) hypothesize that an important characteristic of giftedness is the interaction between the level of metacognition and the availability and flexibility of cognitive styles; that it is usual in the gifted to see a repertoire of approaches to a task, as well as the ability to monitor one's own performance. Whitmore (1988) has found that a risk factor in underachievement among gifted may be the interaction between the child's learning style and opportunities available to meet his or her educational needs.

Carr and Borkowski (1987), studying the relationship of that portion of metacognition classified as metamemory (knowledge about memory processes), found a significant link between flexible, divergent thinking and metamemory, with a significant correlation remaining when the influence of IQ was removed, but not when the influence of achievement was removed. "Gifted children who understand their memory capabilities possess a mature metamemorial knowledge and were more likely to achieve academically, irrespective of IQs, than gifted children with less mature metamemories" (Carr & Borkowski, 1987, 42). They concluded that metamemory provides cognitive flexibility and specific knowledge in approaching difficult tasks, and that metacognitive training provides an alternative approach to the usual problem-solving tasks provided to improve divergent or convergent performance, and may enhance academic achievement, intelligence and creative problem-solving.

Young gifted children can be introduced to methods to enhance cognitive functioning by such simple means as understanding the usefulness of applying a taxonomy such as Bloom's (1969) to a children's story, Little Red Riding Hood: Why did Red Riding Hood go into the woods? (knowledge); Why did Red Riding Hood believe it was not Grandmother in the bed? (comprehension); What should we remember when we meet strangers? (application); What does your grandmother look like? (analysis); Tell a story about a visit to your grandmother (synthesis); or Describe other things which may be scary to you and tell why (evaluation).

Applying a taxonomy or any structured approach to cognitive activities, such as mnemonics to create associations for memory tasks, demonstrates for gifted students that personal control can be acquired to enhance skills in critical thinking and problem-solving. However, Wheatley (1989) cautions that methods work best when they evolve during the problem-solving process, rather than taught as "new rules." The efficacy of a self-generated plan was demonstrated during a math class for gifted, when confusion over which rule should be used to convert units of time from smaller to larger units (e.g., Do you multiply or divide to change minutes to hours?) was coded by one seventh-grade boy as "the SaLaD rule": to change a Smaller unit to Larger, you Divide."

Motivation

Renzulli et al. (1977), in constructing the Scales for Rating Behavioral Characteristics of Superior Students, has described motivational characteristics of this population supported by later research (Renzulli & Hartman, 1981; Renzulli, 1983) which may appear to reflect both strengths and deficits:

1. Becomes absorbed and truly involved in certain topics or problems; is persistent in seeking task completion. (It is sometimes difficult to get him or her to move on to another topic.)
2. Is easily bored with routine tasks.
3. Needs little external motivation to follow through in work that initially excites him or her.
4. Strives toward perfection; is self-critical; is not easily satisfied with his or her own speed or products.
5. Prefers to work independently; requires little direction from teachers.
6. Is interested in many "adult" problems such as religion, politics, sex, race—more than usual for age level.
7. Often is self-assertive (sometimes even aggressive); stubborn in his or her beliefs.
8. Likes to organize and bring structure to things, people, and situations.
9. Is quite concerned with right and wrong, good and bad; often evaluates and passes judgment on events, people, and things (Renzulli et al., 1977).

Highly creative students share these traits and, combined with the independence and high energy as well as the nonconformity and unconventionality which may be intrinsic to creativity, may appear to be more troublesome to some teachers if their behaviors are viewed only as motivational deficits; unnecessary stubbornness, resisting authority, sloppiness, lacking interest in details, challenging directives, and unduly critical (Davis & Rimm, 1989).

However, these behaviors are often reflective of a strength which distinguishes even younger gifted from other learners: an inner locus of control. This ability to follow through in a task, selected because of the child's interest, requires little external motivation. In fact, the reward is the sense of responsibility and control over the activity, attributes needed for success, achievement and a sense of well-being in adult life (Clark, 1988).

Comparing the qualitative results of problem-solving tasks completed by eighty-nine young (ages 4 to 8) children, Kanevsky (1990) found that the high IQ children studied had a more accurate conception of the problem, preferred to "own" their solution to the problem and were more willing to learn from mistakes. And this need for self-directed learning continues throughout the school experience, as demonstrated in a study of one hundred and forty-six winners of the 1983 Westinghouse Science Talent Search. Subotnik (1988) found that a majority of both male and female adolescent scientists listed as their primary motivation for conducting research "curiosity" rather than "aesthetics," "bettering the human condition," or "prestige."

The educational implications of these motivational strengths in gifted and talented include reducing routine, redundant tasks and rechanneling their natural energy and enthusiasm into constructive, self-directed experiences, with guidance and resources provided to support their need to be productive and in control of their efforts.

Attributions

Achieving gifted students generally endorse internal attributions (their innate abilities and efforts) to account for their success, including under-achieving students who may demonstrate less realistic self-understanding by attributing success to ability and failure to bad luck (Laffoon et al., 1989).

Research on the attributions which gifted female students make for their success and failure is similar to the gender-related tendency of non-gifted females to attribute successes to variables such as hard work or luck, while failures are attributed only to lack of ability, as popularized in the *imposter phenomena* which adds the dimension that some females fear that their lack of capability will be found out. Males, on the other hand, tend to reverse attributional thinking and blame others or bad luck for failures and accept successes as evidence of their own high abilities (Subotnik, 1988). In addition, adolescent gifted females may develop what may be called "a motive to avoid success"—perceived negative peer and cultural consequences for females (Freeman, 1974, 29), which does not appear to have been mitigated by developing opportunities for women.

Self-Concepts of Gifted and Talented Students

General Self-Concepts

Feelings of adequacy and self-esteem which accompany personal success would seem to be typical characteristics of the gifted and talented. However, the gifted child is often sensitive and self-critical and may continually measure himself or herself by the standards of the environment: by teacher or parent expectation and evaluation, as well as by personal standards of excellence, and perceiving strengths and comparative weaknesses as competence or failure.

Past studies of the gifted support characteristic emotional stability and positive self-concept within the population (Terman, 1951). Increased identification of gifted as well as opportunities for educational support have produced a proliferation of recent studies on the emotional adjustment of this population. Results of these studies suggest that some gifted children exhibit a variety of emotional problems: from low self-esteem, especially among young boys (Loeb & Jay, 1987), or a sense of isolation from peers (Whitmore, 1980), to depression and suicide (Whitmore, 1980). However, the majority of children with superior intelligence are not viewed as clinically unstable or exhibiting evidence of psychopathology, but rather they may experience some frustration and interpersonal isolation if limited in access to superior-functioning peers (Gallucci, 1988).

Gifted children may erode their strengths and abilities with undue stress, a tendency towards perfectionism, and an unclear sense of personal identity, or, as Morrison and Hershey (1988) state, they can become victims of their talents and hostages to their special abilities. Webb et al. (1982) suggest that a major key in helping gifted children function successfully is the use of stress-reduction techniques, such as developing the ability to communicate feelings related to difficulties or problems, acquiring decision-making skills, understanding that "failure" is often part of a process towards success, and active responsibility for meeting personal goals. These techniques may often be acquired through child's typical strengths in quick comprehension of concepts and good verbal and conceptual ability:

> ... more important than being gifted is feeling good about oneself, feeling that what one does is important, and that one fits with the world. A goal for gifted children is to help them realize that though they are different, they have much in common with others. Gifted children have the same basic human

feelings and needs for belonging and self-respect as other children, although the gifted child may feel these needs more keenly and may want emotional satisfaction more intensely than other children. Certainly they are children and cannot be expected to "find their own way". They need special guidance and help (Webb et al., 1982, 30, 115–117).

Self-Concepts of Academic Achievement

Achieving and Nonachieving Gifted. Clark (1988) describes the impact of self-esteem on individual functioning:

> Children with high self-esteem more often acquire a sense of independence, exhibit exploratory behavior, assert their own rights, develop a strong inner locus of control, and express more self-trust. These traits lead them to personal happiness and more effective functioning.
>
> Low self-esteem results in higher levels of anxiety, more frequent psychosomatic symptoms, less effectiveness, and more destructive behavior. Children with low self-esteem find it hard to believe that any personal action can have favorable outcomes. Instead, they believe themselves powerless and unworthy of love or attention (Clark, 1988, 100).

These descriptions of high self-esteem and low self-esteem may underscore the descriptions of achieving and nonachieving gifted, especially non-achieving gifted boys. Powell (1982) observes that a gifted child's discrepancy between the ideal self (aptitude) and the real self (achievement) may impose a high degree of self-inflicted misery. In a study by Loeb and Jay (1987), 227 gifted children between the ages of 9 and 12 were compared with nongifted peers on three paper and pencil measures of self-concept. Although teacher ratings indicate that while gifted students generally had fewer problems in almost all areas studied, gifted girls had substantially fewer problems in the areas of aggressiveness, depression, lack of confidence, schoolwork, and getting along with other children. While academic success and the label gifted may provide the more verbally gifted females with a positive self-concept and control over the learning environment, gifted boys may see the label gifted as a threat to developing masculine identity in the feminized world of elementary education. And while gifted boys demonstrate less aggressiveness than nongifted boys, perceived lack of physical power may underscore increased concern with living up to the masculine image modeled by peers as male gifted mature. The impact of peer pressure has been cited as a factor in gifted boys continuing in gifted programs beyond elementary school (Ford, 1978).

Culturally Diverse Gifted. Recent studies related to the underrepresentation of minority and disadvantaged children in gifted and talented programs have focused on the relationship of self-esteem and achievement. Minorities have generally suffered from lower expectations for achievement, and in their cultural isolation, gifted may exaggerate behaviors that are offensive to more conforming peers, while at the same time sharing affective similarities with other gifted:

> The gifted child is extraordinarily sensitive and therefore experiences life intensely. To suffer prejudice is painful to everyone, but gifted children from racial minority groups may experience the pain of discrimination more intensely than their peers of average abilities. This pain may be exacerbated by the characteristic perfectionism and the expectation of moral order that is so blatantly unrealized in their daily lives. Because gifted children tend to feel responsible for problems in their lives and chastise themselves mercilessly, gifted children from minority cultures may blame themselves for the "failures" and missed opportunities that are inherent in the experience of living under the yoke of discrimination (Lindstrom & Van Sant, 1986, 584)

The impact of cultural isolation results in part from educational programs which are in conflict with some culturally specific learning styles (Hillard, 1991). American education typically utilizes a stimulus-centered, analytical, "left-brain" approach which may conflict with the more relational, global and "right-brain" approach characteristic of many culturally identifiable minority gifted.

Intelligence is often defined in terms of cultural priorities and character, and the American academic tradition mirrors Western concepts such as rational thought and conformity, and often gifted minority students' talents lie in areas valued within their own minority culture may conflict with peer relationships as well as family values (Schmitz & Galbraith, 1985).

Culturally diverse students, while needing to integrate analytic skills into their processing repertoire, should, as should all children, have access to opportunities which draw from and enhance creativity; a tolerance for diversity and imagery, a memory for essence vs. detail, activities such as improvisation and, in general, a more humanistic and inductive educational program (Hillard, 1991).

Gifted Females. Peer relationships and traditional values also impact on the expectations of gifted females:

> ... in junior and senior high school, girls are exposed to many deep-seated cultural taboos which make it difficult for them to comfortably display their intelligence and pursue excellence as aggressively as boys. The result of this

inhibition can be long-term depression and very low self-esteem (Schmitz & Galbraith, 1985, 33).

As former Quiz Kid Ruth Feldman notes, "it is no fun being labelled a 'brain,' especially for a girl" (Feldman, 1985, 4). Adolescent females are aware of those achieving women, frequently their own mothers, who mirror similar conflicts in managing professional and family responsibilities. Some seeking careers in fields such as law, medicine or other time-intensive professions often choose to limit their sexuality by rejecting traditional child-rearing goals, thus sacrificing this aspect of female self-esteem in order to achieve. Others attempt to juggle motherhood with a career, often with the realization summarized by the self-deprecatory comment these women make of "needing a wife" in order to fulfill myriad responsibilities. To avoid these pitfalls, the adolescent gifted female needs access to career counseling which avoids sex-stereotyped fields, as well as direction in setting priorities and delegating responsibilities: essential skills for the more perfectionistic gifted.

Gifted Handicapped. Handicapped and gifted students, including learning-disabled gifted, are often underidentified because the handicap masks the gifted ability. History is replete with individuals such as Helen Keller (deaf, blind and mute) or Stevie Wonder (blind), whose extraordinary giftedness surfaced despite severe sensory deprivation. Recognition that a handicap may exist with giftedness is an obstacle which many learning-disabled gifted encounter in educational settings. Reduced academic pressures and opportunities to express feelings and problems, as well as providing successful adult role models who have overcome a disability, are strategies which may mitigate the frustration resulting from the disability.

SUMMARY

Ruth Feldman, who participated as a nine-year-old in the radio presentation, *Quiz Kids,* summarizes from experience the impact of a label such as gifted on children:

Children, like the Quiz Kids, who are accustomed to easy success and who are praised for work requiring modest effort, may not develop discrimination or learn to meet a challenge. Children held to impossibly high standards and deprived of praise may get caught in a cycle of hopelessness, of misdirected perfectionism, trying to please parents, teachers, or bosses who can never be satisfied. Either way, praise becomes the point of the endeavor, obscuring internal motivation and self-evaluation. The result can be a gnawing fear of failure that inhibits creative risk-taking and personal goal setting.

A child who is exceptional in any way should accept it as nothing to be embarrassed about or inordinately proud of—it just simply is (Feldman, 1985, 5).

APPENDICES

Appendix 1

SOCIAL/EMOTIONAL DEVELOPMENT: SENSORIMOTOR STAGE

Age	Behaviors
0–3 mos.	*Social:* Infant communicates by crying. Smiles spontaneously to mother's face, voice, smile. Responds to person-to-person contact with adults and children. *Play:* Practice play begins with sensory exploration of own body. Repeats satisfying bodily actions (e.g., movement, vocalizations). *Emotional:* Joy (delight), distress (frustration or pain), surprise, interest.
4–9 mos.	*Social:* Enjoys being near people and played with. Responds gaily to play interactions with others. Cries, smiles, kicks, coos, laughs to attract social attention. Responds differently to strangers (stranger anxiety — 8 mos.). Shouts for attention (8 months); rejects confinement. Cries if other child cries. *Play:* Learns that actions affects objects by manipulating objects. Grasps dangling toys within reach. Shakes/bangs toys/spoons to make different sounds. Uncovers hidden toy. Plays a "game" with adult assistance. Fights for disputed toy (9 months). *Emotions:* Enjoyment, protest, fear, anger, humor, teases, shyness.
10–12 mos.	*Social:* Pays attention to his own name. Recognizes different tones of voice and responds. Able to interpret the emotional expression of familiar adults. Copies simple actions of others. Recognizes himself as an individual apart from mother. Learning to cooperate; shows guilt at wrongdoing. Actively seeks to maintain interactions with adult. Tries to alter mother's plans through persuasion or protest. Displays separation anxiety when apart from mother. Fears strange people and places. Developing a sense of humor. Teases and tests parental limits. Can demonstrate affection. Discriminates positive and negative attention. *Play:* Applies learned movements to new situations. Stacks rings on a peg. Holds crayon — imitating scribbling. Attempts to play with another child. Rolls ball in imitation of adult. *Emotional:* Anxiety, fear, affection, persuasion, protest, guilt, negativism.

Age	Behaviors
1–2 yrs.	*Social:* Recognizes self in mirror or picture, and refers to self by name. Beginning to become independent. Cooperates by helping to put things away. May become angry if activities are interrupted. Responds to simple commands by adult. Begins to realize that he can't have everything his own way. Social relationships with other children are awkward. May hit, bite, or fight over a toy. Engages in social laughter. Shows anger through aggressive behavior.
13–18 mos.	*Play:* Engages in experimentation and ritualized play. Solitary or onlooker play. Plays by self, imitating own play, initiates own play. Deliberately throws/drops toys and watches them fall.
19–24 mos.	Emergence of symbolic play. Rides a broom for a horse; plays house. Imitates adult behaviors in play. Moves (dances to music). Begins to play with other children. *Emotions:* Almost complete store of emotional expressions.

REFERENCES: Crow & Crow, 1953; Caplan, 1973; Fallen & Umansky, 1985; Lerner et al., 1987; Helms & Turner, 1976; Biehler & Hudson, 1986; Jones, 1988.

Appendix 2

SOCIAL/EMOTIONAL DEVELOPMENT: EARLY CHILDHOOD

(AGES 2-5 YEARS)

Age	Behaviors

Two Years Old

SOCIAL: Defends own possessions, but is beginning to share.
Asks for wants.
Knows gender identity.
Participates in simple group activity—singing, dancing.
Little interaction with other children.
Mother continues to be very important to child.
Sometimes makes special friend by age 3.

PLAY: Parallel play or onlooker play.
Imaginative play.
Symbolically uses objects and self in play (plays house).
Beginning cooperative play.
Enjoys imitating mother and using miniature equipment.
Participates in simple group activities.

EMOTIONAL: Gentle, friendly person.
Expresses affection warmly.
Emotionally calm, sure, balanced.
Lovable, engaging, enthusiastic, and appreciative.

Age 2½ Years   Explosive, tense, rigid, insecure, easily frustrated.
Ritualistic, routinized.
Screams, throws temper tantrums for little cause.

Three Years Old

SOCIAL: Friends becoming more interesting than adults.
Shares toys; takes turns with assistance.
Father increasingly important to child.
Beginning to learn to take responsibility.
Shows affections for younger siblings.
Associative group play begins.

PLAY: Joins in play with other children (associative play).
Begins dramatic play—acting out whole scenes.
Uses imaginative play with dolls.
Enjoys imaginary companions.
Often silly in play, doing things wrong purposefully.

EMOTIONAL: Interprets emotions from facial expressions and intonation.
Calm, collected, secure, capable, friendly.
Interested in other children's feelings.
Conforms easily, eager to please.

169

Age	Behaviors

Developing ability to stand frustration; emotions in control.

Age 3¹/₂   Insecure, anxious, inwardized, often bossy.

Self-willed, refuses to obey.

Inconsistent in behaviors.

Four Years Old

SOCIAL: Plays and interacts with other children.

Improving in turn-taking and cooperating.

Spurred on by rivalry in activity.

Understands social problem-solving.

Shows interest in exploring sex differences.

Developing self-responsibility; enjoys doing things for self.

Plays outside with little supervision; likes to be trusted.

Sense of property is developing.

Still home and mother-oriented.

PLAY: Dramatic play, closer to reality.

Plays dress up; very imaginative with self and others.

Loves adventure and anything new.

Plays in groups of 2–5 children.

EMOTIONAL: Exhibits definite personality.

Shows concern and sympathy.

Calm, secure, balanced.

Loves adventure, excitement, anything new.

Age 4¹/₂   Bosses and criticizes; exaggerates and boasts.

Extremes in behaviors: loves a lot, hates a lot.

May prevaricate and use profanity.

Five Years Old

SOCIAL: Wants to do what is expected.

Respects reasonable authority.

Willing to play with most other children in the class.

Engages with other children in cooperative play; fair play.

Engages with other children in role assignments.

Chooses own friends; friendships change rapidly.

One or two best friends of same sex.

Awareness of sex roles begins.

PLAY: Plays simple table games; competitive games.

Plays games with rules.

Plays in small groups, not too highly organized.

Play changes rapidly.

EMOTIONAL: Enjoys life, secure; consistently sunny and happy.

Self-limiting, protects self from overstimulation.

Expresses emotions freely and openly.

Age 5¹/₂   Quarrels are frequent, short duration, forgotten quickly.

Anger outbursts are frequent; ready to disobey.

Jealousy among classmates is common.

Hesitant, dawdling, overdemanding, explosive.

Extremes: shy/bold; affectionate/antagonistic.

REFERENCES: Ames & Ilg, 1976a; Ames & Ilg, 1976b; Ames & Ilg, 1976c; Ames & Ilg, 1979; Biehler & Hudson, 1986; Biehler & Snowman, 1986; Caplan, 1973; Cole & Cole, 1989; Crow & Crow, 1956; Fallen & Umansky, 1985; Healy et al., 1978; Helms & Turner, 1976; Lerner et al., 1987.

Appendix 3

SOCIAL/EMOTIONAL DEVELOPMENT: PRIMARY GRADES

(1ST–3RD GRADES, 6–8 YEARS)

Age	Behaviors

Six Years Old

SOCIAL: Relationship with mother is one of greatest problems.
Best and worst with primary caretakers.
Problems with siblings; competitive, combative nature.
Jealous of siblings; bossy with younger children.
Quarrels frequently.

EMOTIONAL: Bipolarity; wants both of any two opposites.
Stubborn; finds it hard to make up mind and hard to change.
Center of own universe.
Wants to be best and first at everything.
Beginning to separate from mother.
Frequently warm with both parents.
Sensitive to criticism or ridicule; needs frequent praise.
Insecure; difficulty adjusting to failure.
Demanding, difficult, argumentative, oppositional, tantrumy.

Age 6½   Delightful, amusing, good sense of humor.
Lively intellectually.
Loves exploration.
Boundless enthusiasm for any new activity.

Seven Years Old

SOCIAL: Sometimes engages mother in battle of wills.
Usually withdraws rather than fights.
Good with much younger siblings and much older.
Plays more harmoniously than at age 6.
Boys begin discrimination against girls.
Anxious to be accepted by group; slow to accept others.
Highly sociable; makes little trouble in social situations.
Fairness is very important.

EMOTIONAL: Increasing reasonableness.
Ethical—wants to do things right.
No sense of humor.
Emotionally withdrawn and calmer than age 6.
Feels people do not like him/her and are mean.
Often moody, morose, and melancholy.
Displays worries and fears; easily disappointed.
Extremely self-absorbed.

Age	Behaviors

Increasing control of temper.
Becoming sensitive to friends' attitudes.

Eight Years Old

SOCIAL: Friendly; selective in choice of friends.
Permanent "best friend" and semipermanent "enemy."
Likes organized games in small groups.
Overly concerned with rules of games.
Gets carried away with team spirit.
Quarrels frequently.
Likes to help; enjoys responsibility.
Uses language as the medium of interaction.
Knowledge of peer group norms.
Eager to please teacher.

EMOTIONAL: Sensitive to criticism and ridicule; needs frequent praise.
Sensitive to feelings of others.
Knows that each person has a private subjective self.
Risk-taking, underestimates danger.
Gentle, affectionate, comfortable, secure.
Happy much of the time; acceptant of self.

REFERENCES: Ames & Ilg, 1979; Biehler & Hudson, 1986; Cole & Cole, 1989; Skolnick, 1986; Ames & Haber, 1985; Kegan, 1985; Oden, 1988; Harter, 1983.

Appendix 4

SOCIAL/EMOTIONAL DEVELOPMENT: INTERMEDIATE GRADES

(4TH–6TH GRADES; 9–12 YEARS)

SOCIAL BEHAVIORS:
Social Perspective-Taking (Role-Taking):
    Increased social perspective-taking abilities.
    Recognizes and shows concern about how others feel.
    Expresses concern for others.
    Knowledge and inferences about characteristics of people.
    Anticipates how other's personality will affect own behavior (social inferences).
    Developing more insight into reciprocal nature of social interactions.
    Developing ability to observe self and others and engage in social comparison.
    Developing a more mature self-portrait using social comparisons.
Social Regulation and Moral Development:
    Conforms to several sets of rules regarding moral codes and behaviors.
    Assumes certain roles based on unrestrained responses of others.
    Aware of nuances of written and unwritten rules and codes of conduct.
    Current understanding of the social world.
    Learns through indirect socialization techniques such as discussion.
    Increased ability to get along with people.
    Regulating own behavior according to social rules and rule-governed play.
    Growing understanding of self and others in social interactions.
    Participates in activities requiring public comparison and competition.
    Understands appropriate behavior differs in various social settings.
    Sensitive to negative reactions by others.
    Self-shame as a reaction to antisocial conduct or lack of moral behavior.
Social Problem-Solving:
    Developing more sophistication in using social problem-solving skills.
    Sensitive to social problems and social consequences.
    Understands causal thinking (cause-effect) relationships in social problems.
    Understands the importance of goal-setting in the problem-solving strategy.
    Understands the social strategy repertoire.
Social Relationships: Peers:
    Re-establishes self-concept in relation to peers rather than family.
    Emerging independence from parents and growing dependence on peers.
    Experiences emotional conflict between group code and adult rules.
    Interacts with peers in unsupervised situations.
    Membership in appropriate group provides norms of dress, social skills, etc.
    Adequacy is defined by one's relationship to the social group.
    Friendships more important, more intense, and fewer in number.
    Sex-role parameters defined in sexually segregated clubs and activities.
    Learning self-control in dealing with group pressure: avoiding trouble.

Negotiating and apologizing.

Social Relationships: Other Relationships:

Parents and children "co-regulate" child's behaviors.

Both boys and girls turn to father for advice; attempting to cut "apron strings."

Sibling harmony better with older and younger siblings than near same age.

Relationships with grandparents continue to be reciprocally warm.

EMOTIONAL BEHAVIORS:

Self-Knowledge

Increased understanding of self.

Development of a self-theory or a self-definition.

Increased understanding of own personal, emotional characteristics.

Understands how own behavior affects another's actions/reactions to self.

Self-Competence/Self-Evaluation

Able to make global evaluations of self-worth.

Increased ability to control one's emotions and related behaviors (self-control).

Self-concept based on competence—athletic, intellectual, academic, artistic, etc.

Self-pride as an emotional response to an evaluation of competence.

Understanding of trait stability or consistency of attributes that define the self.

REFERENCES: Biehler & Hudson, 1986; Berger, 1986; Harter, 1988, 1985; Greenwald, 1980; Cole & Cole, 1989; Dweck & Elliot, 1983; Rose-Krasnor, 1983; McGinnis & Goldstein, 1984.

Appendix 5

SOCIAL/EMOTIONAL DEVELOPMENT: ADOLESCENCE

MATURE SOCIALLY AND PHYSICALLY:
  Understand and accept biological changes that change body image.
  Become comfortable with adult body; responsibilities associated with sexuality.
  Cope with social problems of sex differences.
  Coping with interpersonal dynamics of dating.
  Understanding psychosocial developmental changes and identity confusion.
FUNCTIONING AS A RESPONSIBLE CITIZEN:
  Internalizing the conventional level of moral development.
  Learning to simultaneously fulfill duties to society and own conscience.
  Developing responsibility for own beliefs, commitments, and attitudes.
  Learning parameters of adult autonomy and responsibility.
  Learning and practicing skills of the "work world" through getting a job.
MAKING CAREER/VOCATIONAL CHOICES:
(Understanding Social Factors in Career Decision-Making):
  Understanding influences of parents' socio-economic status on career choices.
  Understanding effects of level of parental education on career/job choice.
  Understanding effects of attitude and academic achievement on career choice.
  Recognizing the influences of school and curriculums on career choice options.
  Understanding degree of peer group decisions on own career/job decisions.
  Understanding the effect of desire for economic independence on job choice.
SOCIAL INTERACTIONS (PEER GROUP) AND FRIENDSHIPS:
  Earning status and functioning in social arena of school.
  Learning to function within chosen adolescent peer subculture.
  Forming friendships from same socio-economic background (life-style, values).
  Understands the element of choice in peer group membership.
  Understanding the functions of friendship: companionship of familiar partner, source
      of information, physical and ego support, social comparison, trusting relation-
      ship.
  Effects of social development, peer group, friendships influence mate selection, occupa-
      tional choice, sense of self, quality of adult social life.
DESATELLIZE FROM HOME:
  Become less physically, psychologically, and emotionally dependent on parents.
  Developing responsibility, independence, and self-confidence.
  Participating in achievement and independence training.
  Understanding and accepting noncontingent positive regard.
DEVELOP REALISTIC SELF-CONCEPT:
  Constructing an integrated self-portrait.
  Realistically evaluating one's intellectual competence, physical competence, physical
      attractiveness and sex-typing characteristics, social competence, leadership abilities,
      moral beliefs, and sense of humor.

175

Develops the ability to use the perspective of the "universal person."
Uses the self-concept as a standard for evaluating and predicting performance.
Maintains a reasonably positive self-concept.

REFERENCES: Coleman et al., 1974; Elder, 1962; Elkind, 1970; Erikson, 1968; Flavell, 1977; Fowler, 1976; Havighurst, 1952; Johnson, 1963; Kohlberg, 1976; Manaster, 1989; McCandless & Coop, 1979; Santrock, 1990.

BIBLIOGRAPHY

Ames, L. & Haber, C.: *Your Seven-Year-Old.* New York: Dell, 1985.

Ames, L. & Ilg, F.: *Your Two-Year-Old.* New York: Dell, 1976a.

Ames, L. & Ilg, F.: *Your Three-Year-Old.* New York: Dell, 1976b.

Ames, L. & Ilg, F.: *Your Four-Year-Old.* New York: Dell, 1976c.

Ames, L. & Ilg, F.: *Your Five-Year-Old.* New York: Dell, 1976d.

Ames, L. & Ilg, F.: *Your Six-Year-Old.* New York: Dell, 1979.

Anderson, E., Dunlea, A. & Kekelis, L.: Blind children's language: Resolving some differences. *Journal of Child Language,* 11: 646–656, 1984.

Andrews, G., Craig, A., Feyer, A., Hoddinott, S., Howie, P. & Neilsen, M.,: Stuttering: A review of research findings and theories circa 1982. *Journal of Speech and Hearing Disorders,* 48: 226–246, 1983.

Arnold, R. & Hornett, D.: Teaching idioms to children who are deaf. *Teaching Exceptional Children,* 22 (4): 14–17, 1990.

Asarnow, J. & Bates, S.: Depression in child psychiatric inpatients: Cognitive and attributional patterns. *Journal of Abnormal Child Psychology,* 16 (6): 601–615, Dec. 1988.

Asher, S. & Renshaw, P.: Children without friendships: Social knowledge and social skill training. In S.R. Asher & J. Gottman (Eds.), *Development of Children's Friendships.* New York: Cambridge University Press, 1981.

Austin, G.F.: Knowledge of selected concepts obtained by an adolescent deaf population. *American Annals of the Deaf,* 120: 360–370, 1975.

Bachara, G., Raphael, J. & Phelan, W. III: Empathy development in deaf pre-adolescents. *American Annals of the Deaf,* 125: 38–41, 1980.

Baska, L.K.: Characteristics and needs of the gifted. In J. Feldhusen, J. Van Tassel-Baska, & K. Seeley, *Excellence in Educating the Gifted,* Denver: Love, 1989.

Becker, S.: The performance of deaf and hearing children on a logical discovery task. *Volta Review,* 76: 537–545, 1974.

Benbow, C. & Stanley, J.: Sex differences in mathematical reasoning ability: More facts. *Science,* 222: 1029–1031, 1983.

Berger, K.: *The Developing Person Through Childhood and Adolescence.* New York: Worth, 1986.

Best, S., Bigge, J. & Sirvis, B.: Physical and health impairments. In N. Haring & L. McCormick (Eds.) *Exceptional Children and Youth* (5th Ed.). Columbus, OH: Merrill, 1990.

Biehler, R. & Hudson, L.: *Developmental Psychology.* Boston: Houghton Mifflin, 1986.

177

Biehler, R. & Snowman, J.: *Psychology Applied to Teaching (5th ed.).* Boston: Houghton Mifflin, 1986.

Bjorklund, D.F.: *Children's Thinking: Developmental Function Individual Differences.* Pacific Grove, CA: Brooks/Cole, 1989.

Blackwell, P., Egen, E., Fischgrung, J. & Zarcadolas, C.: *Sentences and Other Systems.* Washington, DC: Bell Association for the Deaf, 1978.

Blaesing, L.L.: *Perceptual, Active, and Cognitive Perspective-Taking in Deaf and Hearing Children.* Unpublished doctoral dissertation. University of NC at Chapel Hill, 1978.

Bloom, B.: *Taxonomy of Educational Objectives.* New York: McKay, 1969.

Borkowski, J. & Varnhagan, C.: Transfer of learning strategies: Contrast of self-instructional and traditional formats with EMR children. *American Journal of Mental Deficiency,* 83: 369–379, 1884.

Brackett, P. & Hennings, M.: Communicative interaction of preschool hearing impaired children in an integrated setting. *Volta Review,* 78: 276–285, 1976.

Brazelton, T.B.: The truth about child development. *Family Circle,* 103 (1): 72–74, 1990.

Brown, A.: The role of strategic behavior in retardate memory. In N.R. Ellis (Ed.) *International Review of Research in Mental Retardation,* Vol. 7. New York: Academic Press, 1974.

Bruno, R., Johnson, J. & Simon, S.: Perception of humor by regular class students and students with learning disabilities or mild mental retardation, *Journal of Learning Disabilities,* 20: 568–570, 1987.

Bryan, T.: Learning disabled children's comprehension of nonverbal communication, *Journal of Learning Disabilities,* 10: 501–506, 1977.

Bryan, T.: Self-concept and attributions of the learning disabled, *Learning Disabilities Focus,* 1(2): 82–89, 1986.

Bryan, T., Donahue, M. & Pearl, R.: Learning disabled children's peer interactions during a small group problem-solving task. *Learning Disability Quarterly,* 4: 13–22, 1981.

Bryan, T. & Pflaum, S.: Social interactions of learning disabled children: A linguistic, social, and cognitive analysis, *Learning Disability Quarterly,* 1: 70–79, 1978.

Bryan, T., Sherman, R. & Fisher, A.: Learning disabled boys' nonverbal behaviors with a dyadic interview, *Learning Disability Quarterly,* 3: 65–72, 1980.

Bryan, T., Werner, M. & Pearl, R.: Learning disabled students' conformity responses to prosocial and antisocial situations, *Learning Disability Quarterly,* 5: 344–352, 1982.

Calhoun, M. & Howisher, M.: *Teaching and Learning Strategies for Physically Handicapped Students.* Baltimore: University Park Press, 1979.

Calvert, D.: Articulation and hearing impairment. In N. Lass, L. McReynolds, J. Northern & D. Yoder (Eds.), *Speech, Language, and Hearing.* Philadelphia: Saunders, 1982.

Campione, J. & Brown, A.: Memory and metamemory development in educable retarded children. In R.V. Kail, Jr. & J.W. Hagen (Eds.), *Perspectives on the Development of Memory and Cognition.* Hillsdale, NJ: Erlbaum, 1977.

Cantor, N., Markus, H., Neidenthal, P., & Nurius, P.: On motivation and the self-concept. In R.M. Sorrentino & E. T. Higgins (Eds.), *Handbook of Motivation and Cognition: Foundations of Social Behavior.* New York: Guilford Press, 1986.

Caplan, F.: *The First Twelve Months of Life.* New York: Gosset & Dunlap, 1973.

Carr, M. & Borkowski, J.G.: Metamemory in gifted Children. *Gifted Child Quarterly,* 31 (1): 40–44, 1987.

Carter, J.: Intelligence and reading achievement of EMR in three educational settings. *Mental Retardation,* 13 (5): 26–27, 1975.

Cartwright, G., Cartwright, C. & Ward, M. *Educating Special Learners, (3rd Ed.).* Belmont, CA.: Wadsworth, 1989.

Chapman, J.: Cognitive-motivational characteristics and academic achievement of learning disabled children: A longitudinal study. *Journal of Educational Psychology,* 80(3): 357–365, 1988.

Cicci, R.: Reading, writing, and phonology. *Harvard Educational Review,* 40: 287, 1970.

Clark, B.: *Growing Up Gifted.* Columbus, OH: Merrill, 1988.

Clark, R.: Differences in self-concept among students identified as ED, EMR, and normal. *Dissertation Abstracts International,* 36, (5A): 2708, Nov. 1975.

Cline, R.: A description of self-esteem measures among educable mentally retarded children and their nonretarded peers. *Dissertation Abstracts International,* 36: 2133A, 1975.

Coady, E.: *Social Problem Solving Skills and School Related Social Competency of Elementary Age Deaf Students: A Descriptive Study.* Unpublished doctoral dissertation, University of Washington, 1984.

Cohen, G.: *The Psychology of Cognition* (2nd Ed.). New York: Academic Press, 1983.

Cohen, S. & Plaskon, S.: *Language Arts for the Mildly Handicapped.* Columbus, OH: Merrill, 1980.

Coker, G.: A comparison of self-concepts and academic achievement of visually handicapped children enrolled in a regular school and in a residential school. *Education of Visually Handicapped,* 11 (3): 67–74, Fall 1979.

Cole, M. & Cole, S.: *The Development of Children.* New York: W. H. Freeman, 1989.

Coleman, J. et. al.: *Youth: Transition to adulthood.* Report of the Panel on Youth of the President's Science Advisory Committee. Chicago: University of Chicago Press, 1974.

Crow, L. & Crow, A.: *Child Psychology.* New York: Barnes & Noble, 1953.

Cullinan, D. & Epstein, M.: Behavior disorders. In N. Haring & L. McCormick (Eds.). *Exceptional Children and Youth: An Introduction to Special Education* (Fifth edition). Columbus, OH: Merrill, 1990.

Davis, G. & Rimm, S.: *Education of the Gifted and Talented* (2nd Ed.). Englewood Cliffs, NJ: Prentice-Hall, 1989.

Davis, J., Elfenbein, J., Schum, R. & Bentler, R.: Effects of Mild and Moderate Hearing Impairments on Language, Educational, and Psychological Behavior of Children. *Journal of Speech and Hearing Disorders,* 51: 53–62, 1986.

Derr, A.: How learning disabled adolescent boys make moral judgments, *Journal of Learning Disabilities,* 19: 160–164, 1986.

Deshler, D. & Schumaker, J.: Social skills of learning-disabled adolescents: A review of characteristics and intervention, *Topics in Learning and Learning Disabilities,* 3: 15–23, 1983.

Deshler, D., Schumaker, J., Alley, G., Warner, M. & Clark, F.: An epidemiological study of learning disabled adolescents in secondary schools: Academic self-image and attributions. (Research Report No 14), Lawrence: University of Kansas, Institute for Research in Learning Disabilities, 1980.

Dodge, K. & Frame, C.: Social cognitive biases and deficits in aggressive boys. *Child Development,* 53: 620–635, 1982.

Donahue, M.: Interactions between linguistic and pragmatic development in learning-disabled children: Three views of the state of the union. In S. Rosenburg (Ed.) *Advances in Applied Psycholinguistics: Vol. 1. Disorders of First-Language Development.* Cambridge: Cambridge University Press, 1987.

Douglas, V.: Attentional and cognitive problems. In M. Rutter (Ed.), *Developmental Neuropsychiatry.* New York: Guilford Press, 1983.

Dowaliby, R., Burke, N. & McKee, B.: A comparison of hearing impaired and normally hearing students on locus of control, people orientation, and study habits and attitudes. *American Annals of the Deaf,* 128: 53–59, 1981.

Drew, C., Logan, D. & Hardman, M.: *Mental Retardation: A life Cycle Approach* (4th Ed.). Columbus, OH: Merrill, 1988.

Dudley-Marling, C., Snider, V. & Tarver, S.: Locus of control and learning disabilities: A review and discussion. *Perceptual and Motor Skills,* 54: 503–504, 1982.

Dweck, C. & Elliot, E.S.: Achievement motivation. In E.M. Hetherington (Ed.) *Handbook of Child Psychology: Socialization, Personality, and Social Development* (Vol. 4). New York: Wiley, 1983.

Edgerton, R. (Ed.): *Lives in process: Mentally retarded adults in a large city.* Washington, DC: American Association on Mental Deficiency, 1984.

Edwards, J. & Edwards, D.: Rate of behavior development: Direct and continuous measurement. *Perceptual & Motor Skills,* 31: 633–634, 1970.

Eisenson, J.: *Aphasia in Children.* New York: Harper & Row, 1972.

Elder, G.H.: Structural variations in the child-rearing relationship, *Sociometry,* 25: 241–262, 1962.

Elkind, D.: *Children and Adolescents: Interpretative Essays on Jean Piaget.* New York: Oxford University Press, 1970.

Ellis, N.: Memory processes in retardates and normals. *International Review of Research in Mental Retardation,* 4, 1970.

Epanchin, B.: Aggressive behavior in children and adolescents. In B. Epanchin & J. Paul (Eds.) *Emotional Problems of Childhood and Adolescence: A Multidisciplinary Perspective.* Columbus, OH: Merrill, 1987.

Epstein, M. & Cullinan, D.: Academic performance of behaviorally disordered and learning disabled pupils, *The Journal of Special Education,* 17: 303–307, 1983.

Epstein, M., Polloway, E., Patton, J., & Foley, R.: Mild retardation: Student characteristics and services. *Education & Training of the Mentally Retarded,* 24 (1): 7–16, 1989.

Erikson, E.H.: *Identity: Youth and Crisis.* New York: Norton, 1968.

Fallen, N. & Umansky, W.: *Young Children With Special Needs,* 2nd ed. Columbus, OH: Merrill, 1985.

Falvey, M.S.: *Community-Based Curriculum: Instructional Strategies for Students With Severe Handicaps.* Baltimore: Brookes, 1986.

Farnham-Diggory, S.: Self, future, and time: A developmental study of the concepts of psychotic brain-damaged, and normal children. *Child Development Monographs,* 31(1): 1–63, 1966.

Farrugia, D. & Austin, G.: A study of social emotional adjustment patterns of hearing impaired students in different educational settings. *American Annals of the Deaf,* 110:456–478, 1980.

Federal Register: Implementation of Part B of the Education of All Handicapped Children Act, 42, August, 23, 1977.

Feldman, R.D.: The promise and pain of growing up gifted. Gifted/Creative/Talented, May/June 1985.

Feldman, R.S., White, J.B. & Lobato, D.: Social skills and nonverbal behavior. In R.S. Feldman (Ed.) *Development of Nonverbal Behavior in Children.* New York: Springer-Verlag, 1982.

Flavell, J.H.: *Cognitive Development,* (2nd ed). Englewood Cliffs, N.J.: Prentice Hall, 1985.

Fleming, M. & Malone, M.: The relationship of student characteristics and student performance in science as viewed by meta-analysis research. *Journal of Research in Science Teaching,* 20: 481–495, 1983.

Ford, B.: Student attitudes toward special programming and identification. *Gifted Children Quarterly,* 22(4): 481–497, 1978.

Fowler, J.W.: Stages in Faith: The structural developmental approach. In F. Hennessey (Ed.) *Values and Moral Development and Behavior: Theory, Research, and Social Issues.* New York: Holt, Rinehart & Winston, 1976.

Gagne, F.: Giftedness and talent: Reexamining a reexamination of the definitions. *Gifted Child Quarterly,* 29: 103–112, 1985.

Gallucci, N.T.: Emotional adjustment of gifted children. *Gifted Child Quarterly,* 32(2): 273–276, 1988.

Gardner, H.: *Frames of Mind.* New York: Basic Books, 1983.

Gearheart, B., Weishahn, M. & Gearheart, C.: *The Exceptional Student in the Regular Classroom,* (4th ed.). Columbus, OH: Merrill, 1988.

Gelfand, D., Jenson, W. & Drew, C.: *Understanding Child Behavior Disorders,* (2nd ed.). New York: Holt, Rinehart & Winston, 1988.

Goertzel, V. & Goertzel, M.: *Cradles of Eminence.* Boston: Little, Brown, 1962.

Goertzel, M., Goertzel, V. & Goertzel, T.: *Three Hundred Eminent Personalities.* San Francisco: Jossey-Bass, 1978.

Goetz, T. & Dweck, C.: Learned helplessness in social situations. *Journal of Personality and Social Psychology,* 39: 246–255, 1980.

Goldfarb, W.: Self-awareness in schizophrenic children. *Archives of General Psychology,* 8 (1): 47–60, 1963.

Goodstein, L.: Functional speech disorders and personality: A survey of the literature. *Journal of Speech and Hearing Impaired Research,* 1: 359–376, 1958.

Greenberg, M. & Kusche, C.: Cognitive, personal, and social development of deaf children and adolescents. In M. Wang, M. Reynolds & H. Walberg (Eds.) *Handbook of Special Education: Research and Practice, Vol. 3, Low Incidence Conditions.* New York: Pergamon, 1989.

Greenspan, S.: Defining social competence in children: A working model. In B. K. Keogh (Ed.). *Advances in Special Education (Vol. 3): Socialization Influences on Exceptionality.* Greenwich, CT: JAI Press, 1981.

Greenwald, A.G.: The totalitarian ego: Fabrication and revision of personal history, *American Psychologist,* 7: 603–618, 1980.

Gregory, J., Shanahan, T. & Walberg, H.: Orthopaedically handicapped students in public and private high schools, *The Exceptional Child,* 34 (2): 85–92, July 1987.

Gresham, F.: Social competence and motivational characteristics of learning disabled students. In M. Wang, M. Reynolds, & H. Walberg (Eds.), *Handbook of Special Education: Research and Practice, Vol. 2, Mildly Handicapped Conditions.* New York: Pergamon, 1988.

Gresham, F. & Reschly, D.: Social skills and peer acceptance differences between learning disabled and nonhandicapped students, *Learning Disability Quarterly,* 9: 23–32, 1986.

Griffin, G.: Childhood predictive characteristics of aggressive adolescents. *Exceptional Children,* 54 (3): 246–252, 1987.

Grossman, H.: *Teaching the Emotionally Disturbed: A Casebook.* New York: Holt, Rinehart & Winston, 1965.

Grossman, H. (Ed.): *Manual on Terminology and Classification in Mental Retardation.* Washington, DC: American Association on Mental Deficiently, Special Publication No. 2, 1973 and 1977.

Grossman, H. (Ed.): *Classification in Mental Retardation.* Washington, DC: American Association on Mental Deficiency, 1983.

Guess, D. & Siegel-Causey, E.: Students with severe and multiple disabilities. In E. Meyen & T. Skrtic (Eds.) *Exceptional Children and Youth: An Introduction* (3rd ed.). Denver: Love, 1988.

Hallahan, D., Gajar, A., Cohen, A. & Tarver, S.: Selective attention and locus of control in learning disabled and normal children. *Journal of Learning Disabilities* 11: 47–52, 1978.

Hallahan, D. & Kauffman, J.: *Exceptional Children: Introduction to Special Education,* (4th ed.). Englewood Cliffs, NJ: Prentice Hall, 1988.

Hallahan, D., Kauffman, J. & Lloyd, J.: *Introduction to Learning Disabilities,* (2nd ed.). Englewood Cliffs, NJ: Prentice-Hall, 1985.

Hansen, V., Shankweiler, P. & Fischer, F.: Determinants of spelling ability in deaf and hearing adults: Access to linguistic structure. *Cognition,* 14: 323–344, 1983.

Hardt, J.: How passive-aggressive behavior in emotionally disturbed children affects peer interactions in a classroom setting. (ERIC Documents ED297518), 1988.

Hardman, M., Drew, C., Egan, M. & Wolf, B.: *Human Exceptionality,* (3rd ed.). Boston: Allyn & Bacon, 1990.

Haring, N. & McCormick, L.: *Exceptional Children and Youth,* (5th ed.), Columbus, OH: Merrill, 1990.

Harter, S.: The development of the self-esteem. In M. Heatherington (Ed.), *Handbook of Child Psychology: Social and Personality Development* (Vol. 4). New York: Wiley, 1983.

Harter, S.: Competence as a dimension of self-evaluation: Toward a comprehensive model of self-worth. In R. Leahy (Ed.), *The Development of the Self.* Orlando: Academic Press, 1985.

Harter, S.: Processes underlying the construction, maintenance and enhancement of the self-concept in children. In J. Suls & A. Greenwald (Eds.), *Psychological Perspectives on the Self.* (Vol. 3, 136–182). Hillsdale, NJ: Erlbaum, 1986.

Harter, S.: Developmental processes in the construction of the self. In T. Yawkey & J.E. Johnson (Eds.), *Integrative Processes and Socialization: Early to Middle Childhood.* Hillsdale, NJ: Erlbaum, (1988).

Harvey, D. & Greenway, A.: The self-concept of physically handicapped children and their nonhandicapped siblings: An empirical investigation. *Journal of Child Psychology and Psychiatry,* 25: 273–284, 1984.

Harvey, M.: Public school treatment of low income children. *Urban Education,* 15: 279–323, 1980.

Havighurst, R.: *Developmental Tasks and Education.* New York: Longmans, Green, 1952.

Healy, A., McAreavey, P., Von Hippel, C.S., Jones, S.H.: Chart of normal development: Infancy to six years of age. In *Maintaining Preschoolers: Children with Health Impairments.* Washington D.C.: U.S. Department of Health, Education, & Welfare, Office of Human Development Services, Administration for Children, Youth and Families, Head Start Bureau, 1978.

Helms, D. & Turner, J.: *Exploring Child Behavior.* Philadelphia: Saunders, 1982.

Hess, T. & Radtke, R.: Processing and memory factors in children's reading comprehension skill. *Child Development,* 52: 479–488, 1981.

Heward, W. & Orlansky, M.: *Exceptional Children* (3rd ed.). Columbus, OH: Merrill, 1988.

Higginbotham, D., Baker, B. & Neill, R.: Assessing the social participation and cognitive play abilities of hearing-impaired preschoolers. *The Volta Review,* 82: 261–270, 1980.

Higginbotham, D. & Baker, B.: Social participation and cognitive play differences in hearing impaired and normally hearing preschoolers. *The Volta Review,* 83: 135–149, 1983.

Hillard, A.: Learning styles and cultural diversity. Seminar presented at the 71st Annual National Meeting of the Association of Teacher Educators, New Orleans, 1991.

Hollinger, C.: Toward an understanding of career development among gifted/talented female adolescents. *Journal of the Education of the Gifted,* 12(1): 62–69, 1988.

Hung, D., Tzeng, O. & Warren, D.: A chronometric study of sentence processing in deaf children. *Cognitive Psychology,* 13: 583–610, 1987.

Hymes, D.: On communicative competence. In J. Pride & J. Holmes (Eds.) *Sociolinguistics* Baltimore: Penguin, 1972.

Jackson, N.E.: Precocious reading ability: What does it mean? *Gifted Child Quarterly,* 32 (1): 200–204, 1988.

Jaeger, J., Borod, J.C. & Peselow, E.: Facial expression of positive and negative emotions in patients with unipolar depression. *Journal of Affective Disorders,* 11: 43–50, 1986.

Jankowski, L. & Evans, J.: The exercise capacity of blind children. *Journal of Visual Impairment and Blindness,* 75: 248–251, 1981.

Johnson, D. & Blalock, J.: *Young adults with learning disabilities.* New York: Grune & Stratton, 1987.

Jones, C.J.: Analysis of the self-concepts of handicapped children, *Remedial and Special Education,* 6: 32–36, Sept./Oct. 1985.

Jones, C.J.: *Evaluation and Educational Programming of Deaf-Blind/Severely Multihandi-capped Students: Sensorimotor Stage.* Springfield, IL: Charles C Thomas, 1988.

Jones, C.J.: *Enhancing Self-Concepts and Achievement of Mildly Handicapped Students: Learning Disabled, Mildly Mentally Retarded, Behavior Disordered, and Speech/Language Impaired.* Springfield, IL: Charles C Thomas, 1992.

Jurkovic, G. & Selman, R.: A developmental analysis of intrapsychic understanding: Treating emotional disturbances in children. In R.L. Selman & R. Yando (Eds.) *New Distinctions for Child Development, No. 7, Clinical-Developmental Psychology.* San Francisco: Jossey-Bass, 1980.

Kanevsky, L.: Pursuing qualitative differences in the flexible use of problem-solving strategy by young children. *Journal for the Education of the Gifted,* 13 (2): 115–140, 1990.

Karchmer, M.: Demographics and deaf adolescents. In G. Anderson & D. Wilson (Eds.) *The Habilitation and Rehabilitation of Deaf Adolescents.* Washington DC: Gallaudet College Press, 1985.

Kauffman, J., Cullinan, D. & Epstein, M.: Characteristics of students placed in special programs for the seriously emotionally disturbed. *Behavior Disorders,* 12: 175–184, 1987.

Kazdin, A.E.: *Conduct disorders in childhood and adolescence.* Beverly Hills, CA: Sage, 1987.

Kegan, R.: The loss of Pete's dragon: Developments of the self in the years five to seven. In R. Leahy (Ed.) *The Development of the Self.* Orlando: Academic Press, 1985.

Keith, C.: Pervasive developmental disorders. In B. Epanchin & J. Paul (Eds.) *Emotional Problems of Childhood and Adolescence: A Multidisciplinary Perspective.* Columbus, OH: Merrill, 1987.

Kekelis, L. & Sacks, S.: Mainstreaming visually impaired children into regular education programs: The effects of visual impairment on children's interaction with peers. In S. Sacks, L. Kekelis & R. Gaylord-Ross (Eds.) *The Development of Social Skills by Visually Impaired Children.* San Francisco: San Francisco State University, 1988.

King, R.: Differentiating conduct disorder from depressive disorders in school age children. Paper presented at the Annual Meeting of the American Educational

Research Association (70th, San Francisco, CA. (ERIC Document Number: ED269683), April 16–20, 1986.

Kirk, S. & Gallagher, J.: *Educating Exceptional Children* (6th ed.). Boston: Houghton Mifflin, 1989.

Kneeder, R.: The use of cognitive training to change social behaviors. *Exceptional Children Quarterly,* 1: 65–73, 1980.

Knight-Arest, I.: Communicative effectiveness of learning disabled and normally achieving 10 to 13-year old boys, *Learning Disability Quarterly,* 7: 237–245, 1984.

Knobloch, P.: Psychological considerations of emotionally disturbed children. In W. Cruickshank (Ed.) *Psychology of Exceptional Children and Youth.* Englewood Cliffs, NJ: Prentice Hall, 1971.

Kohlberg, L.: Moral stages and moralization: The cognitive developmental approach. In T. Lickona (Ed.) *Moral Development and Behavior: Theory, Research, and Social Issues.* New York: Holt, Rinehart & Winston, 1976.

Kramer, J. & Engle, R.: Teaching awareness of strategic behavior in combination with strategy training: Effect on children's memory performance. *Journal of Experimental Child Psychology,* 32: 513–530, 1981.

Kramer, J., Piersel, W. & Glover, J.: Cognitive and social development of mildly retarded children. In M. Wang, M. Reynolds, & H. Walberg (eds.). *Handbook of Special Education: Research and Practice, Volume 2 Mildly Handicapped Conditions.* Oxford: Pergamon, 1988.

Kusche, C.: Linguistic processing, encoding capacities, and reading achievement in deaf children and adolescents. In D.S. Martin (Ed.) *International Symposium on Cognition, Education, and Deafness,* Vol. 2, Washington, DC: Gallaudet College, 1984.

Kusche, C., Greenberg, M. & Garfield, T.: Nonverbal intelligence and verbal achievement in deaf adolescents: An examination of heredity and environment. *American Annals of the Deaf,* 128 (4): 458–466, 1983.

Ladd, G. & Oden, S.: The relationship between peer acceptance and children's ideas about helpfulness. *Child Development,* 50: 402–408, 1979.

Lafoon, K.S., Jenkins-Friedman, R. & Tollefson, N.: Causal attributions of underachieving gifted, achieving gifted, and nongifted students. *Journal for the Education of the Gifted,* 13 (1): 4–21, 1989.

Land, S. & Vineberg, S.: Locus of control in blind children. *Exceptional Children,* 31: 257–260, 1965.

Landau, M. & Olsezewski-Kubilius, P.: Gender differences in participation in math/science activities. Paper presented at the Annual Conference of The National Association for Gifted Children, Orlando, FL, 1988.

Lang, H.: Academic development and preparation. In M. Wang, M. Reynolds & H. Walberg (Eds.) *Handbook of Special Education Research and Practice, Vol. 2, Mildly Handicapped Conditions.* New York: Pergamon, 1989.

Lawrence, E. & Winschel, J.: Self-concept and the retarded: Research and issues. *Exceptional Children,* 39: 310–319, 1973.

Lawrence, E. & Winschel, J.: Locus of control: Implications for special education. *Exceptional Children,* 41: 483–490, 1975.

Lederberg, A.: Peer interaction in young deaf children: The effect of partner hearing status and familiarity. *Developmental Psychology,* 22(5): 691–700, Sept. 1986.

Lee, P. & Mak, F.: Locus of control: Teachers' ratings and task performance of physically handicapped children. *Exceptional Child,* 31(2): 128–133, July, 1984.

Lerner, J.: *Learning Disabilities: Theories, Diagnosis, and Teaching Strategies.* (5th ed.). Boston: Houghton Mifflin, 1989.

Lerner, J., Mardell-Czudnowski, C. & Goldenberg, D.: *Special Education for the Early Childhood Years* (2nd ed.). Englewood Cliffs, NJ: Prentice Hall, 1987.

Lerner, R. & Shea, J.: Social behavior in adolescence. In B. Wolman (Ed.) *Handbook of Developmental Psychology.* Englewood Cliffs, NJ: Prentice Hall, 1982.

Levanthal, T. & Sills, M.: Self-image in school phobia. *American Journal of Orthopsychiatry,* 34(4): 685–689, 1964.

Levine, E.: *The Psychology of Deafness.* New York: Columbia University Press, 1960.

Levine, E. & Wagner, G.: Personality patterns of deaf persons. *Perceptual and Motor Skills* (Monograph Supplement 4-V39), 1974.

Levine, J.: *Secondary Instruction: A Manual for Classroom Teaching.* Boston: Allyn & Bacon, 1989.

Levine, M.: *Developmental Variations and Learning Disorders.* Cambridge, MA: Educators Publishing Service, 1987.

Levitt, E.: *The Psychology of anxiety* (2nd Ed.). Hillsdale, NJ: Earlbaum, 1980.

Levitt, H.: Speech and hearing in communication. In M. Wang, M. Reynolds & H. Walberg (Eds.) *Handbook of Special Education: Research and Practice, Vol. 3, Low Incidence Conditions.* New York: Pergamon, 1989.

Lindstrom, R. & Van Sant, S.: Special issues in working with gifted minority adolescents. *Journal of Counseling and Development,* 64: 583–585, 1986.

Lloyd, J.: Academic instruction and cognitive behavior modification: The need for attack strategy training. *Exceptional Education Quarterly,* 1: 53–64, 1980.

Loeb, R.C. & Jay, G.: Self-Concept in gifted children: Differential impact in boys and girls. *Gifted Child Quarterly,* 31 (1): 9–14, 1987.

Loeb, R. & Sarigiani, P.: The impact of hearing impairment on self-perceptions of children. *The Volta Review,* 88(2): 89–100, 1986.

Logan, D. & Rose, E.: Characteristics of the mentally retarded. In P.T. Cegelka & H. J. Prehm (Eds.), *Mental Retardation: From Categories to People.* Columbus, OH: Merrill, 1982.

Loper, A.: Metacognitive development: Implications for cognitive training. *Exceptional Education Quarterly,* 1: 1–8, 1980.

Lowenbraun, S.: Hearing impaired. In E. Meyen & T. Skrtic (Eds.) *Exceptional Children and Youth: An Introduction* (3rd ed.). Denver: Love, 1988.

Lowenfeld, B.: Psychological considerations. In B. Lowenfeld (Ed.) *The Visually Handicapped Child in School.* New York: John Day, 1973.

Lovitt, T.: *Introduction to Learning Disabilities.* Boston: Allyn & Bacon, 1989.

Luchow, J. et. al.: Learned helplessness: Perceived effects of ability and effort on academic performance among EH and LD/EH children. Paper presented at the

Annual Convention of the Council for Exceptional Children (63rd, Anaheim, CA, April 15–19, 1985). (ERIC Reproduction (No. ED257264), 1985.

Ludlow, C.: Children's language disorders: Recent research advances. *Annals of Neurology,* 7: 497–507, 1980.

Luftig, R.: The effect of differential educational placements on the self-concept of retarded pupils. Paper presented at the annual meeting of the American Educational Research Assn. (ERIC Document Reproduction Service No. ED 196198), 1980.

Maccoby, E.: *Social Development.* New York: Harcourt Brace, 1980.

MacMillan, D.: *Mental Retardation in School and Society* (2nd ed.). Boston: Little, Brown, 1982.

MacMillan, D. & Morrison, G.: Correlates of social status among mildly handicapped learners in self-contained classes. *Journal of Educational Psychology,* 72: 437–444, 1980.

Manaster, G.J.: *Adolescent Development: A Psychological Interpretation.* Itasca, IL: F.E. Peacock, 1989.

Mann, L. & Sabatino, D.: *Foundations of Cognitive Process in Remedial and Special Education.* Rockville, MD: Aspen, 1985.

Margalit, M. & Zak, I.: Anxiety and self-concept of learning disabled children. *Journal of Learning Disabilities,* 17 (9):537–539, Nov. 1984.

Marland, S.P., Jr.: Education of the Gifted and Talented, Vol. 1, Report to the Congress of the United States by the US Commissioner of Education. Washington, DC: US Government Printing Office, 1972.

Martinson, R.: *The Identification of the Gifted and Talented.* Reston, VA: Council for Exceptional Children, 1981.

Mattingly, I.G.: Reading, the linguistic process, and linguistic awareness. In J. Kavanagh & I.G. Mattingly (Eds.) *Language By Ear and By Eye: The Relationship Between Speech and Reading.* Cambridge: The MIT Press, 1972.

Maurer, H. & Newbrough, J.R.: Facial expressions of mentally retarded and nonretarded children: I. Recognition by mentally retarded and nonretarded adults. *American Journal of Mental Deficiency,* 91: 505–510, 1987.

McCandless, B. & Coop, R.: *Adolescents: Behavior and Development* (2nd ed.). New York: Holt, Rinehart & Winston, 1979.

McConnell, F.: Children with hearing disabilities. In L.M. Dunn, *Exceptional Children in the Schools.* New York: Holt, Rinehart & Winston, 1973.

McCormick, L.: Communication disorders. In N. Haring & L. McCormick (Eds.) *Exceptional Children and Youth* (Fifth Ed.). Columbus, OH: Merrill, 1990.

McCoy, K. & Prehm, H.: *Teaching Mainstreamed Students: Methods and Techniques.* Denver: Love, 1987.

McFarland, W. & Simmons, B.: The importance of early intervention with severe childhood deafness. *Pediatric Annals,* 9: 13–19, 1980.

McGinnis, E. & Goldstein, A.P.: *Skillstreaming the Elementary School Child: A Guide for Teaching Prosocial Skills.* Champaign, IL: Research Press, 1984.

Meadow, K.P.: *Deafness and Child Development.* Berkely, CA: University of California Press, 1980.

Meadow, K.P.: Social adjustment of preschool children: Deaf and hearing, with and without other handicaps. *Topics in Early Childhood Special Education,* 3: 27–40, 1984.

Meadow-Orlans, K.: An analysis of the effectiveness of early intervention programs for hearing impaired children. In M. Guralnick & F. Bennett (Eds.) *The Effectiveness of Early Intervention for At-Risk and Handicapped Children.* New York: Academic Press, 1987.

Mercer, C.: *Students with Learning Disabilities* (3rd ed.). Columbus, OH: Merrill, 1987.

Mercer, C. & Mercer, A.: *Teaching Students with Learning Problems* (3rd ed.). Columbus, OH: Merrill, 1989.

Meyer, E.: Psychological and emotional problems of deaf children. *American Annals of the Deaf,* 98: 472–477, 1953.

Millar, S.: Crossmodal and intersensory perception and the blind. In R. Walk & H. Pick, Jr. (Eds.) *Intersensory Perception and Sensory Integration.* New York: Pergamon, 1987.

Monson, L. & Simeonsson, R.: Normal child development. In B. Epanchin & J. Paul (Eds.) *Emotional Problems of Childhood and Adolescence: A Multidisciplinary Perspective.* Columbus, OH: Merrill, 1987.

Moores, D.: *Educating the Deaf: Psychology, Principles, and Practice* (2nd ed.). Boston: Houghton Mifflin, 1982.

Morgan, S.: Locus of control in children labeled learning disabled, behaviorally disordered, and learning disabled/behaviorally disordered. *Learning Disabilities Research,* 2 (1): 10–13 (ERIC Reproduction No. ED 350866), 1986.

Morrison, B. & Hershey, M.: Are we meeting the emotional needs of the gifted? *Challenge,* 31: 9–12, 1988.

Morrison, G.: Mentally retarded. In E. Meyen & T. Skrtic (Eds.) *Exceptional Children and Youth: An Introduction* (3rd ed.). Denver: Love, 1988.

Mullins, J. B.: *A Teacher's Guide to Management of Physically Handicapped Students.* Springfield, IL: Charles C Thomas, 1979.

Myers, P. & Hammill, D.: *Learning Disabilities Basic Concepts, Assessment Practices & Instructional Strategies.* Austin, TX: PRO–ED, 1990.

Neville, H. & Bellugi, U.: Patterns of cerebral specialization in congenitally deaf adults. In P. Siple (Ed.) *Understanding Language Through Sign Language Research.* New York: Academic Press, 1978.

Nippold, M.: Comprehension of figurative language in youth. *Topics in Language Disorders,* 5(3):1–20, 1985.

Nowicki, S. & DiGirolamo, A.: The association of external locus of control, nonverbal processing difficulties, and emotional disturbance. *Behavioral Disorders,* 15 (1): 28–34, 1989.

Obiakor, F., Stiles, S., Muller, D.: Diminished self-concept of the visually impaired: Fact or fiction? (ERIC Documents Reproduction No. ED 300942), 1987.

Oden, S.: Alternative perspectives on children's peer relationships. In T. Yawkey & J.E. Johnson (Eds.), *Integrative Processes and Socialization: Early to Middle Childhood.* Hillsdale, NJ: Erlbaum, 1988.

Odom, P., Blanton, R. & Laukhuf, C.: Facial expressions and interpretation of emotion arousing situations in deaf and hearing children. *Journal of Abnormal Child Psychology,* 1: 139–151, 1973.

Ollendick, H., Balla, D. & Zigler, E.: Expectancy of success and the probability learning performance of retarded children. *Journal of Abnormal Psychology,* 77: 275–281, 1971.

Oyer, H., Crowe, B. & Hass, W.: *Speech, Language, & Hearing Disorders: A Guide for the Teacher.* Boston: Little, Brown, 1987.

Parsons, S.: Locus of control and adaptive behavior in visually impaired children. *Journal of Visual Impairment and Blindness,* 81 (9): 429–432, 1987.

Patton, J., Beirne-Smith, A., Payne, J.: *Mental Retardation* (3rd ed.). Columbus, OH: Merrill, 1990.

Patton, J. & Polloway, E.: Mild mental retardation. In N. Haring & L. McCormick (Eds.) *Exceptional Children and Youth: An Introduction to Special Education* (5th ed.). Columbus, OH: Merrill, 1990.

Paul, R.: The comprehension of multimeaning words from selected frequency levels by deaf and hearing subjects. Unpublished doctoral dissertation, University of Illinois at Champaign-Urbana, 1984.

Peckham, C.: Speech defects in a national sample of children aged seven years. *British Journal of Disorders of Communication,* 8: 2–8, 1973.

Pendergrass, R. & Hodges, M.: Deaf students in group problem solving situations: A study of the interactive process. *American Annals of the Deaf,* 121: 327–330, 1976.

Perna, S. et. al.: The relationship of internal locus of control, academic achievement, and IQ in emotionally disturbed boys, *Behavioral Disorders,* 9 (1): 36–42, 1983.

Politino, V.: Attitude toward physical activity and self-concept of normal and emotionally disturbed children. *Dissertation Abstracts International,* 40 (8A): 4476, Feb. 1980.

Polloway, E., Epstein, M., Patton, J., Cullinan, D. & Luebke, J.: Demographic, social and behavioral characteristics of students with educable mental retardation. *Education and Training of the Mentally Retarded,* 21: 27–34, 1986.

Polloway, E. & Smith, J.: Current status of the mild mental retardation construct: Identification, placement, and programs. In M. Wang, M. Reynolds, & H. Wahlberg (Eds.), *The Handbook of Special Education: Research and Practice.* Oxford: Pergamon, 1987.

Powell, P.: Seduction of ideas. *Roeper Review,* 3(4): 3–4, 1982.

Pray, Jr., B.S., Kramer, J. & Camp, C.: Training recall readiness skills to retarded adults: Effects on skill maintenance and generalization. *Human Learning,* 3: 43–51, 1984.

Prinz, P. & Ferrier, L.: "Can you give me that one?": The comprehension, production and judgment of directives by language-impaired children. *Journal of Speech and Hearing Disorders,* 48: 44–54, 1983.

Pullis, M.: Affective and motivational aspects of learning disabilities. In D. K. Reid, *Teaching the Learning Disabled A Cognitive Developmental Approach.* Boston: Allyn & Bacon, 1988.

Purkey, W.: *Self-Concept and School Achievement.* Englewood Cliffs, NJ: Prentice Hall, 1970.

Quigley, S. & Kretschmer, R.: *The Education of Deaf Children: Issues, Theory, and Practice.* Baltimore, MD: University Park Press, 1982.

Quigley, S. & Paul, P.: English language development. In M. Wang, M. Reynolds & H. Walberg (Eds.) *Handbook of Special Education Research and Practice, Vol. 2, Mildly Handicapped Conditions.* New York: Pergamon, 1989.

Ratner, N.: Atypical language development. In J. Gleason (Ed.) *The Development of Language.* Columbus, OH: Merrill, 1989.

Reid, D.K.: *Teaching the Learning Disabled: A Cognitive Developmental Approach.* Boston: Allyn & Bacon, 1988.

Renzulli, J.S.: What makes giftedness? Reexamining a definition. *Phil Delta Kappan,* 60: 180–184, 261, 1978.

Renzulli, J.S.: Rating the behavioral characteristics of superior students. G/C/T, 30–35, 1983.

Renzulli, J.S.: The three ring conception of giftedness: A developmental model for creative productivity. In R.J. Sternberg & J.E. Davidson (Eds.) *Conceptions of Giftedness.* Cambridge, MA: Cambridge University Press, 1986.

Renzulli, J.S. & Delcourt, M.: The legacy and logic of research on the identification of gifted persons. *Gifted Child Quarterly,* 30(1): 20–23, 1986.

Renzulli, J.S. & Hartman, R.K.: Scale for rating the behavioral characteristics of superior students. In W.B. Barbe & J.S. Renzulli (Eds.) *Psychology and Education of the Gifted* (3rd ed.). New York: Irvington, 1981.

Reschly, D.: Learning characteristics of mildly handicapped students: Implications for classification, placement, and programming. In M. Wang, M. Reynolds, & H. Wolberg (Eds.), *Handbook of Special Education: Research and Practice. Vol. I, Learner Characteristics and Adaptive Education.* New York: Pergamon, 1987.

Rice, M.: Speech and language-impaired. In E. Meyen & T. Skrtic (Eds.) *Exceptional Children and Youth: An Introduction* (3rd ed.). Denver: Love, 1988.

Rizzo, J. & Zabel, R.: *Educating Children and Adolescents with Behavioral Disorders: An Integrative Approach.* Boston: Allyn & Bacon, 1988.

Robinson, S. & Deshler, D.: Learning Disabled. In E. Meyen & T. Skrtic (Eds.), *Exceptional Children and Youth: An Introduction* (3rd ed.). Denver: Love, 1988.

Robinson, H. & Robinson, N.: *The Mentally Retarded Child: A Psychological Approach.* New York: McGraw-Hill, 1976.

Rogers, H.: An exploration of selected affective characteristics of learning disabled children. Master's Thesis, University of Saskatchewan, 1983.

Rogers, H. & Saklofske, D.: Self-concepts, locus of control and performance expectations of learning disabled children, *Journal of Learning Disabilities* 18 (5): 273–278, 1985.

Rose-Krasnor, L.: Social cognition. In T. Yawkey & J.E. Johnson (Eds.), *Integrative Processes and Socialization: Early to Middle Childhood.* Hillsdale, NJ: Earlbaum, 1988.

Rosenberg, M.: *Conceiving the Self.* New York: Basic Books, 1979.

Saccuzzo, D. & Michael, B.: Speed of information processing and structural limitations by mentally retarded and dual-diagnosed retarded-schizophrenic persons. *American Journal of Mental Deficiency,* 89: 187–194, 1984.

Sacks, S., Rosen, S. & Gaylord-Ross, R.: Visual Impairment. In N. Haring & L. McCormick (Eds.) *Exceptional Children and Youth* (5th ed.). Columbus, OH: Merrill, 1990.

Santrock, J.: *Adolescence.* Dubuque, IA: Brown, 1990.

Schloss, P.: Dimensions of students' behavior disorders: An alternative to medical model classification. *Diagnostique,* 11 (11): 21–30, Fall 1985.

Schmitz, C. & Galbraith, J.: *Managing the Social and Emotional Needs of the Gifted: A Teacher's Survival Guide.* Minneapolis, MN: Free Spirit, 1985.

Scholl, G.: Education of visually handicapped children and youth: An introduction. In M. Wang, M. Reynolds & H. Walberg (Eds.) *Handbook of Special Education: Research and Practice, Vol. 3, Low Incidence Conditions.* Oxford: Pergamon, 1989.

Schumaker, J. & Hazel, J.: Social skills assessment and training for the learning disabled: Who's on first and what is on second? Part I. *Journal of Learning Disabilities,* 17: 422–431, 1984.

Seiler, P.: Social aspects of educating deaf persons: Perspectives of a deaf professional. *Deafness Monograph No. 2, Social Aspects of Educating Deaf Persons.* Washington, DC: Gallaudet College, 1982.

Seligman, M. & Peterson, C.: A learned helplessness perspective on childhood depression. In M. Rutter, C. Izard, & P. Read (Eds.) *Depression in Young People: Developmental and Clinical Perspectives.* New York: Guilford, 1986.

Shea, T.: *Teaching Children and Youth with Behavior Disorders.* St. Louis: C.V. Mosby, 1978.

Sherrill, D.: Peer, teacher, and self perceptions of children with severe functional articulation disorders. *Dissertation Abstracts,* 28 (2A): 507–508, 1967.

Shore, B. & Dover, A.: Metacognition, intelligence and giftedness. *Gifted Child Quarterly,* 31: 37–39, 1987.

Shriberg, I.: Developmental phonological disorders. In T. Hixon, I. Shriberg & J. Saxman (Eds.) *Introduction to Communication Disorders.* Englewood Cliffs, NJ: Prentice Hall, 1980.

Silverman, R. & Zigmond, N.: Self-concept in learning disabled adolescents. Paper presented at the annual meeting of the American Educational Research Association, Los Angeles, CA, 1981.

Silverman, R., Zigmond, N. & Sansone, J.: Teaching coping skills to adolescents with learning problems. In E. Meyen, G. Vergason, & R. Whelan (Eds.) *Promising Practices for Exceptional Children Curriculum Implications.* Denver: Love, 1983.

Singh, N.: Facial recognition and production of facial expressions of emotion by people with mental retardation. Paper presented at the annual meeting of the American Association on Mental Retardation, Atlanta, GA, May 1990.

Sirvis, B.: Physical disabilities. In E. Meyen & T. Skrtic (Eds.) *Exceptional Children and Youth* (3rd ed.). Denver: Love, 1988.

Skolnick, A.: *The Psychology of Human Development.* San Diego: Harcourt, Brace, Jovanovich, 1986.

Smollar, J. & Youniss, J.: Adolescent self-concept development. In R. Leahy (Ed). *The Development of the Self.* Orlando: Academic Press, 1985.

Song, I. & Hattie, J.: Home environment, self-concept, and academic achievement: A causal modeling approach. *Journal of Educational Psychology,* 76, 6: 1269–1281, 1984.

Spekman, N.: Dyadic verbal communication abilities of learning disabled and normally achieving fourth grade and fifth grade boys. *Learning Disability Quarterly,* 4: 139–151, 1981.

Spitz, H.: Beyond field theory in the study of mental deficiency. In N.R. Ellis (Ed.) *Handbook of Mental Deficiency: Psychological Theory and Research* (2nd ed.). Hillsdale, NJ: Erlbaum, 1979.

Spriger, S.: The development of conservation of number in deaf and hearing children. Paper presented at Canadian Psychological Association, April, 1979.

Stanley, J.: Use of general ability and specific aptitude measures in identification: Some principles and certain cautions. *Gifted Child Quarterly,* 284: 177–180, 1984.

Stangvik, G.: *Self-Concept and School Segregation.* Goteborg, Sweden: ACTA, UNIVERSITATIS GOTHOBURGENSIS, 1979.

Stephens, B. & Grube, C.: Development of Piagetian reasoning in congenitally blind children. *Journal of Visual Impairment and Blindness,* 76: 133–143, 1982.

Sternberg, M.: Communication with deaf-blind children. Proceedings: Workshops for Serving the Deaf-Blind and Multihandicapped Child: Identification, Assessment, and Training. California State Department of Education, Sacramento: Southwestern Region Deaf-Blind Center (ERIC Document Reproduction No. 179039), 1979.

Sternberg, R.J.: *Beyond IQ: A Triarchic Theory of Human Intelligence.* Cambridge, MA: Cambridge University Press, 1986.

Sternberg, R.J. & Davidson, J.E. (Eds.): *Conceptions of Giftedness.* Cambridge, MA: Cambridge University Press, 1986.

Stevenson, D. & Romney, D.: Depression in learning disabled children. *Journal of Learning Disabilities,* 17: 579, 1984.

Strang, L., Smith, M. & Rogers, G.: Social comparison, multiple reference groups, and the self-concepts of academically handicapped children before and after mainstreaming. *Journal of Educational Psychology,* 70: 487–497, 1978.

Subotnik, R.: The motivation to experiment: A study of gifted adolescents' attitudes toward scientific research. *Journal of the Education of the Gifted,* 11(3): 19–35, 1988.

Sullivan, P.: Administration modifications on the WISC–R performance scale with different categories of deaf children. *American Annals of the Deaf,* 127: 780–788, 1982.

Suppes, P.: Computer-assisted instruction for deaf students. *American Annals of the Deaf,* 116: 500–508, 1971.

Suter, D. & Wolf, J.: Issues in the identification and programming of the gifted/learning disabled child. *Journal for the Education of the Gifted.* 10 (3): 227–237, 1987.

Sweeney, M. & Zionts, P.: The "second skin": Perceptions of disturbed and non-disturbed early adolescents on clothing, self-concept, and body image. *Adolescence,* 24 (94): 411–420, Sum. 1989.

Telford, C. & Sawrey, J.: *The Exceptional Individual.* Englewood Cliffs, NJ: Prentice Hall, 1977.

Terman, L.: The discovery and encouragement of exceptional talent. In W.B. Barbe & J.S. Renzulli (Eds.) *Psychology and Education of the Gifted* (3rd ed.). New York: Irvington, 1981.

Terman, L. & Odin, M.: The gifted child grows up. In L. Terman (Ed.) *The Genetic Studies of Genius* (Vol. IV). Stanford, CA: Stanford University Press, 1947.

Terman, L. & Odin, M.: The Stanford studies of the gifted. In P. Witty (Ed.) *The Gifted Child.* Boston: D.C. Heath, 1951.

Thelan, E.: Determinants of amount of stereotyped behavior in normal human infants. *Etiology & Sociobiology,* 1: 141–150, 1980.

Thomas, C. & Patton, J.: Mild and moderate retardation. In J. Patton, J. Payne & M. Bierne-Smith *Mental Retardation* (3rd ed.). Columbus, OH: Merrill, 1990.

Trybus, R. & Karchmer, M.: School achievement scores of hearing impaired children: National data on achievement, status, and growth patterns. *American Annals of the Deaf,* 122: 62–69, 1979.

Turiel, E., Killen, M. & Helwig, C.C.: Morality: Its structure, functions, and vagaries. In J. Kegan & S. Lamb (Eds.), *The Emergence of Morality.* Chicago: Chicago University Press, 1987.

Tuttle, D.: Visually impaired. In E. Meyen & T. Skrtic (Eds.). *Exceptional Children and Youth: An Introduction* (3rd ed.). Denver: Love, 1988.

Vallecorsa, A.: An investigation of self-concept in elementary school age students in learning disabilities classrooms. *Dissertation Abstracts International,* 40 (8A): 4536, 1980.

Vandell, D. & George, L.: Social interaction in hearing and deaf preschoolers: Successes and failures in initiation. *Child Development,* 52: 627–635, 1981.

Van Kleeck, A.: Metalinguistic skills: Cutting across spoken and written language and problem-solving abilities. In G. Wallach & K. Butler (Eds.) *Language Learning Disabilities in School-Age Children.* Baltimore, MD: Williams & Wilkins, 1984.

Wallace, G., Cohen, S. & Polloway, E.: *Language Arts: Teaching Exceptional Students.* Belmont, CA: A Wodsworth, 1989.

Walthall, J.: An investigation of reported self-concept among EMR subjects. *Dissertation Abstracts International,* 36 (7A): 4411, 1976.

Warren, C. & Hasenstab, S.: Self-concept of severely to profoundly hearing impaired children. *Volta Review,* 88 (6): 289–295, Oct.–Nov., 1986.

Webb, J., Mceckstroth, E. & Tolan, S.: *Guiding the Gifted Child.* Columbus, OH: Ohio Psychology Publishing, 1982.

Weiss, E.: Learning disabled children's understanding of social interactions of peers. *Journal of Learning Disabilities,* 17: 612–615, 1984.

Wheatley, G.: Instructional methods for the gifted. In J. Feldhusen, J. Van Tassel-Baska & K. Seeley, *Excellence in Educating the Gifted.* Denver: Love, 1989.

Whelan, R.: Emotional disturbance. In E. Meyen & T. Skrtic (Eds.) *Exceptional Children and Youth: An Introduction* (3rd ed.). Denver: Love, 1988.

Whitmore, J.: *Giftedness, Conflict and Underachievement.* Boston: Allyn & Bacon, 1980.

Whorton, J. & Algozzine, R.: Comparison of intellectual, achievement, and adaptive behavior levels for students who are mentally retarded, *Mental Retardation,* 16: 320–321, 1978.

Wiig, E.: Learning disabilities in school-age children and youth. In G. Shames & E. Wiigs (Ed.) *Human Communication Disorders* (2nd ed.). Columbus, OH: Merrill, 1986.

Wiig, E. & Roach, M.: Immediate recall of semantically varied "sentences" by learning disabled adolescents. *Perceptual and Motor Skills,* 40: 119–125, 1975.

Wiig, E. & Semel, E.: *Language Assessment and Intervention for the Learning Disabled* (2nd ed.). Columbus, OH: Merrill, 1984.

Wilczenski, F.: Facial emotional expressions of adults with mental retardation. *Education and Training in Mental Retardation,* 26 (3): 319–324, Sept. 1991.

Wiley, J.: A psychology of auditory impairment. In W. Cruickshank (Ed.) *Psychology of Exceptional Children and Youth.* Englewood Cliffs, NJ: Prentice Hall, 1971.

Withrow, F.: Immediate memory span of deaf and normally hearing children. *Exceptional Children,* 35: 33–41, 1968.

Witty, P.: "Who are the gifted?" In N. Henry (Ed.) *Education of the Gifted, Part II.* Fifty-Seventh Yearbook of the National Society for the Study of Education. Chicago: University of Chicago Press, 1958.

Wolery, M. & Haring, T.: Moderate, severe, and profound handicaps. In T. Haring & L. McCormick (Eds.) *Exceptional Children and Youth: An Introduction to Special Education* (5th ed.). Columbus, OH: Merrill, 1990.

Wood, D., Wood, H. & Howarth, P.: Mathematical abilities of deaf school leavers. *British Journal of Developmental Psychology,* 1: 67, 1983.

Wood, F. & Johnson, A.: Coopersmith Self-Esteem Inventory scores for boys with severe behavior problems. *Exceptional Children,* 38: 739, 1972.

Wright, B.: *Physical Disability: A Psychosocial Approach* (2nd ed.). New York: Harper & Row, 1983.

Youniss, J.: The nature of social development: A conceptual discussion of cognition. In H. McGurk (Ed.) *Issues in Childhood Social Development.* London: Methuen, 1978.

Zigmond, N.: A prototype of comprehensive service for secondary students with learning disabilities: A preliminary report. *Learning Disability Quarterly,* 1: 39–49, 1978.

Ziv, A. & Gadish, O.: Humor & giftedness. *Journal for the Education of the Gifted,* 13 (4): 332–345, 1990.

Zunich, M. & Ledwith, B.: Self-concept of visually handicapped and sighted children. *Perceptual and Motor Skills,* 21: 771–774, 1965.

INDEX